The
Complete
Book of
Confederate
Trivia

J. Stephen Lang

Burd Street Press

This Burd Street Press publication
was printed by
Beidel Printing House, Inc.
63 West Burd Street
Shippensburg, PA 17257 USA

In respect for the scholarship contained herein, the acid-free paper used in this book meets the guidelines for permanence and durability of the Committee on Production Guidelines for Book Longevity of the Council on Library Resources.

For a complete list of available publications
please write
Burd Street Press
Division of White Mane Publishing Company, Inc.
P.O Box 152
Shippensburg, PA 17257 USA

Library of Congress Cataloging-in-Publication Data

Lang, J. Stephen.
    The complete book of Confederate trivia / J. Stephen Lang.
        p.   cm.
    Includes bibliographical references.
    ISBN 1-57249-007-1 (alk. paper)
    1. Confederate States of America--Miscellanea.
    2. United States--History--Civil War, 1861-1865--Miscellanea.
    I. Title.
    E487.L36   1996
    973.7'13--dc20   95-52054
                                                                    CIP

PRINTED IN THE UNITED STATES OF AMERICA

To
William McCluskey
8th Tennessee Infantry
C.S.A.
and
John Lang
9th Alabama Infantry
C.S.A.

two forebears of mine

Table of Contents

Part 8: Daily Life in Wartime

Part 9: The Criminal Life

Introduction

Can we speak of *the Confederacy* and *trivia* in the same breath? After all the serious books, essays, songs, movies, artworks, and monuments inspired by the Confederacy, can it be *trivial?* In spite of its short life—barely over four years—the Confederate States of America still inspires fascination and even reverence. Many people—including several of this author's ancestors—lost their lives defending the Lost Cause. So how can the Confederacy provide quizzical readers with leisure—and even laughter?

Well, it can, and for the simple reason that millions of people are still fascinated by the Southern Confederacy, even by minute details of it. To look at the South from 1861 to 1865 is to look at an earthy, very human collection of characters and incidents that cannot help but amuse (as well as enlighten) a reader. I do not need to convince Civil War buffs of this. But even the "unconverted" may find this collection of questions and answers to be a treasure trove of fascinating people and occurrences.

The story of the Confederacy throbs with human life. It is full of sublime events—and sometimes pathetic, sometimes amusing pictures of human failings. The old South evokes tears and laughter, repulsion and admiration. Probing its many characters and incidents reveals to us much about present-day America, about ourselves.

This is not the first collection of questions and answers about the Civil War, and it probably will not be the last. However, the focus here is not on the war itself, but on the new Southern nation. Military matters are, naturally, important. But the book you are holding also looks at the whole spectrum of human life in the newborn nation. The soldiers and the battles are here, but so is everyday life, political life, indeed, all of life in the four years of the Confederacy.

Most previous books of Civil War trivia seem to have focused on the seriousness of the matter, neglecting the possibilities of finding things to chuckle over and cry over. Too many of these volumes have been painfully dry.

I have tried to avoid dryness at all costs. I have also aimed for a *larger* book than any of the previous efforts, large enough to cover everything from Robert E. Lee's horse to the sad fate of the world's first submarine. The arrangement here is topical, with such topics as "The Confederacy on Screen" (movies, that is), "Star Men: The Generals," "Notable Women," "Ridin' the Rails," "Bars and Stripes Forever: Prison Life," "Bang, Pow, Boom: Weaponry," "They Spied," "Soldier Talk," and many others. One can't include every subject in the book, of course, but the range is wide—famous quotations, battles, notable nicknames, politicians, food (and famine), music, flags, religious revivals, crime and punishments, medicine, and many, many more. Readers of my previous books of trivia have been pleased with the arrangement of having the answers on the back sides of the question pages, so we have used that arrangement here. (It's much easier than having to flip to a separate answer section at the back of the book.)

The various topical sections are arranged under nine sections of questions and answers. However, despite the attempt at organization, the book is for browsing. It was made to fill up your time commuting on the train, the hour you spend waiting at the dentist's office, the few minutes before dinner is on the table, the hours on the freeway when you and the other two commuters in the back seat are in the mood for a game of "quiz me." In short, the book is designed to be read randomly, anywhere, and with no preparation of any kind. It is designed to entertain the person who unashamedly likes to be entertained—and challenged. It is designed for the lifelong Civil War buff, for anyone who loves American history, and for the newcomer who has yet to discover just exactly *why* so many people are still obsessed with people and events of the 1860s. For the newcomer who cannot enjoy all four volumes of Freeman's renowned biography of Robert E. Lee, I humbly offer a pleasant and painless way to meet the old South.

The author would like to hear from any person who is able to correctly (and without peeking at the answers on the back of each page) answer every question in this book. In doing the research for this book, the author himself learned quite a bit, but not enough to answer every question correctly—at least, not yet.

Happy reading! I hope you enjoy getting better acquainted with that fascinating place—and time—known as the Confederacy.

Part 1

A Cast
of
Thousands

ᛒ Going to Extremes

War, it is said, brings out the best and worst in human beings. It could be said that it leads men to extremes. Below are questions about some of the extremes—some serious, some not—of the Confederacy and its people.

1. Which Confederate general was believed to have personally killed more men than any other American general?
2. Which general, weighing in at 290 pounds, was the Big Man of the Confederacy?
3. What Confederate cemetery contains the graves of more than 12,000 Union soldiers?
4. What was the Confederacy's bloodiest one-day battle?
5. What was the Confederacy's costliest victory in the war?
6. What was the "Queen City" of the Confederacy?
7. Who was the Confederacy's best friend in Europe?
8. What is the world's best-selling novel about the Confederacy?
9. Who was the Supreme Villain of the Confederacy?
10. And who might run a close second?
11. What was the Confederate army's most far-flung attack?
12. What radical idea was proposed for drafting more soldiers for the Confederate army?
13. What great American hero was forced out of office because he opposed his state's entry into the Confederacy?
14. What Southern capital received the pitiful name of "Chimneyville"?
15. What was the most hated law of the Confederacy?
16. What was the most noted massacre of the Civil War?
17. What was the motive behind Gen. Wade Hampton's capture of 2,500 at a Yankee camp in Coggins Point, Virginia?
18. Why did President Jefferson Davis go to see captured Union soldier David Van Buskirk?
19. What Confederate officer had been an officer as far back as the War of 1812?
20. What Mississippi tree was literally whittled away to nothing by Union soldiers?
21. What future general had himself buried alive in order to leave New York and head south for the war?

✎ Going to Extremes (answers)

1. Rambunctious Nathan Bedford Forrest, called "that devil Forrest" by the Union. The hard-bitten cavalryman had even killed one of his own officers in a brawl.
2. Gen. Sterling "Pap" Price, the former Missouri governor who threw in his lot with the Confederacy.
3. Andersonville National Historic Site in Georgia. The prison was noted for deplorable sanitation and the high mortality rate of prisoners.
4. Antietam, Maryland (September 17, 1862). In the space of a single day over 23,000 soldiers were killed, wounded, or missing.
5. Probably the Battle of Chancellorsville (Va.), a Confederate victory, but the site of Thomas "Stonewall" Jackson's death by friendly fire.
6. Richmond, Virginia, which is why it was chosen as the final capital. It had more prestige, though New Orleans was actually larger and wealthier.
7. Henry Hotze, publisher of the London *Index*, a pro-South newspaper financed by the Confederate government. Hotze's paper won many Europeans to the Southern side in the war.
8. *Gone with the Wind*, what else? Published in 1936, it still sells well in the U.S. and abroad.
9. Union Gen. William T. Sherman, whose destructive march through Georgia in 1864 made his name a by-word for cruelty.
10. Gen. Benjamin F. Butler, military governor of Union-occupied New Orleans in 1862. Rumor has it that New Orleans residents had his portrait painted on the bottoms of their chamber pots. He was nicknamed "Spoons" for allegedly stealing Confederates' silverware.
11. Probably the October 1864 raid on St. Albans, Vermont, the Confederates pouring in from Canada.
12. Drafting slaves. First proposed by Gen. Patrick Cleburne, the plan was adopted by the Confederate Congress in 1864. It was assumed that slaves who fought would eventually be given their freedom.
13. The great Sam Houston, who was governor of Texas when it seceded in 1861.
14. Jackson, Mississippi, after being torched by Union Gen. William T. Sherman. There were a lot of chimneys standing, but not many buildings attached to them. (Historians assure us that there were, in fact, many Chimneyvilles in the beaten Confederacy.)
15. The infamous Order 28 issued by Union Gen. Benjamin Butler, mentioned in Question 10. Governor of Yankee-occupied New Orleans, "Beast" Butler issued an order which stated that local women in any way harassing Union soldiers would be treated as common prostitutes.
16. The Fort Pillow massacre in 1864. Fort Pillow, in Tennessee, was held by 295 white and 262 black Federals. Under Gen. Nathan B. Forrest, the fort was taken, with 231 men killed. According to Union accounts, the killing took place *after* the fort had already surrendered.
17. Hunger. The 2,500 were cattle, not soldiers. Hampton's 7th Virginia Cavalry was trying to scrounge up some much-needed food for Robert E. Lee's famished soldiers.
18. The 380-pound soldier stood 6 foot 11 inches—the biggest Union prisoner in Richmond, and possibly the biggest soldier in the army.
19. David Twiggs of Texas, born in 1790.
20. The "Pemberton Oak" at Vicksburg, under which Confederate Gen. Pemberton and Union Gen. Grant discussed terms of surrender. The men wanted pieces of the tree for a keepsake.
21. Gustavus Smith, who was New York City's street commissioner. Fearing the reaction if the locals learned he was joining the Confederacy, he faked an illness and had a coffin (containing bricks) buried. Smith slipped out of town in disguise.

⚐ By Any Other Name: Notable Nicknames

Some noted Confederates were almost as well-known by their nicknames as by their given names. As you answer these, keep in mind that some figures had more than one nickname.

1. "Stonewall"
2. "Marse Robert"
3. "Dizzy Miss Lizzy"
4. "Fitz"
5. "Old Pete"
6. "Prince John"
7. "Rooney"
8. "The Gallant Pelham"
9. "Little Billy"
10. "The Fighting Bishop"
11. "Old Blue Light"
12. "Old Pap"
13. "Pathfinder of the Seas"
14. "The Last Cavalier"
15. "Fightin' Joe"
16. "Lee's War Horse"
17. "Prince Rupert"
18. "Old Baldy"
19. "The Bad Old Man"
20. "Shanks"
21. "Uncle Joe"
22. "The Grand Creole"
23. "Stonewall Jackson of the West"
24. "Savior of the Valley"

✎ By Any Other Name: Notable Nicknames (answers)

1. Gen. Thomas Jonathan Jackson, who was said to stand firm as a stone wall at the First Battle of Bull Run. (Here is an interesting case of the nickname being better known than the man's actual name.)
2. Gen. Robert E. Lee, of course. As a plantation head, he would qualify as a "marse" ("master," that is), but the title seems to be rooted in the affection his troops felt for him.
3. Noted spy for the Union, Elizabeth Van Lew. From one of Richmond's prominent families, she was nonetheless a valuable spy for the Union. Acting addle-brained help her conceal her espionage.
4. Gen. Fitzhugh Lee, nephew of Robert E. Lee and a renowned soldier in his own right.
5. Gen. James Longstreet.
6. Gen. John Magruder, called "Prince" because of his courtly manner and his reputation for entertaining lavishly.
7. Gen. William Henry Fitzhugh Lee, Robert E. Lee's second son.
8. Major John Pelham, the handsome Alabama boy who Robert E. Lee described as "gallant," a name that stuck for eternity.
9. Gen. William Mahone, who was on the short side, or Gen. William Henry Whiting, also short.
10. Gen. Leonidas Polk, who was Episcopal bishop of Louisiana before becoming a general.
11. Another name for Thomas "Stonewall" Jackson. The general's eyes were a piercing blue, even more so (so it was said) when he was ready for battle.
12. Gen. Sterling Price. At 290 pounds, "Pap" probably did seem rather large and fatherly.
13. The Confederate navy's Matthew Fontaine Maury, noted oceanographer and the first man to identify the Gulf Stream.
14. Gen. J. E. B. Stuart, notable for his chivalry, especially in regard to women. Actual, the general's usual name "Jeb" was itself a nickname, his full name being James Ewell Brown Stuart.
15. Gen. Joseph Wheeler, noted for his aggressiveness and hard-hitting tactics.
16. Another nickname for Gen. James Longstreet, who Lee relied on greatly.
17. Another nickname for Jeb Stuart. The original Rupert was a great hero and was a dashing, elegant military man in the English Civil Wars of the 1640s. Stuart was considered the Confederacy's embodiment of the same chivalry.
18. Gen. Richard Ewell, who was, indeed, bald.
19. Gen. Jubal Early. The name originated with Lee, who (like everyone else) couldn't help but notice Early's profanity, his contempt for religion, his careless dress, and his sarcastic smile.
20. Gen. Nathan Evans, noted for his thinness.
21. Another nickname for Gen. Joseph E. Johnston.
22. Gen. P. T. G. Beauregard, a bit pompous and descended from the old French (Creole) aristocracy of Louisiana.
23. Irish-born Gen. Patrick Cleburne, active west of the Mississippi.
24. Gen. Thomas Rosser, noted for his actions in the Shenandoah Valley of Virginia.

25. "Old Jack"
26. "Old Straight"
27. "Father of the Confederacy"
28. "Old Borey"
29. "Mudwall"
30. "Old Jube"
31. "Long Blade"
32. "Bloody Bill"
33. "Old Reliable"
34. "Wizard of the Saddle"
35. "Spoons"
36. "The Sphinx of the Confederacy"
37. "Old Allegheny"
38. "Granny"
39. "Extra Billy"
40. "Spy of the Cumberland"
41. "Slow Coach"
42. "Grumble"
43. "Poet-Priest of the Confederacy"
44. "Father of Secession"
45. "Old Rock"
46. "Swamp Fox of the Confederacy"
47. "Poet Laureate of the Confederacy"
48. "Old Blizzards"
49. "Old One Wing"
50. "Ramrod"
51. "The Gray Ghost"
52. "Dutch Sergeant"
53. "Billy Fixing"
54. "Make Laws"
55. "Daughter of the Confederacy"
56. "Bald Eagle"
57. "Jubilee"

25. Still another nickname for Thomas "Stonewall" Jackson. While "Stonewall" was Jackson's most widely used nickname, "Old Jack" was more commonly used by the admiring soldiers under his command.
26. Gen. Alexander Peter Stewart, notable in the Tennessee campaigns.
27. George Washington, who, being a Virginian and a leader in a Revolution, was regarded by some as the Confederacy's guiding spirit.
28. Gen. P. G. T. Beauregard.
29. Gen. William Jackson, a cousin and one-time staff member of the great "Stonewall," and certainly less famous.
30. Another nickname for Gen. Jubal Early, who was a 44-year-old bachelor when the war began, already stooped with arthritis.
31. The dashing German-born cavalry officer Heros von Borcke, who reputedly carried the heaviest sword in the Confederacy. His other nickname, also related to the sword, was "Major Armstrong."
32. Guerrilla leader William Anderson, famous for his massacre in Centralia, Missouri.
33. Gen. William J. Hardee.
34. Cavalry general Nathan Bedford Forrest.
35. Benjamin Butler, the Union general who governed occupied New Orleans. The Confederates accused him of being low enough to steal silverware.
36. President Jefferson Davis, so called because of his reserve.
37. Gen. Edward Johnson, noted for his activity in western Virginia.
38. Believe it or not, this was an earlier nickname for Robert E. Lee, and not an affectionate one. Before he made his reputation and became the revered "Marse Robert," Lee was not expected to amount to much.
39. Virginia governor William Smith.
40. Noted spy and actress Pauline Cushman.
41. Secretary of War Leroy P. Walker, noted for shirking responsibility.
42. Gen. William Edmondson Jones, noted for his sharp tongue and cantankerousness.
43. Abram Joseph Ryan, Catholic chaplain and noted writer of patriotic Confederate poetry.
44. South Carolina secessionist agitator Robert Barnwell Rhett.
45. Gen. Henry Lewis Benning of Georgia.
46. Jeff Thompson, the self-titled "general" who operated in the swampy areas of Missouri.
47. Henry Timrod, poet who waxed lyrical about the birth of the new Confederate nation.
48. Gen. William W. Loring, noted for his feud with "Stonewall" Jackson.
49. Gen. James Green Martin, who had lost his right arm in the Mexican War.
50. Gen. Richard L. Page, who had a brilliant career in both army and navy.
51. Partisan ranger John S. Mosby.
52. Henry Wirz, commandant of Andersonville Prison.
53. Gen. Cadmus Marcellus Wilcox.
54. Lafayette McLaws, noted as a stickler for regulations.
55. Varina Ann Jefferson Davis, daughter of the president, born in 1864, who became a fairly well-known novelist.
56. Gen. Martin Gary, noted for his sharp features and bald pate.
57. Still another nickname of Gen. Jubal Early (who was "Jubal E."—get it?).

⚑ Quotable Quotes

1. What general's last words were, "Let us cross over the river and rest under the shade of the trees"?
2. Who, speaking of President Jefferson Davis, said, "The man and the hour have met"?
3. Who said, "I would sooner die a thousand deaths than betray a friend or be false to duty"?
4. What leader said, "We ask nothing; we want nothing; we have no complications"?
5. What Union general gave his troops orders to "live off the country" while in Mississippi?
6. What year was the Richmond *Examiner* referring to when it said, on December 31, "Today closes the gloomiest year of our struggle"?
7. When Robert E. Lee said "I can scarcely think of him without weeping," what general was he speaking of?
8. In July 1864, President Jefferson Davis wrote to Robert E. Lee that "Johnston has failed. It seems necessary to relieve him." What was Johnston's notable failure?
9. In what Southern bay did Union naval man David Farragut utter his famous words "Damn the torpedoes! Full speed ahead!"?
10. Who made a speech stating "I see no chance for Sherman to escape from a defeat or a disgraceful retreat"?
11. Who, through the generosity of Union General Sherman, were the pastors of occupied towns allowed to pray for?
12. Who proposed to Gen. Grant in March 1865 that the "unhappy difficulties" be resolved by a military convention?
13. Who received a note from General Joseph Johnston, asking for a "temporary suspension of hostilities"?
14. What Confederate official was arrested by the Federals and charged with instigating "piratical expeditions"?
15. What governor stated "Tennessee will furnish not a single man for the purpose of coercion"?
16. To what general did President Jefferson Davis send an angry telegram asking, "Will you surrender Atlanta without a fight"?
17. What Confederate official said to Lincoln's face, "Is there no way of putting an end to the present trouble?"?
18. What egotistical general did President Jefferson Davis accuse of "trying to exalt yourself at my expense"?
19. What general said, "I don't believe we can have an army without music"?

✎ Quotable Quotes (answers)

1. Thomas "Stonewall" Jackson's, May 10, 1863.
2. Noted secessionist William L. Yancey.
3. Confederate spy Sam Davis, executed by the Union at age 21.
4. President Jefferson Davis.
5. U. S. Grant. The soldiers did, stripping the countryside bare.
6. It referred to 1863—indeed, a bad year for the Confederacy.
7. Cavalryman J. E. B. Stuart, just killed at Yellow Tavern, Virginia.
8. He had withdrawn his army all the way to Atlanta, leaving the path open for Sherman's Union troops.
9. Mobile Bay, Alabama.
10. President Jefferson Davis. He was proven wrong.
11. President Jefferson Davis. Sherman stated, "Jeff Davis and the devil both need it."
12. Robert E. Lee. Grant replied that he had no authority to hold such a conference.
13. Union General William T. Sherman.
14. Navy Secretary Stephen Mallory.
15. Isham Harris.
16. Joseph E. Johnston, who was then replaced by the more aggressive John Hood.
17. Vice-president Alexander Stephens, part of the informal "peace conference" that met with Lincoln at Fort Monroe, Virginia.
18. P. G. T. Beauregard. Both men were being a bit vain.
19. Robert E. Lee.

20. What state's government sent a message to Lincoln saying, "The people of this commonwealth are freemen, not slaves"?
21. What Union general issued the famous campaign order "Wherever Lee goes, there you will go also"?
22. What Tennessee congressman was censured by Congress for making "treasonous overtures" to the Federal government?
23. What was Union Gen. George McClellan holding when he said, "Here is a paper with which if I cannot whip Bobbie Lee I will be willing to go home"?
24. What type of soldiers were sometimes referred to as "a nuisance and an evil to the service" by regular officers?
25. At what battle in Virginia did Gen. Thomas "Stonewall" Jackson shout, "The Stonewall Brigade never retreats! Follow me!"?
26. What type of soldier boasted that he was "First at Bethel, last at Appomattox"?
27. What anti-slavery amendment was called by Lincoln "the king's cure for all evils"?
28. What renowned South Carolina advocate of states' rights said, as his dying words, "The South, the poor South"?
29. Who announced, on February 18, 1861, "We have changed the constituent parts, but not the system of government"?
30. What cavalry general's motto was "Get there first with the most"?
31. What English statesman, speaking of the Confederacy, stated, "They have made a nation"?
32. What general published a prayer asking that God "will give us a name and place among the nations of the earth"?
33. What devout general had as his personal motto, "Duty is ours, consequences are God's"?
34. What did Jefferson Davis call the "noblest of human conquests"?
35. Who claimed that secession was "the most glorious event in the history of Florida"?
36. What Confederate official's favorite expression was *Tout va bien*?
37. What Confederate Cabinet member was called by Jefferson Davis, "the most accomplished statesman I have ever known"?
38. Who, on April 2, 1865 sent a message to President Jefferson Davis saying, "I think it is absolutely necessary that we should abandon our position tonight"?
39. What Confederate agent has been called "the greatest scoundrel of the Civil War"?
40. To what brave officer did Robert E. Lee say, "My noble soldier, I thank you from the bottom of my heart"?
41. What courageous general's last words before he died at Gettysburg were "Give them the cold steel!"?

20. Arkansas.
21. U. S. Grant.
22. Henry Foote, President Jefferson Davis's longtime critic and adversary.
23. The infamous "Lost Order," containing Lee's plan for the invasion of Maryland. It had been found by a Union private wrapped around 3 cigars.
24. The partisan rangers, who were often paid well for the goods they captured in their raids.
25. Port Republic.
26. The Tarheels of North Carolina.
27. The Thirteenth Amendment, abolishing all slavery in the U.S.
28. John C. Calhoun, former U.S. vice-president.
29. Jefferson Davis, in his inaugural address in Montgomery.
30. Nathan Bedford Forrest. He is sometimes quoted as saying "firstest with the mostest."
31. William Gladstone, who later became prime minister.
32. Robert E. Lee.
33. Thomas "Stonewall" Jackson.
34. "A victory over yourselves."
35. Florida's governor, John Milton.
36. Diplomat Pierre Rost, working in France. *Tout va bien* is "all goes well," the unrealistic response Rost gave to Europeans' inquiries about the Confederate war effort.
37. Judah Benjamin, who held three different positions in the Cabinet.
38. Robert E. Lee. "Our position" refers to Richmond.
39. Jacob Thompson, who made off with all the Confederate funds stashed in Canadian banks. He lived in high style in Paris for several years.
40. Richard "Fightin' Dick" Anderson.
41. Lewis Addison Armistead.

42. What happened to cavalry leader Turner Ashby after he shouted "Forward, my brave boys!"?
43. Who said "God's will be done" at the time of his capture?
44. What Georgia general died at First Manassas, his last words being "They have killed me, boys, but never give up the field"?
45. What cavalry general stated that his philosophy was "War means fightin' and fightin' means killin'"?
46. How did Gen. William W. Loring get his nickname "Old Blizzards"?
47. Who received a gold jewel-studded sword inscribed, "To General Robert E. Lee, from his British sympathizers"?
48. What cavalry raider's exploits led Lincoln to send a message to the Union troops, "They are having a stampede in Kentucky. Please look to it"?
49. What officer ran afoul of Jefferson Davis for referring to Mrs. Davis as "an old squaw"?
50. David Farragut demanded that Fort Morgan in Alabama surrender "to prevent the unnecessary sacrifice of human life." What reply came from the fort's defender, Richard L. Page?
51. What statesman, who had turned against President Jefferson Davis, stated, "Our liberties, once lost, may be lost forever"?
52. What act of Lincoln did Jefferson Davis call "the most execrable measure recorded in the history of guilty man"?
53. What proposal was Robert E. Lee referring to when he said "I think the measure not only expedient but necessary"?
54. What did Florida governor John Milton do after announcing that "death would be preferable to reunion"?
55. Whose tombstone reads "Here lie my two sons. Only God knows which was right"?
56. What noted politician never asked for a pardon from the U.S., replying "Pardon for what? I haven't pardoned you all yet!"?
57. At what battle did Gen. Winfield Scott Featherston yell, "Charge, Mississippians! Drive them into the Potomac or into eternity!"?

42. He was struck by a bullet and killed instantly.
43. Jefferson Davis.
44. Francis Bartow.
45. Nathan Bedford Forrest.
46. Telling his men to fire on Union troops, he had yelled, "Give them blizzards, boys!"
47. Not General Lee. The sword was taken by the Union from a captured Confederate blockade runner.
48. John Hunt Morgan.
49. Abraham C. Myers, who apparently was referring to Varina Davis's dark complexion. Myers regretted the remark.
50. "I am prepared to sacrifice life, and will only surrender when I have no means of defense."
51. Vice-president Alexander Stephens.
52. The Emancipation Proclamation.
53. Arming slaves for the Confederate army.
54. Killed himself.
55. The Terrill brothers of Virginia. William was a Union general, James a Confederate general. Both died in the war, and the father buried them in a single grave.
56. Robert Tombs, who had served in the U.S. Senate. By not asking for pardon, he was never able to hold national office again.
57. Ball's Bluff, where his men did a lot of both.

⚑ Career Changes: Pre-War to War

Many Confederate leaders began their careers in standard fashion for the mid-1800s: fighting in the Mexican War and/or fighting the Indians in Florida and the West. In fact, the Mexican War was, career-wise, the overture to the Civil War. But there were some curious exceptions.

1. What general was an Episcopal bishop before the war came?
2. Who taught (rather badly) at the Virginia Military Institute before assuming a post in the Confederate army?
3. Who had served as secretary of war under President Franklin Pierce?
4. Who was a former U.S. vice-president?
5. Who was superintendent of the U.S. Military Academy at West Point just before the Civil War?
6. Who was superintendent of West Point in the 1850s?
7. Who was, besides being a Louisiana plantation lord, commissioner of the board of public works for the state?
8. Who was a real estate broker and slave dealer in his home state of Tennessee?
9. Who was a cavalryman in the French army?
10. Who was a cavalry professor at West Point?
11. Who headed an expedition to restore order among the Mormons in Utah?
12. Who was a math instructor at West Point and, later, a fighter against the Comanche Indians in Texas?
13. Who had served in the fight between Britain and America over the territory that is now Washington State?
14. Who was a former governor of Missouri?
15. Who had been an actor before becoming a noted spy for the Confederacy?
16. Who had been an Indian fighter in Kansas?
17. Who was a U.S. senator and lawyer in Louisiana?
18. Who had been a Georgia congressman before becoming second man in the Confederacy?
19. Who had been a Virginia congressman before joining Jefferson Davis's cabinet?
20. Who was a mere 17-year-old Virginia girl when she began a spying career?
21. Who was a U.S. senator from Florida and, earlier, a judge?
22. Who was organizer of the Lexington Rifles, a militia group in Kentucky?

✎ Career Changes: Pre-War to War (answers)

1. Leonidas Polk, a West Point graduate, consecrated a bishop at age thirty-two. When war broke out, he was serving as bishop of Louisiana. (The Union never ceased ribbing the Confederacy about having a bishop for a general.)
2. Thomas Jonathan Jackson, better known as "Stonewall." (And, to some VMI cadets who found Jackson a bit odd, he was known as "Tom Fool.")
3. Jefferson Davis, the Confederacy's first (and only) president.
4. John Breckinridge, vice-president under James Buchanan, and later a Confederate general and cabinet member.
5. P. G. T. Beauregard, who held the position only a short time before entering the Confederate army as a general.
6. The beloved Gen. Robert E. Lee, who greatly improved the academy during his time there.
7. Braxton Bragg, later a noted general.
8. Nathan Bedford Forrest, who became the great cavalry general, the "wild man" of the Confederate cavalry.
9. William Joseph Hardee, later a dashing general in the western part of the Confederacy.
10. John Bell Hood, the great general from Kentucky, active especially in Tennessee.
11. Albert Sidney Johnston, the great general who, to the great loss of the Confederacy, died at the Battle of Shiloh, 1862.
12. Edmund Kirby Smith, general, active in the western Confederacy (which was often referred to as "Kirby Smith-dom").
13. George E. Pickett, general, leader of the famous cavalry charge at Gettysburg.
14. Sterling Price, general in the western Confederacy.
15. James Harrison, who passed on vital information before the Battle of Gettysburg.
16. The dashing James Ewell Brown Stuart ("Jeb"), noted general in the Confederate cavalry.
17. Judah P. Benjamin, later holder of several positions in the Confederate cabinet.
18. Alexander Stephens, vice-president of the Confederacy.
19. James Seddon, who was one of several men serving as Secretary of War in the cabinet. He had the distinction of serving longer than any of the others.
20. The famous Belle Boyd, the most noted of Confederate spies.
21. Stephen Mallory, secretary of the navy, the only notable Confederate born on the island of Trinidad.
22. John Hunt Morgan, general, active in the Tennessee cavalry campaigns.

23. Who was a renowned oceanographer, the first man to describe the Gulf Stream and the man who standardized the logs kept by ship captains?

24. Who was a treaty negotiator for the Cherokee Indians and also publisher of a Cherokee newspaper?

25. What Robert E. Lee lookalike was an Episcopal minister and school principal before becoming a general in the artillery?

26. Who had been a respected Washington hostess before her career as a spy for the Confederacy?

27. Who studied law while in jail for shooting a fellow student at the University of Virginia?

28. Who was commissioner of streets for the city of New York?

29. Who was a lawyer and congressman before becoming the Confederacy's ambassador to France?

30. What elderly plantation patriarch was a noted authority on agriculture before firing the first shot at Fort Sumter?

31. What blockade runner and, later, cabinet member of the Confederacy had spent years as a cotton merchant?

32. What general had run against Abraham Lincoln for president?

33. What head of the Union's spying on Confederates had been head of a famous Chicago detective agency?

34. What noted Union spy, born in the South, had been a stage actress?

35. Who had been a naval commander in the Mexican War?

36. Who was a frontier gambler and petty thief before heading a band of pro-Confederate bushwhackers?

37. What U.S. Secretary of War resigned and became a Confederate general?

38. What Irish-born general had been a pharmacist, a lawyer, and a soldier in the British army?

23. Matthew Fontaine Maury, the great figure in the Confederate navy, often called the "Pathfinder of the Seas."
24. Stand Watie, the Indian who became a Confederate general.
25. William Pendleton, who, during the war, was preaching when he wasn't directing the Confederacy's guns. His physical resemblance to Lee, by the way, was amazing.
26. Rose O'Neal Greenhow, who wormed secrets out of the Union politicians she entertained.
27. John S. Mosby, leader of the famous Partisan Rangers who were such a thorn in the Union's side.
28. Gen. Gustavus Smith.
29. John Slidell.
30. Edmund Ruffin, zealous secessionist from Virginia.
31. George Trenholm, secretary of the treasury.
32. John Breckinridge (remember Question 4?), who had been vice-president under Lincoln's predecessor, James Buchanan. With four presidential candidates, Breckinridge came in second. Curiously, Breckinridge received more electoral votes than Lincoln's more famous opponent, Stephen Douglas. Douglas did, however, receive more popular votes than Breckinridge.
33. Allan Pinkerton.
34. Pauline Cushman.
35. Raphael Semmes, who became commander of the Confederate navy.
36. The notorious William Quantrill.
37. John Floyd.
38. Patrick Cleburne.

⚑ Career Changes: War to Post-War

How does a person adjust to life after loss? Most Confederate leaders tried their darndest, some becoming college presidents, some going into politics, some continuing in the military, and so on. Some adjusted very badly, as you will see.

1. What general became president of Virginia's Washington College?
2. What Louisiana general became president of a railroad and also the manager of the Louisiana State Lottery?
3. Who fled to Cuba after the war and traveled there and in Europe for several years?
4. Who became president of a railroad and, incidentally, had some connection with the founding of the Ku Klux Klan?
5. Who was both a senator from Georgia and governor of Georgia?
6. Who became a congressman representing Richmond and, later, commissioner of U.S. railroads for President Grover Cleveland?
7. Who became chancellor of the University of Nashville and, later, professor of mathematics at the University of the South?
8. Who served as U.S. minister to Turkey under President Hayes?
9. Who became a general in the army of Emperor Maximilian of Mexico, serving him until the poor emperor's execution?
10. Who spent the rest of his days as a life insurance agent in Richmond?
11. What naval man practiced law in Mobile, Alabama, until his death?
12. What Confederate spy became a noted actress and public speaker, attracting attention because of her colorful spy tales?
13. Who spent two years in prison in Fort Monroe, Virginia, and later wrote *The Rise and Fall of the Confederate Government?*
14. Who became a physics professor at the Virginia Military Institute, and a nationally renowned expert on oceanography?
15. Who served as president of the University of the South and of the University of Alabama?
16. Who served as a newspaper editor, a college president, and an author of an algebra textbook and religious tracts?
17. What leader of a band of raiders became briefly unpopular in the South for supporting Grant for president?
18. What general went on to fight in the Spanish-American War and in the Philippines?
19. What Confederate cabinet member fled to England, where he built up a lucrative law practice and became Queen's Counsel?
20. What former governor became chief justice of the Georgia Supreme Court and later a senator from Georgia?

✎ Career Changes: War to Post-War (answers)

1. Robert E. Lee. The college is now Washington and Lee University, and Lee and his horse are buried on its campus.
2. P. G. T. Beauregard.
3. Gen. John C. Breckinridge, former U.S. vice-president.
4. Nathan Bedford Forrest, who, according to some sources, was a Grand Wizard in the Klan.
5. Gen. John B. Gordon.
6. Gen. Joseph E. Johnston.
7. Gen. Edmund Kirby Smith.
8. Gen. James Longstreet.
9. Gen. John B. Magruder.
10. Gen. George E. Pickett.
11. Raphael Semmes, head of the Confederate navy.
12. The infamous spy, Belle Boyd.
13. President Jefferson Davis.
14. Matthew Fontaine Maury, the Confederate navy's noted "Pathfinder of the Seas."
15. Josiah Gorgas, the Confederacy's chief of ordnance.
16. Gen. Daniel Harvey Hill.
17. John Mosby, leader of the infamous Partisan Rangers that wildly harassed Union troops.
18. Joseph ("Fightin' Joe") Wheeler.
19. Judah P. Benjamin, who had held more than one position in Jefferson Davis's cabinet.
20. Joseph Brown.

21. What aged Southern agitator committed suicide shortly after the Confederacy's surrender?
22. What state governor served as senator, then governor, then senator again?
23. What Indian leader became a planter and tobacco manufacturer?
24. What general and secretary of state fled to Cuba and England, then returned to the South to practice law?
25. What kinsman of Robert E. Lee served as governor of Virginia and later a general in the Spanish-American War?
26. What general served as governor of Kentucky and was later a vice-presidential candidate?
27. Who became park commissioner of the Chickamauga and Chatta-nooga National Military Parks?
28. Who was executed by the Federal government for allowing the deplorable conditions of the Confederacy's Andersonville prison?
29. What Tennessee governor became a six-term senator from the state?
30. What general served as Episcopal minister, just as he had before (and during) the war?
31. What Confederate admiral became, ironically, president of an agricultural college?
32. What courageous naval commander became an admiral in the navy of Peru?

21. Edmund Ruffin, the Virginia planter credited with firing the first shot on Fort Sumter.
22. North Carolina's Zebulon Vance.
23. Stand Watie, the Cherokee general of the Confederacy.
24. Robert A. Toombs.
25. Fitzhugh Lee, Robert's nephew, and a noted general in his own right.
26. Simon Bolivar Buckner.
27. Gen. Alexander Stewart, who had been involved in the Chickamauga and Chattanooga campaigns.
28. Henry Wirz, commandant of Andersonville. His was the only execution that resulted from the Civil War.
29. Isham Harris.
30. Gen. William Pendleton.
31. Franklin Buchanan, president of Maryland State Agricultural College. (An interesting change, from seawater to land cultivation.)
32. John Randolph Tucker.

⚐ Some Major Personal Losses

War is wasteful. While we romanticize the glory of fighting and dying for the Cause, we must admit that war is a tremendous loss of resources, human and otherwise. Some of the South's brightest and best did not survive the war.

1. What gritty general had to be strapped to his saddle after losing a leg and the use of one arm?
2. What beloved general died from friendly fire wounds after a glorious victory?
3. What bodily loss occurred shortly before his death?
4. Which general died for "violating the sanctity of the home"?
5. What bishop (and general) died instantly at Pine Mountain, Georgia, after cannon shot passed through his chest?
6. Which valiant general died fighting near Petersburg, Virginia, just one week before Lee surrendered to Grant?
7. What capable general died at Shiloh after a minié ball severed an artery in his leg?
8. What Alabama general was shot after surrendering to Union troops?
9. What general died singing "Rock of Ages" after being wounded in a skirmish north of Richmond?
10. What gallant blond Alabama lad was posthumously promoted to lieutenant colonel after being killed at Kelly's Ford?
11. What Confederate bushwhacker was fatally wounded by Union troops while on his way to assassinate Lincoln?
12. What general was killed by a Union man named Speed Fry after shooting Fry's horse?
13. What 29-year-old general died after being mortally wounded at Gettysburg?
14. What general's death at Gettysburg is commemorated by a monument on the spot where he fell?
15. What general, later a prison head, was executed by the Union for his ill treatment of prisoners?
16. What grizzled secession agitator committed suicide when the Confederacy surrendered?
17. What general died at the First Battle of Bull Run after bestowing the name "Stonewall" on Thomas J. Jackson?
18. What was the "Battle of the Generals"?
19. Who was the only fatality in the Union navy's bombardment of Fort McAllister?
20. What general's boot filled with blood while he ignored a leg wound and bled to death on a battlefield?

🔖 Some Major Personal Losses (answers)

1. The gallant Gen. John B. Hood of Tennessee, who lost the use of his left arm at Gettysburg and had his right leg amputated after Chickamauga.
2. Thomas "Stonewall" Jackson, victor at Chancellorsville, 1863.
3. His left arm was amputated.
4. Earl Van Dorn, who was shot at Spring Hill, Tennessee, by a Dr. Peters, who claimed the general had violated the sanctity of his home. Van Dorn's friends claimed that the doctor shot him purely for political reasons.
5. The "Fighting Bishop" of the Confederacy, Gen. Leonidas Polk.
6. Ambrose Powell Hill.
7. Gen. Albert Sidney Johnston, one of the earliest and greatest losses to the Confederacy.
8. John Hunt Morgan. According to one version of the story, he was treacherously shot after surrendering. In another version, he was merely surprised and killed by the Union troops.
9. The dashing cavalry Gen. Jeb Stuart.
10. John Pelham, known as "the gallant Pelham."
11. The notorious raider William Quantrill.
12. Tennessean Felix Zollicoffer.
13. William Pender, who survived his wounding by about two weeks.
14. Lewis Armistead, who led the charge that day waving his hat on top of his sword.
15. Henry Wirz, the sole execution of the war, condemned because of the horrible conditions at Andersonville prison.
16. Edmund Ruffin, the Virginia plantation lord who had the honor of firing the first shot on Fort Sumter.
17. Barnard Bee. In trying to rally his own troops, Gen. Bee supposedly uttered the immortal words, "Look at Jackson's bridge! It stands like a stone wall! Rally behind the Virginians!" Some versions of the story have Bee proclaiming that Jackson himself stood like a stone wall. At any rate, Bee gave an immortal nickname to a great general. Bee himself died the day after the battle.
18. The Battle of Franklin, November 30, 1864. Six Confederate generals died in the battle.
19. Tom Cat, the garrison's mascot.
20. Albert Sidney Johnston at the Battle of Shiloh, April 1862.

21. What devout general died, as he had always wished, on a Sunday?
22. What was the fate of Horace Hunley, creator of the Confederacy's only submarine?
23. What caused the death of President Jefferson Davis's five-year-old son Joe in 1864?
24. Why was Gen. Stephen Dodson Ramseur wearing a white flower when he was fatally wounded at Cedar Creek?
25. Who died at the Virginia home of Bessie Shackelford in March 1863?
26. Why is there a monument to Lt. Col. John Quincy Marr at Fairfax Courthouse, Virginia?
27. What minor injury at Gettysburg led to the death of William Dorsey Pender?
28. What courageous general's last words before he died at Gettysburg were "Give them the cold steel!"?
29. What governor died at the Battle of Shiloh in Tennessee?
30. What Southern governor committed suicide rather than surrender to the Union?
31. What longtime advocate of Southern nationalism died before the Confederacy did?
32. What brilliant Georgia lawyer bled to death from a thigh wound he received at Fredericksburg in December 1862?
33. What port city had 10 percent of its population die from a yellow fever epidemic in 1862?
34. What was the irony of the popular sentimental ballad "The Drummer Boy of Shiloh"?
35. What was the Bloody Pond at the Battle of Shiloh?
36. Who died in the office building of a plantation called Fairfield?
37. What much-loved general died instantly when a Federal cannon shot struck him in the chest at Pine Mountain, Georgia?
38. In what peculiar fashion did 200 Rebel soldiers die in Petersburg, Virginia, on July 30, 1864?
39. Who died with a bag of $2,000 in gold around her neck?
40. What famous Rebel horseman was fatally wounded by a man on foot?
41. What Southern governor died just as his state was gearing up for war?
42. What 61-year-old Tennessean was promoted to major general after his death?
43. What general's death led to a warmer relationship between Robert E. Lee and James Longstreet?
44. What brave general died in Alabama when he fell from his horse because of a broken stirrup?

21. Thomas "Stonewall" Jackson.
22. He died in a sinking (not the final one) of his creation.
23. He fell from a balcony at the Confederate White House.
24. In honor of his firstborn child, whom he never saw.
25. Her fiancé, cavalry hero John Pelham, the "Gallant Pelham."
26. Marr, killed by a stray bullet from a Federal rifle, was the first Confederate to die in the war.
27. He was struck in the leg by a shell fragment and ignored it. Many days later, infection had set in, and even after amputation it was too late to save him.
28. Lewis Addison Armistead.
29. Kentuckian George W. Johnson, who joined the Confederate army after the Union armies had taken control of Kentucky.
30. John Milton of Florida, who died April 1, 1865.
31. William L. Yancey, who died in July 1863.
32. Thomas Cobb, brother of noted statesman Howell Cobb.
33. Wilmington, North Carolina.
34. The boy who died at Shiloh was actually a Yankee, though this is not mentioned in the ballad.
35. A small pond where the wounded of both sides came to drink and bathe their wounds. Men and horses died there, coloring the water a dark red.
36. Thomas "Stonewall" Jackson.
37. Leonidas Polk, who had been Episcopal bishop of Louisiana.
38. They were killed in the Crater explosion, in which a 586-foot tunnel had been dug by the Union under the Confederate entrenchments and packed with gunpowder.
39. Noted spy Rose O'Neal Greenhow, who drowned when her boat capsized.
40. The dashing J. E. B. Stuart, shot at Yellow Tavern, Virginia.
41. North Carolinian Gov. John W. Ellis.
42. Daniel Donelson, who had distinguished himself at Stone's River.
43. Thomas "Stonewall" Jackson's. Jackson and Longstreet had always been somewhat hostile.
44. Mississippi Gen. William Edwin Baldwin.

45. What Georgia general died at First Manassas, his last words being "They have killed me, boys, but never give up the field"?
46. What general died of dysentery contracted during the long siege of Vicksburg?
47. What Kentucky general, later governor of the state, died in 1914 at the age of 91?
48. What French-born general died in poverty at Richmond's Confederate Soldiers' Home in 1896?
49. What did 24-year-old Gen. James Dearing die from, three days before the Appomattox surrender?
50. What fate befell 51-year-old Louisiana general Adley Hogan Gladden at the Battle of Shiloh?
51. What Ohio-born general died at Seven Pines just eight days after being made brigadier general?
52. What tough cavalryman from Florida died after being shot through the heart at Pea Ridge?
53. What burden of guilt can probably be attached to the 18th North Carolina regiment?
54. What Tennessee college professor was mortally wounded at the Battle of Franklin, one of six Confederate generals dying there?
55. What gallant North Carolina general was mortally wounded at Spotsylvania in May 1864?
56. What non-combat death did Gen. Lucius Walker meet with?
57. What brigadier general's gory death by an exploding shell went unlamented by his own men?
58. What general who died at Gettysburg was brother of a Confederate naval hero?
59. What brave Tennessee general died in an insane asylum at the age of 85?
60. What was the only casualty in the famous *Monitor-Merrimack* battle?

45. Francis Bartow. The Confederate Congress adjourned for one day in his honor.
46. John Stevens Bowen, buried at the Confederate Cemetery at Vicksburg.
47. Simon Bolivar Buckner.
48. Raleigh Colston, former professor at VMI.
49. A fatal wound from a duel with a Union officer, who also died.
50. Being wounded in the arm, his arm was amputated, but he died on the field anyway.
51. Robert Hopkins Hatton.
52. James McIntosh, who fell the same day as his close friend Ben McCulloch.
53. The fatal shooting of Thomas "Stonewall" Jackson after the Battle of Chancellorsville.
54. John Carpenter Carter.
55. Junius Daniel.
56. He was killed in a duel with Gen. John S. Marmaduke.
57. Charles Winder, commander of the Stonewall Brigade, despised by the men.
58. Paul Jones Semmes, brother of Raphael Semmes.
59. Thomas Benton Smith, whose brain was laid open by a Union officer's saber when Smith was captured at Nashville.
60. A Confederate shell hit one of the *Monitor*'s viewing slits, temporarily blinding the commander, John Worden.

⚑ They Did It First

1. What was the first Confederate capitol building?
2. What was the South's first ironclad ship?
3. At what battle was the infamous "Rebel yell" first heard?
4. What honor was given to 67-year-old secessionist Edmund Ruffin on April 12, 1861?
5. What was Robert E. Lee's first official post in the Confederacy?
6. What dubious distinction did Gen. Robert Garnett have in the Civil War?
7. Where was "Stonewall" Jackson's first military command?
8. What innovative weapons were first deployed in July 1861 in the Potomac River?
9. What state was the scene of the first military reconnaissance by balloon?
10. Where was the first successful invasion of Confederate territory?
11. Who were the first five full generals named by the Confederacy?
12. Who was the first Confederate buried in Richmond's Hollywood Cemetery, the great resting place of famous Confederates?
13. What elected body met officially for the first time in Richmond in February 1862?
14. What was the first major Southern city to be permanently occupied by Union troops?
15. What innovative weapon saw its first use in Middleburg, Virginia, in 1862?
16. What became of the first Confederate flag ever made?
17. What South Carolina city was the first Southern place to see the Union's first all-black regiment?
18. What innovative item arrived in Charleston in August 15, 1863?
19. What momentous event in the world's naval history occurred on February 17, 1864?
20. What was the first combined army-navy operation in the war?
21. Which badly divided border state saw first blood spilled in the riots of March 1861?
22. When President Jefferson Davis issued his first call for troops, how many did he ask for?
23. What Virginia area was the site of the first aircraft carrier?
24. What new object was raised over the Capitol in Montgomery on March 4, 1861?
25. Where was the first use of land mines by the Confederacy?
26. Who was Virginia's first martyr in the war?
27. What was the first aggressive act of the pro-secession government in Arkansas?
28. What state saw the first real fighting in the war, with an exchange of fire in early January 1861?

🔖 They Did It First (answers)

1. The Alabama State House in Montgomery.
2. The CSS *Virginia*, built from the captured USS *Merrimack*.
3. The First Battle of Manassas, July 21, 1861.
4. Firing the first shot on Fort Sumter.
5. Commander of the defenses of Virginia.
6. He was the first general to be killed.
7. At Harper's Ferry, Virginia (later West Virginia).
8. Mines, at that time called "torpedoes." The Confederates were first to use them.
9. Virginia.
10. At Hatteras in North Carolina, where Confederates tried to keep the inlet clear for their blockade runners. They failed.
11. Samuel Cooper, Albert Sidney Johnston, Robert E. Lee, Joseph E. Johnston, and P. G. T. Beauregard.
12. Former President John Tyler, who had been elected to the Confederate Congress before he died in 1862.
13. The Confederate Congress.
14. Nashville, Tennessee.
15. The early form of machine gun, used by the Union against Confederate troops.
16. It draped the casket of Thomas "Stonewall" Jackson.
17. Port Royal. The 54th Massachusetts Volunteers arrived in June 1863. (This was seen in the movie *Glory*.)
18. The Confederacy's first submarine, the *Hunley*.
19. The first combat sinking of a ship by a submarine. The CSS *H. L. Hunley* sank the USS *Housatonic*.
20. The Union's capture of the Confederate forts guarding the important Hatteras Inlet in North Carolina.
21. Maryland. The Baltimore Riots were quite violent.
22. He asked for 100,000.
23. Hampton Roads, where the Union ship *Fanny* had a reconnaissance balloon launched from its deck in August 1861.
24. The first Confederate flag, the original Stars and Bars.
25. The Battle of Yorktown in 1862.
26. Alexandria hotel manager James T. Jackson, who killed Union Col. Elmer Ellsworth for removing the Confederate flag from Jackson's hotel. A private in Ellsworth's regiment then killed Jackson.
27. Seizing the Federal arsenal at Little Rock.
28. Florida, where state troops seized Fort Marion near St. Augustine and Forts McCree and Barrancas near Pensacola.

29. What noted general's first command was Commander of the Department of Florida?
30. What was the first Northern state to send volunteers to fight the Confederacy?
31. What Confederate city ranked first in manufacturing?
32. What was the first Confederate state to ratify the 13th Amendment, ending slavery?
33. What well-known song was first performed at 1861 at a variety show in Jackson, Mississippi?
34. What was the first Indian tribe to declare itself on the Confederate side?
35. What body met for the first time on February 18, 1862?
36. What type of soldier boasted that he was "First at Bethel, last at Appomattox"?
37. Who received the first Thanks of the Confederate States Congress in February 1861?
38. Who was the first general to receive a Thanks of Congress from the Confederacy?
39. What was the first Confederate victory to produce panic in Washington?
40. What Southern state is mentioned first in the unofficial Confederate anthem, "The Bonnie Blue Flag"?
41. Who was the first Confederate general to commit suicide in the war years?
42. What was the first convention at which South Carolina proposed secession of all Southern states?
43. What Louisiana general had graduated first in his class at West Point?
44. What Virginia Military Institute graduate was the first Confederate to die in the war?
45. What contribution did Clement Stevens make to military history?
46. What naval officer had been the first head of the U.S. Naval Academy at Annapolis?
47. According to tradition, what Union officer at Fort Sumter fired the first shot against the Confederacy?
48. What member of the distinguished Lee family graduated first in his class at West Point?
49. What was Nicola Marschall famous for?
50. What noted Confederate scientist was the first man to identify the Gulf Stream?
51. What historic deed was done by the USS *Sabine* in Pensacola, Florida, in April 1861?
52. What was the first title of the song "Dixie"?
53. What was the first Northern state to make the offer of men and money to fight the secession states?

29. Robert E. Lee. This is a forgotten stage of his career.
30. Pennsylvania.
31. Richmond.
32. Tennessee.
33. "The Bonnie Blue Flag," written by English-born entertainer Harry McCarthy.
34. The Choctaws, February 1861.
35. A bicameral Confederate Congress.
36. The Tarheels of North Carolina.
37. The state of Alabama, for loaning $500,000 to the Confederacy.
38. P. G. T. Beauregard for his action in the taking of Fort Sumter.
39. Bull Run, which put the victorious Rebels very near the city.
40. South Carolina—the first to secede, of course.
41. Philip St. George Cocke, who killed himself in December 1861.
42. The Nashville Convention, 1850, a meeting of delegates from the slave states to discuss Southern unity.
43. Paul Hébert, a classmate of William T. Sherman and George Thomas.
44. John Quincy Marr, who was killed by a random bullet from Federals firing at Fairfax Courthouse, Virginia.
45. He designed an iron-plated battery near Charleston, possibly the first armored fortification in the world.
46. Franklin Buchanan.
47. Abner Doubleday, who is also credited with inventing baseball.
48. Custis Lee, Robert E. Lee's eldest son.
49. She designed the Stars and Bars, the first official Confederate flag.
50. Oceanographer Matthew F. Maury, the "Pathfinder of the Seas."
51. It was the first Union ship to blockade a Southern port—a key component in the South's defeat.
52. "I Wish I Was in Dixie's Land." Thankfully, it was shortened.
53. Massachusetts. This was appropriate, since it was the state with the most outspoken abolitionists.

♫ What's That Name Again?

Not every noted Confederate was named John, Robert, Mary, or Sarah. Test your knowledge of these unusual names, and keep in mind that these are real names, not nicknames.

1. What general's name was a statement of the Southern cause?
2. What Tennessee general's unusual name is last in any list of noted Confederates?
3. What noted Creole general had the longest name of any Confederate officer?
4. What unusually named Cherokee lawyer represented his people in the Confederate congress?
5. What general was also a bishop in the Episcopal church?
6. What governor of North Carolina was named for one of the twelve tribes of Israel?
7. What general was named for renowned American general Winfield Scott?
8. What Virginia general emigrated to Cuba after the war?
9. What general and chief of ordnance was name for an Old Testament king?
10. What Georgia general was named for a Roman emperor?
11. What were the first and middle names of Gen. "Rob" Wheat?
12. What was the last name of Alabama general James Thadeus ——?
13. What biblical name was the first name of Mr. Hotchkiss, Stonewall Jackson's noted map-maker?
14. What was the first name of Ohio-born Confederate general Johnson?
15. What were the first and middle names of Mr. Lamar, Confederate diplomat to Russia?
16. What was the first name of Gen. Law, noted for his feud with Gen. Longstreet?
17. What general was nephew of Robert E. Lee?
18. Who was the only Indian to become a Confederate general?
19. What oddly named general, born in Rhode Island, was noted for helping compile the Official Records of the Union and Confederate Armies?
20. What very young Alabama general bore the entire name of Southern orator John C. Calhoun?
21. What strangely named Kentucky governor allowed Confederate recruiters to operate in his state?
22. What German was a member of Jefferson Davis's cabinet?
23. What governor shared his name with a famous English poet?

✎ What's That Name Again? (answers)

1. States Rights Gist (1831–1864) of South Carolina.
2. Felix Zollicoffer.
3. Pierre Gustave Toutant Beauregard.
4. Elias Cornelius Boudinot (whose name is French, not Cherokee).
5. Leonidas Polk.
6. Zebulon Vance.
7. Winfield Scott Featherston of Tennessee.
8. Birkett Davenport Fry.
9. Josiah Gorgas.
10. Henry Constantine Wayne (Constantine, not Henry, was the emperor, but you knew that already.)
11. Chatham Roberdeau.
12. Holtzclaw.
13. Jedediah, who was usually just "Jed."
14. Bushrod.
15. Lucius Quintus Cincinnatus.
16. Evander.
17. Fitzhugh Lee, usually called "Fitz."
18. Stand Watie.
19. Lunsford Lindsay Lomax.
20. John Caldwell Calhoun Sanders, one of the Confederacy's youngest generals.
21. Beriah Magoffin. (Beriah is an Old Testament name, by the way.)
22. Christopher Gustavus Memminger, Secretary of the Treasury.
23. John Milton, governor of Florida.

24. What cantankerous man was the Confederacy's commissary general?
25. What general joined the Mexican army after the war and was killed in battle?
26. What general was named for the Great Liberator of Latin America?
27. What general was nephew of Louisiana general Leonidas Polk?
28. What general was named for a biblical angel?
29. What were the first and middle names of controversial Gen. Robertson?
30. What Georgia general was named for the French soldier who aided George Washington's army?
31. What Massachusetts-born Mississippi general was also noted as a professor?
32. What was the first name of Admiral Semmes?
33. What general was named for a leader in the 16th-century Protestant Reformation?
34. What were the first and middle names of Gen. Stevenson of Virginia?
35. What Georgia general had a very Roman-sounding name?
36. What Ohio-born Tennessee general was named for a lesser-known Roman emperor?
37. What was President Jefferson Davis's middle name?
38. What English-born Confederate general had served in the British army before leading a North Carolina regiment?
39. What general was named for a noted Swedish king and military leader?
40. What Tennessee general was named for the father of the prophet Samuel in the Bible?
41. Who was the war governor of Tennessee?
42. What were the names of Gen. C. M. Wilcox of North Carolina?
43. What Georgia general, named for an emperor, was made general after his death?
44. What Maine-born Confederate general was named for one of the twelve tribes of Israel?
45. What was the first name of Gen. Holmes, a North Carolina man and classmate of Robert E. Lee?
46. What was the feminine-sounding first name of Virginia Gen. Hunton?
47. Who had the sappiest name of any Confederate general?
48. Can you give the full name of the German-born cavalry officer who was the close friend of J. E. B. Stuart?
49. What Welshman made his reputation in the Confederate navy?
50. What Tennessee general had the first name of an Old Testament soldier and the last name that would remind you of sleep?

24. Lucius Bellinger Northrop.
25. Mosby Monroe Parsons.
26. Simon Bolivar Buckner of Kentucky.
27. Lucius Polk.
28. Gabriel James Rains of North Carolina.
29. Beverly Holcombe.
30. Lafayette McLaws.
31. Claudius Wistar Sears.
32. Raphael.
33. Martin Luther Smith.
34. Carter Littlepage.
35. Marcellus Augustus Stovall.
36. Otho French Strahl. (If you've heard of Emperor Otho, give yourself an "A plus" in Roman history.)
37. Finis, meaning "the last," since he was the last born of a large brood.
38. Collett Leventhorpe.
39. Gustavus Smith.
40. Elkanah Greer.
41. Isham Harris.
42. Cadmus Marcellus.
43. Claudius Charles Wilson.
44. Zebulon York.
45. Theophilus.
46. Eppa, whose post-war career as a politician was more distinguished than his Confederate military career.
47. Probably John Marmaduke Sappington of Missouri.
48. Johann August Heinrich Heros von Borcke, often called (for obvious reasons) simply "Von," and also known as "Long Blade."
49. Catesby ap Roger Jones. The "ap" is the Welsh equivalent of the "O'" in Irish names and the "Mac" in Scotch and Irish names.
50. Gideon Pillow.

⚑ Brother Against Brother, and Other Family Matters

Did brothers literally fight against brother in the Civil War? Indeed they did, in some cases at the higher echelons. Just as often, of course, brothers fought beside brothers. In a divided America, family relations became complex and sometimes strained. A Southern man married to a Northern woman aroused suspicions on both sides. So did Southern-born men who fought on the Union side.

1. What dashing Confederate general was married to the daughter of a Union general?
2. What relation was Gen. Richard Taylor to President Jefferson Davis?
3. What Confederate cavalry general had a grudge against the Union because his brother had been murdered by a Union patrol?
4. What senator (and father of a Confederate general and Union general) worked successfully to keep his home state neutral in the war?
5. What Virginia clan had the highest number of Confederate generals in a single family?
6. What general was Gen. A. P. Hill's brother-in-law?
7. What U.S. president was uncle of Tennessee general Lucius Marshall Walker?
8. What relation were Generals Thomas "Stonewall" Jackson and Daniel Harvey Hill?
9. What caused of the death of President Jefferson Davis's five-year-old son Joe in 1864?
10. Why did Abraham Lincoln's family mourn the death of Confederate Gen. Ben Hardin Helm at the Battle of Chickamauga?
11. What general carried a sword that his father had used against the British in the Revolutionary War?
12. What honor did the Confederacy give to the granddaughter of former president John Tyler?
13. What noted Confederate general was uncle of Indian agent Elias Boudinot?
14. What U.S. official, largely responsible for preventing Europe from giving diplomatic recognition to the Confederacy, was the son and grandson of U.S. presidents?
15. What Union general had a son and son-in-law who were Confederate generals?
16. What Georgia statesman was urging his state toward secession while his brother, the governor, urged compromise?

✎ Brother Against Brother, and Other Family Matters

(answers)

1. J. E. B. Stuart, whose father-in-law was Philip St. George Cooke.
2. Brother-in-law. Davis's first wife was Taylor's sister.
3. Turner Ashby.
4. John J. Crittenden of Kentucky.
5. The Lees, of course. Besides Robert E. Lee, there were his sons Custis and "Rooney," and Robert's nephew, Fitzhugh.
6. John Hunt Morgan, brother of Hill's beautiful wife Molly.
7. James K. Polk.
8. Brothers-in-law. Jackson was married to Mary Anna Morrison, sister of Hill's wife Isabella Morrison.
9. He fell from a balcony at the Confederate White House.
10. Helm's wife was the sister of the president's wife.
11. Joseph E. Johnston.
12. Raising the first Confederate flag over the capitol in Montgomery.
13. Stand Watie. Both were Cherokees.
14. Charles Francis Adams, son of John Quincy and grandson of John.
15. Philip St. George Cooke, father of John Cooke, father-in-law of J. E. B. Stuart.
16. Thomas Cobb, brother of Howell Cobb. Both became Confederate generals.

17. What South Carolina soldier had to defend Port Royal against an attack from his brother?
18. What Kentucky general was the brother-in-law of Gen. John Hunt Morgan?
19. What two Alabama brothers were both wounded at Dranesville, Virginia?
20. What relation were Generals James Harrison and Thomas Harrison?
21. What general was married to the daughter of South Carolina governor Francis Pickens?
22. What future general had almost been expelled from West Point by his uncle, the superintendent?
23. What relation was Gen. Leonidas Polk to Gen. Lucius Polk?
24. What North Carolina general had his son serving as his aide?
25. What relation were Gen. Robert Garnett and Gen. Richard Garnett?
26. What relation was Richard L. Page to Robert E. Lee?
27. What Union general was the brother of a Confederate general and son of a great congressional compromiser?
28. What relation were Texas generals Ben McCulloch and Henry McCulloch?
29. What relation was Gen. William L. "Mudwall" Jackson to Thomas "Stonewall" Jackson?
30. What ill-fated general was the brother-in-law of Gen. William Preston?
31. What relation were Gabriel Rains and George Rains, both Confederate generals?
32. What general who died at Gettysburg was brother of a Confederate naval hero?
33. What relation were Confederate Gen. James McIntosh and Union Gen. John McIntosh?
34. What relation were Louisiana generals Louis Hébert and Paul Hébert?
35. What relation was Gen. Walter Stevens to Gen. Paul Hébert?
36. What general fled with his son to Egypt after the war, with both men serving in the Egyptian army?
37. What Confederate official was the son-in-law of a president?
38. What general had a son who survived the wreck of the *Titanic*?
39. What general had introduced U. S. Grant to his cousin Julia Dent, who Grant married?
40. What general was married to the daughter of the chief justice of Pennsylvania?
41. Why did Confederate soldiers in Petersburg, Virginia, light bonfires?

17. Thomas Drayton, whose brother, Union Cmdr. Percival Drayton, commanded the lead Union warship.
18. Basil Duke.
19. John Horace Forney and William Henry Forney.
20. Brothers.
21. Matthew Calbraith Butler.
22. Fitzhugh Lee, nephew of Robert E. Lee.
23. His uncle.
24. Lewis Addison Armistead, who was killed at Gettysburg.
25. They were cousins, both in the same class at West Point.
26. Cousin. They resembled each other a great deal.
27. Thomas L. Crittenden, brother of George Crittenden and son of John J. Crittenden.
28. Brothers.
29. Cousins, both born in the same town, Clarksburg, Virginia (now in West Virginia).
30. Albert Sidney Johnston, who died at Shiloh, was married to Preston's sister.
31. Brothers. Gabriel was the older.
32. Paul Jones Semmes, brother of Raphael Semmes.
33. Brothers.
34. Cousins.
35. Brother-in-law. Stevens had married Hébert's sister.
36. Alexander Reynolds and his son Frank.
37. Jefferson Davis. His first wife was the daughter of Zachary Taylor.
38. Archibald Gracie, Jr., whose son, Archibald III, was a West Point grad as his father was.
39. James Longstreet.
40. Richard Anderson, who aroused some suspicions by having a Yankee wife.
41. In honor of the birth of a son to Gen. George Pickett.

42. What general, brother of a Union general, ruined his military career by drinking on duty?
43. What was the distinction of David Barton of Winchester, Virginia?
44. What Confederate general had the most divided family in the Civil War?
45. What world-famous general alienated his father-in-law, a staunch Unionist and a college president?
46. What painful personal news did President Jefferson Davis receive in June 1863?
47. What Union general issued an order that banished from their home any family with a father, husband, or brother in the Confederate army?
48. What relation was Gen. Robert Vance to North Carolina Gov. Zebulon Vance?
49. What Confederate Cabinet member was a grandson of Thomas Jefferson?
50. Who was the "Daughter of the Confederacy"?
51. What distinction was held by Mrs. Enoch Cook of Alabama?
52. What officer alienated his Virginia family when he turned down a Confederate commission and sided with the Union?
53. What noted U.S. official had three brothers-in-law who were Confederate officers?
54. What was a "cousinwealth"?
55. What fate befell Union Gen. William Terrill and Confederate Gen. James Terrill, who were brothers?
56. What noted author served on the staff of his cousin-by-marriage, J. E. B. Stuart?
57. What relation to President Jefferson Davis was Gen. Joseph Robert Davis?

42. George Crittenden, brother of Thomas Crittenden.
43. He had six sons in the famous Stonewall Brigade.
44. John Rogers Cooke, whose father was Union Gen. Philip St. George Cooke and whose sister Flora married cavalry leader J. E. B. Stuart.
45. Thomas "Stonewall" Jackson. Dr. George Junkin, president of Washington College, was the father of Jackson's first wife Eleanor.
46. His family plantation, Brierfield, had been burned by Federal troops.
47. U. S. Grant. The order was never actually enforced.
48. Brothers. Robert was older.
49. George W. Randolph, Secretary of War.
50. Jefferson Davis's daughter, Varina Anne Jefferson Davis, born in wartime (1864).
51. She had a husband, ten sons, and two grandsons in the Confederate army.
52. George H. Thomas, a native of Southampton County, Virginia.
53. Lincoln.
54. A locally raised military unit, so called because many of the men were related by blood. There were many "cousinwealths" in the Confederate army.
55. Both died in the war, and their father buried them in a single grave.
56. John Esten Cooke, who admired Stuart greatly. Stuart, in turn, referred to Cooke as "an enormous bore."
57. Nephew.

⚐ Quotable Quotes (Part 2)

1. What general uttered the famous words, "There is Jackson standing like a stone wall"?
2. What cavalry general was Lee speaking of when he said, "He never brought me a piece of false information"?
3. What general had taken as his youthful motto, "You may be whatever you resolve to be"?
4. What leader said, at the war's beginning, "We are without machinery, without means, and threatened by a powerful opposition, but I do not despond"?
5. What Union general sent these words to Fort Donelson in Tennessee: "No terms except an unconditional and immediate surrender"?
6. What Union general said, prior to Antietam, "If I cannot whip Bobby Lee, I will be willing to go home"?
7. What battle was Lee lamenting when he said, "This has been a sad day for us, a sad day, but we can't expect always to gain victories"?
8. What Union general, who made his reputation in terrorizing Georgia, is supposed to have said, "War is hell"?
9. What courageous cavalryman said, "All I ask of fate is that I may be killed leading a cavalry charge"?
10. What noble leader said, "It is well war is so terrible, or we should get too fond of it"?
11. What general said before the Battle of Spotsylvania, "I shall come out of this fight a live major general or a dead brigadier"?
12. What Indiana-born general claimed he joined the Confederate army because of his "aristocratic inclinations and admiration for the South"?
13. What Tennessee general was called by Sherman "the most remarkable man our Civil War produced"?
14. What former Confederate soldier later became world famous for tracking down missionary David Livingstone in Africa?
15. What general received a promotion even after bad-mouthing his superior, Gen. Edmund Kirby Smith?
16. What spunky general, seriously wounded at First Manassas, told his surgeon "I don't feel like dying yet" and recovered?
17. What quarrelsome general uttered the famous words "History will award the main honor where it is due—to the private soldier"?
18. What fearless cavalry leader was "Stonewall" Jackson referring to when he said, "As a partisan officer I never knew his superior"?
19. What notorious Union ship was called a "Yankee cheese box on a raft"?

✎ Quotable Quotes (Part 2) (answers)

1. Gen. Barnard Bee, speaking of Thomas J. Jackson at First Manassas. Bee died in the battle.
2. J. E. B. Stuart, who had just been killed.
3. Thomas "Stonewall" Jackson.
4. President Jefferson Davis.
5. U. S. Grant, earning him his nickname, "Unconditional Surrender."
6. George B. McClellan.
7. Gettysburg.
8. William T. Sherman, who also said, "War at best is barbarism."
9. J. E. B. Stuart.
10. Robert E. Lee.
11. Abner Monroe Perrin, who became a dead brigadier.
12. Francis Asbury Shoup.
13. Nathan Bedford Forrest.
14. Henry Morton Stanley (famous for "Dr. Livingstone, I presume?").
15. Richard Taylor, who had called Smith "stupid, pig-headed, and obstinate."
16. Chatham Roberdeau "Rob" Wheat.
17. Braxton Bragg.
18. Turner Ashby, killed in June 1862.
19. The *Monitor*.

20. What Confederate naval hero was given instructions to "do the enemy's commerce the greatest injury in the shortest time"?
21. What war criminal's last words, spoken to his executioner, were "I know what orders are—I am being hung for obeying them"?
22. What statesman referred to West Point graduates who joined the Confederacy as men who "proved false to the land which had pampered them"?
23. What Knoxville, Tennessee, newspaper editor declared that he would "fight the secessionist leaders till hell froze over"?
24. What Confederate Cabinet member was said to look like "a man who has been in his grave a month"?
25. How did North Carolina Gov. John Ellis react to a telegraph from U.S. Secretary of War Simon Cameron, requesting troops for the Union?
26. What green Confederate officer, who later won the nickname "Old Reliable," told his wife "My first drill will be on the battlefield"?
27. What general said, "I cannot consent to place in the control of others one who cannot control himself"?
28. Who stated that his chief military strategy was "always mystify, mislead, and surprise the enemy"?
29. What spunky cavalryman said, after being mortally wounded, "I had rather die than be whipped"?
30. What grumpy, foul-mouthed, hard-drinking general was called "my bad old man" by Robert E. Lee?
31. What general was offered a civil post after he lost both a leg and an arm, but refused?
32. What instructions did former Gen. Richard Ewell give regarding his tombstone?
33. What noble Tennessee general declined an offer to run for governor, saying, "I would feel dishonored in this hour of trial to quit the field"?
34. What Virginia officer was called "the most fearless man I ever knew" by Gen. Daniel Harvey Hill?
35. What prompted Confederate general Simon Bolivar Buckner to ask Kentuckians to "defend their homes against the invasion of the North"?
36. What state's governor complained to the Confederate government that the Confederate cavalry in his state was doing immeasurable harm?
37. What portly Kentucky general was described by Braxton Bragg as doing "some fine running and no fighting"?
38. What general was a soldier describing when he said, "He looked as though he ought to have been and was the monarch of the world"?

20. Raphael Semmes.
21. Henry Wirz, commandant of Andersonville Prison, executed for "impairing the health and destroying the lives of prisoners."
22. Lincoln.
23. William G. Brownlow, one of the South's most famous Unionists.
24. Secretary of War James Seddon, who had a rather gaunt look due to poor health.
25. Ellis replied, "You can get no troops from North Carolina." The state then seceded.
26. John Bratton of South Carolina.
27. Robert E. Lee.
28. Thomas "Stonewall" Jackson.
29. J. E. B. Stuart.
30. Jubal Early, surely one of the Confederacy's crankiest officers.
31. John B. Hood, who replied, "No bombproof place for me."
32. He insisted that "nothing reflecting against the government of the United States is put upon it."
33. William Bate, who, after the war, was twice elected governor.
34. Samuel Garland, Jr., who was mortally wounded at South Mountain, Maryland.
35. The Kentucky legislature's order to expel all Confederate troops from the state.
36. North Carolina. Gov. Zebulon Vance claimed that the cavalry's seizure of horses and food was like "another plague on the Egyptians."
37. Humphrey Marshall, a 300-pounder who gave up soldiering to be a Confederate congressman.
38. Robert E. Lee.

39. What controversial general was described by a subordinate as "either stark mad or utterly incompetent"?
40. What Union general said, "My plans are perfect. May God have mercy on General Lee, for I will have none"?
41. On learning of a certain general's death, Lee said, "I have lost my right arm." Who was he?
42. Who said, quite correctly, "I can make Georgia howl"?
43. What crusty general said, "We haven't taken Washington, but we scared Abe Lincoln like hell"?
44. What Union general said, speaking of the Shenandoah Valley, "Eat out Virginia clear and clean so that crows flying over it will have to carry their fodder with them"?
45. What Confederate Cabinet member described the new nation as "cast upon the winds and waves"?
46. Who described the Confederates as having "unconquered and unconquerable hearts"?
47. What woman, famous for her diary of the war years, described Confederate leaders as having "a knack of hoping"?
48. What two-word phrase did Robert E. Lee always use to refer to Yankees?
49. What noted politician warned of the importance of Fort Sumter with these words: "The firing upon that fort will inaugurate a civil war greater than any the world has yet seen. It is suicide, murder, and will lose us every friend in the North"?
50. What hard-fighting general said at First Manassas, "Sir, we will give them the bayonet"?
51. What vain general described Thomas "Stonewall" Jackson as an "able, fearless soldier"?
52. What portly general did Jefferson Davis call "the vainest man I have ever met"?

39. Braxton Bragg.
40. Gen. Joseph Hooker, whose plans for Chancellorsville were definitely *not* perfect.
41. Thomas "Stonewall" Jackson.
42. William T. Sherman.
43. Jubal Early.
44. U. S. Grant.
45. Attorney General Thomas Bragg, brother of Gen. Braxton Bragg.
46. Jefferson Davis.
47. Mary Chesnut, famous for her *Diary from Dixie.*
48. "Those people."
49. Robert Toombs, who proved to be quite a prophet.
50. Thomas "Stonewall" Jackson.
51. P. G. T. Beauregard, the "Grand Creole."
52. Sterling Price of Missouri.

♭ Notable Women, and Some Less Notable

You won't find many statues or monuments to Confederate women, alas, but that doesn't mean they were unimportant. True, the men fought the battles and made the laws, but the women—some famous, some less so— kept the new nation humming at home, in the hospitals, and in a few places where you might not expect to find them.

1. Who was the "Daughter of the Confederacy"?
2. What city was the scene of the famous Bread Riot in which a horde of women, angry over high prices and the scarcity of goods, began looting stores?
3. Who was the only woman commissioned in the Confederate army?
4. When Union men looted Southern homes, what did some women use to hide small articles?
5. What group of women held raffles, auctions, and benefit concerts to raise money to build ironclads for the Confederacy?
6. What notorious Confederate spy killed a Union soldier who had insulted her mother?
7. What was the original purpose of the women who started the Richmond Bread Riot?
8. What woman wrote the most famous diary of the Civil War years?
9. What wife of a noted politician became an expert at forging her husband's signature on official documents?
10. What was the gist of the infamous Order No. 28, issued by Benjamin Butler in New Orleans?
11. How did the women of New Orleans respond to Union general Benjamin Butler's infamous Order No. 28?
12. What famous woman gave public readings titled *The Perils of a Spy*?
13. What was the source of the longstanding quarrel between President Jefferson Davis and General Joseph E. Johnston?
14. In what city did the Memorial Day holiday originate?
15. What Scottish-born nurse published *Hospital life in the Confederate Army of Tennessee*?
16. Where would Richmond spy Elizabeth Van Lew obtain the information she passed on to Union officers?
17. What was Nicola Marschall famous for?
18. What honor did the Confederacy give to the granddaughter of former president John Tyler?
19. What noted woman was a close friend of diarist Mary Chesnut?

✎ Notable Women, and Some Less Notable (answers)

1. Jefferson Davis's daughter, Varina Anne Jefferson Davis, born in wartime (1864). She became a novelist.
2. Richmond.
3. Captain Sally Tompkins, the compassionate head of a Richmond hospital.
4. Their hoop skirts.
5. The Ladies' Gunboat Societies.
6. Belle Boyd of Virginia, probably the Confederacy's most famous spy.
7. They had gathered for a church meeting. Their purpose soon changed.
8. Mary Chesnut, wife of Southern politician James Chesnut. Her *Diary from Dixie*, sometimes called *Mary Chesnut's Civil War*, is a classic of Confederate memoirs.
9. Varina Davis, wife of the president. She did this only when Davis was overworked or ill, and with his permission.
10. The "Woman's Order" announced that any woman showing open contempt for a Union soldier would be treated like a common prostitute.
11. They had his likeness painted on the bottom of chamber pots.
12. Belle Boyd.
13. According to rumor, they had a fight over a woman when both men were West Point cadets.
14. Petersburg, Virginia, where the wife of a Union officer saw schoolgirls decorating the graves of Confederate soldiers at Old Blandford Church. Reporting this to her husband, Gen. John Logan, he took steps that ultimately led to the observance of Memorial Day.
15. The energetic Kate Cumming.
16. In Richmond's Libby Prison, where she regularly visited Union prisoners, who gave her information about the Confederate troops they had recently seen.
17. She designed the Stars and Bars, the first official Confederate flag.
18. Raising the first Confederate flag over the Capitol in Montgomery.
19. Varina Davis, wife of Jefferson Davis.

20. What indignity was suffered by Union naval man David Farragut in the streets of New Orleans?
21. What woman wrote a popular book about serving in the Confederate army as a man named Harry Buford?
22. What belle of Richmond society married Gen. John Pegram and became a widow in three weeks?
23. What general had a teen-aged wife named LaSalle?
24. Who ran the famous Robertson Hospital in Richmond?
25. What was the distinction of Flora Cooke?
26. What general issued a stinging proclamation to the men of the South, telling them to rise up and defend the women from the ruffian Federals who treated them like common harlots?
27. What western Virginia spy, captured by Federals in 1862, took her guard's gun and shot him dead?
28. What did the Union do to intimidate fiery Confederate raider Hanse McNeill?
29. What Virginia general had five wives?
30. What major Richmond building exploded in 1863, killing 45 women and children?
31. Why did Abraham Lincoln's family mourn the death of Confederate Gen. Ben Hardin Helm at the Battle of Chickamauga?
32. What caused the Confederate government to begin hiring women, older men, and the disabled for government jobs in 1864?
33. What was the claim to fame of Richmond woman Mary Jackson?
34. How many women were arrested in New Orleans for violating Gen. Benjamin Butler's notorious General Order No. 28?
35. What noted woman had been born at "The Briars" near Natchez, Mississippi?
36. Who was originally supposed to own "Stonewall" Jackson's horse Little Sorrel?
37. Who wrote *A Southern Woman's Story*, a narrative of hospital life in Confederate Richmond?
38. What was John Slidell's chief asset as Confederate diplomat in France?
39. What Union general was mobbed by Southern women, begging his protection from "those Yankees"?
40. What Union spy and actress toasted President Jefferson Davis during one of her performances?
41. To whom did Varina Davis bequeath Beauvoir, the Davises' last home in Mississippi?
42. What was special about the woman guerrilla leader Sue Mundy?
43. What type of "camp servant" was often just a camp prostitute?

20. A local woman emptied a chamber pot on his head.
21. Loreta Janeta Velazquez. Her book *Woman in Battle* is probably more fiction than fact.
22. The lovely Hetty Cary. She and Pegram married in Richmond's St. Paul's Church. Three weeks later, his funeral was held there.
23. Gen. George Pickett.
24. Sally Tompkins. During her 45 months at the hospital, only 73 men died.
25. She was the wife of cavalry general J. E. B. Stuart, sister of infantry general John Rogers Cooke, and daughter of *Union* general Philip Cooke.
26. P. G. T. Beauregard.
27. Nancy Hart. Historians now wonder if Nancy Hart was real or fictitious.
28. Captured his wife and children and imprisoned them in Ohio.
29. John Daniel Imboden. (He had only one at a time, of course.)
30. The Confederate State Laboratory, part of the Richmond arsenal.
31. Helm's wife was the sister of the president's wife.
32. Shortage of army manpower. Able-bodied men in government jobs were needed to join the dwindling Confederate army.
33. She led the notorious "Bread Riot" in April 1863, in which women looted stores and marched on Capitol Square.
34. Only one. Thus the order, stating that any woman insulting a Union soldier would be treated like a prostitute, was highly effective.
35. Varina Davis, wife of the president.
36. It was to be a gift for his wife, Anna. Jackson took such a liking to the 11-year-old horse that he kept it for himself.
37. Phoebe Pember, one of the South's most respected nurses.
38. His marriage to a French Creole woman.
39. William T. Sherman, when he occupied Savannah, Georgia.
40. Pauline Cushman.
41. To the state, for use as a Confederate veterans' home.
42. "She" was actually a petite, long-haired man, Marcellus Clark. The Louisville newspaper who reported the Sue Mundy story hoped to embarrass the Union army.
43. A laundry woman. An order was issued stating that laundresses not actually doing laundry must be discharged.

44. What was the "flock of black sheep"?
45. What manufacturing facility produced Confederate uniforms?
46. What were the Confederacy's "silk dress balloons"?
47. What was the biggest complaint Confederate prisoners made about Union nursing chief Dorothea Dix?
48. What woman received a full military funeral when she died in Richmond in 1916?
49. What woman doctor, working for the Union, spent four months in a Confederate prison?
50. What Union nurse, who followed her husband on his marches, nursed both Confederates and Federals while in New Bern, North Carolina?
51. How could a Southern man in a Union-occupied area avoid taking the oath of loyalty to the Union?
52. In what sort of outfits did the women of Montgomery dress their children in spring 1861?
53. What general referred to his wife as "Mrs. Brown" (though *his* name wasn't Brown)?
54. What noted Confederate nurse constantly urged the South's women to care for wounded and disabled soldiers before and after the war?
55. What led Pennsylvania-born Josiah Gorgas to go South and head the Confederacy's ordnance corps?
56. What Confederate official was the son-in-law of a president?
57. What two Ohio sisters were noted as couriers, carrying messages between Confederate officers and pro-Southern politicians in the North?
58. What happened after the seriously wounded Gen. William S. Walker dictated his deathbed letters to his wife and friends?
59. What Baltimore belle defiantly waved the Rebel flag from her window as Union troops went by?
60. What controversial general's letters to his young wife are titled *Heart of a Soldier*?
61. What general was Gen. A. P. Hill's brother-in-law?
62. What general, imprisoned after Lee's surrender, was released because his wife had some clout with President Andrew Johnson?
63. What general was married to the daughter of the chief justice of Pennsylvania?
64. Without women as dance partners, how did the Confederate soldiers stage dances?
65. What talented woman wrote the 2-volume *Jefferson Davis: Ex-President of the Confederate States of America*?

44. The horde of blacks—mostly women and children—that had followed Sherman's armies through the Carolinas. Observers called them "black sheep."
45. None did. It was a "cottage industry" involving devoted Confederate women who turned Confederate-made cloth into finished uniforms.
46. Observation balloons made of colorful dress silk. (Contrary to a common belief, the balloons weren't actually made of women's dresses.)
47. That she only employed ugly women as nurses.
48. "Captain Sally," beloved hospital administrator Sally Tompkins.
49. Mary Edwards Walker. Oddly, she was captured while treating a Confederate soldier on a battlefield.
50. Kady Brownell.
51. Have his wife take the oath, thus allowing her the privileges of buying and selling which came with taking the oath.
52. The flashy Zouave outfits worn by some Southern soldiers, including some from Alabama.
53. Richard Ewell, who had married the widowed Mrs. Brown and continued to call her by that name.
54. Kate Cumming of Alabama.
55. His wife was an Alabamian, plus Gorgas thought of abolitionists as extremists.
56. Jefferson Davis. His first wife was the daughter of Zachary Taylor.
57. The Moon sisters, Lottie and Ginnie.
58. He recovered, thanks to a Union surgeon, and went on to fight more battles.
59. Hetty Cary. According to the tale, the Union officer thought her "too beautiful to arrest."
60. George Pickett's. His wife LaSalle was about half his age.
61. John Hunt Morgan, brother of Hill's beautiful wife Molly.
62. Richard Ewell, whose wife had known Johnson in Tennessee.
63. Richard Anderson, who aroused some suspicions by having a Yankee wife.
64. By just pairing off, which sometimes involved one dance partner donning a bonnet or some other article of women's clothing. Occasionally, of course, women were allowed to visit the camps, and dances involved the usual male-female couples.
65. His wife, Varina Davis.

66. What contribution did Marinda B. Moore make to children's literature?
67. What is the claim to fame of Barbara Fritchie?
68. Who was the "Siren of the Shenandoah"?
69. What relation were Generals Thomas "Stonewall" Jackson and Daniel Harvey Hill?
70. What crippled general died within 24 hours after his wife's funeral?
71. What noted woman died after leaving a captured ship and capsizing in her getaway boat?
72. Who was known as the "Florence Nightingale of the Confederacy"?
73. What general got married during the interval after his humiliating defeat at Gettysburg?
74. What wealthy Baton Rouge girl wrote a popular diary of the Civil War years?
75. What notable woman married the captain of the ship who captured her?
76. According to Mary Chesnut's diary, what were Confederate women almost always doing with their hands?
77. What Confederate general's widow caused an uproar in the Northern press when she visited the White House after her husband's death?
78. What Confederate spy went on to become a Hollywood actress?
79. Who was "Winnie"?
80. What did widow Sarah Anne Dorsey provide for Jefferson Davis after the war?
81. What belle endeared herself to the Confederacy by singing "Maryland, My Maryland" to the troops after the victory of First Manassas?
82. What man did spy Elizabeth Van Lew invite to tea when the Union troops entered Richmond?
83. What famous nurse traveled often through the Confederacy as she attended the Union wounded?
84. What new use did Confederate women find for grapevine?
85. Who married "Lizinka," the wealthy widow who had been his sweetheart in his younger days?

66. She wrote *The Dixie Speller* and *Geographical Reader for the Dixie Children*.
67. According to legend, elderly Barbara Fritchie defiantly waved her Union flag as "Stonewall" and his soldiers marched through her Maryland town. "Stonewall" being a gentleman, he did not shoot her.
68. Confederate spy Belle Boyd, who had a host of colorful nicknames.
69. Brothers-in-law. Jackson was married to Mary Anna Morrison, sister of Hill's wife Isabella Morrison.
70. Richard Ewell.
71. Noted Rebel spy Rose O'Neal Greenhow, who was carrying secret documents at the time.
72. Ella Newsom, a noted hospital administrator. As a wealthy physician's widow, she had both money and medical knowledge to aid in her work.
73. George E. Pickett, who married a woman half his age.
74. Sarah Morgan, whose diary is almost as popular as that of the renowned Mary Chesnut.
75. The great spy, Belle Boyd.
76. Knitting.
77. Emily Todd Helm, widow of Ben Hardin Helm and sister of Mrs. Abraham Lincoln. Emily had to take a loyalty oath to the Union.
78. Ginnie Moon, who, like her sister Lottie, carried messages between Confederate officers and Southern sympathizers in the North.
79. This was the nickname of the "Daughter of the Confederacy," Varina Anne Jefferson Davis.
80. Beauvoir, his Mississippi home during his last twelve years. She also helped Davis write his memoirs.
81. Hetty Cary, who was jestingly made a lieutenant colonel by Gen. Beauregard.
82. Union general U. S. Grant, her employer.
83. Clara Barton, who later founded the Red Cross.
84. In hard times, it served as hoops for skirts, or stays for corsets.
85. Gen. Richard Ewell, who had lost Lizinka Campbell to a rival during his youth.

⚑ Inventors, Scientists, and So Forth

War is a horrible thing, but it does seem to call forth human ingenuity. Confederate scientists and inventors made a contribution to human life, and not only in the military sphere. This is particularly remarkable considering that the South was basically an agricultural society, giving little incentive for scientific creativity.

1. What innovative weapon was invented by Gen. Gabriel Rains?
2. What original weapon was used only once in the Civil War, then retired for several years?
3. What innovative form of transportation arrived in Charleston in August 15, 1863?
4. What novel weapons were first deployed in July 1861 in the Potomac River?
5. What name is given to artillery shot designed to break apart on firing?
6. What role did Joseph Le Compte play in the Confederacy?
7. What Confederate invention was able to fire about 20 rounds per minute at a maximum range of 2,000 yards?
8. What Virginian, a noted secessionist agitator, was also one of the leading agricultural innovators of his day?
9. What invention did J. E. B. Stuart present to the U.S. war department?
10. What Confederate naval man invented a deep-sea sounding apparatus for mapping the ocean bottom?
11. What noted Union weapon was built by Swedish inventor John Ericsson?
12. What is the claim to fame of Robert Parker Parrott?
13. What popular game for soldiers was invented by a Union man who had defended Fort Sumter?
14. Who was a renowned oceanographer, the first man to describe the Gulf Stream and the man who standardized the logs kept by ship captains?
15. What contribution did Clement Stevens make to military history?
16. What general used his background as a chemist to improve the processing of gunpowder?
17. What harmless pursuit was the Prince de Polignac involved in before joining the Confederate army?

🖎 Inventors, Scientists, and So Forth

(answers)

1. The land mine, which many gentleman officers frowned on.
2. The early form of machine gun, used against Confederates in one battle. The gun was later improved by a Mr. Gatling.
3. The Confederacy's first submarine, the *Hunley.*
4. Mines, at that time called "torpedoes." The Confederates were first to use them.
5. Case shot, invented by the Englishman Henry Schrapnel.
6. Pioneering in the field of pharmacy, inventing new medicines and compounds.
7. The Williams rapid-fire gun. They fell out of use after the war.
8. Edmund Ruffin, who developed new ways of fertilizing the soil on his rundown farms.
9. A device for attaching a saber to a cavalry belt.
10. John M. Brooke, who also advocated the use of ironclads by the Confederacy.
11. The ironclad USS *Monitor* famous for its battle in Hampton Roads, Virginia.
12. He invented the widely used Parrott guns, cannons that could fire projectiles from 10 pounds to 250 pounds. Parrott guns, particularly the larger ones, were useful in battering masonry forts.
13. Baseball, supposedly invented by Abner Doubleday, who (according to tradition) fired the first shot in defense of Fort Sumter.
14. Matthew Fontaine Maury, the great figure in the Confederate navy, often called the "Pathfinder of the Seas."
15. He designed an iron-plated battery near Charleston, possibly the first armored fortification in the world.
16. George W. Rains, head of the Confederacy's Niter and Mining Bureau.
17. Studying plant life in Central America.

⚐ Some Major Personal Losses (Part 2)

1. What spunky cavalryman said, after being mortally wounded, "I had rather die than be whipped"?
2. What crippled general died within 24 hours after his wife's funeral?
3. Who was the only person who ever died at the Confederate White House in Richmond?
4. What general's death lead to a flood of sentimental songs and poems being written?
5. What brave North Carolina officer died in 1867 at age 27 from wounds from a Union sharpshooter?
6. What general sent a team to rescue captured partisan fighter Hanse McNeill?
7. What posthumous honor was given to Gen. Frank Paxton, one of "Stonewall" Jackson's "pets"?
8. What Mississippi general received a fatal wound after the assault on the Round Tops at Gettysburg?
9. What general's brigade became lost in the woods at Malvern Hill and suffered 33 casualties without firing a shot?
10. What name is given to Gen. James Fagan's 1864 action against Union Gen. Frederick Steele?
11. What Ohio-born general adopted Tennessee as his home state and died at the Battle of Franklin?
12. What did President Jefferson Davis do with every Confederate deserter condemned to death?
13. What famous general had a leg amputated after the Battle of Groveton in 1862?
14. What amputee general had to be tied to his horse when he took to the field?
15. What occurred at the First Battle of Manassas that horrified the residents of Washington?
16. What Louisiana officer lost his left arm and left foot fighting in Virginia?
17. What Virginia battle resulted in the loss of a leg for William Brandon, though he went on to fight at Gettysburg and Chickamauga?
18. What did South Carolina general James Conner lose at Cedar Creek in Virginia?
19. What did Texas Gen. Matthew Duncan Ector lose while fighting in the Atlanta campaign?
20. What capable general was fitted with a wooden leg after losing his leg at Groveton in 1862?
21. When Gen. William Bate was wounded at Shiloh, doctors insisted on amputating his left leg. How did Bate respond?

❧ Some Major Personal Losses (Part 2)

(answers)

1. J. E. B. Stuart.
2. Richard Ewell.
3. President Jefferson Davis's five-year-old son, Joe, who fell from a balcony.
4. Thomas "Stonewall" Jackson, killed at Chancellorsville in 1863.
5. John Decatur Barry.
6. Jubal Early. McNeill was rescued, but soon died of a wound.
7. He is buried just a few feet from Jackson. Both died at Chancellorsville.
8. William Barksdale, commander of the hard-fighting Barksdale's Mississippi Brigade.
9. Jubal Early.
10. "The slaughter of Mark's Mills," involving 1,600 Union casualties and the capture of 200 Union wagons.
11. Otho French Strahl, one of six Confederate generals who died at Franklin.
12. Commuted his sentence. Davis had a compassionate streak.
13. Richard S. Ewell.
14. John Hood, who had lost a leg and the use of one arm.
15. Wounded men of both armies were hobbling or crawling to the city for help. This impressed both sides with the need for better medical facilities for the armies.
16. Francis R. T. Nicholls.
17. Malvern Hill, in the Peninsula Campaign.
18. His leg, which had already been broken at Gaines' Mill.
19. A leg.
20. Richard S. Ewell, "Old Bald Head."
21. He drew a pistol on them. They did not amputate the leg.

22. What aggressive Ohio-born general lost a leg at Bentonville, one of the war's last battles?
23. Who was responsible for shooting and permanently blinding Gen. Adam Rankin Johnson?
24. What happened to Union general John Sedgwick after he boasted that the Rebels were so far from him that they couldn't shoot an elephant?
25. What general was killed in a rainstorm, wearing a conspicuous white raincoat?
26. What major Tennessee battle of 1862 saw nearly 24,000 men killed, wounded, or missing?
27. What was unusual about the Union drummer who killed a Confederate officer at Chickamauga?
28. What North Carolina general was killed instantly at Antietam by a head wound from a Union sharpshooter?
29. Who was killed at Franklin after raising his cap on his sword and leading his men forward?
30. How long had Victor Jean Baptiste Girardey been a general before he was killed?
31. What chubby New Yorker was killed near Petersburg in 1864, after which his father carried the body home to New York?
32. What courageous young South Carolina general was killed by his own troops in May 1864?
33. What controversial Virginia general was killed at Piedmont and buried on the field by Federals?
34. What Texas general, famous for wearing a black velvet suit, was killed at Pea Ridge in 1862?
35. What general killed Gen. Lucius Walker in a sunrise duel but was never prosecuted?
36. What honor fell to Private John Huff of the 5th Michigan Cavalry?
37. What did Matthew Butler lose at the Battle of Brandy Station?
38. What gritty Alabama general received four wounds at Gettysburg but did not halt his charge till a foot wound stopped him?

22. Daniel Reynolds, who considered Arkansas his adopted state.
23. His own troops—by accident, of course.
24. He was killed instantly, shot through the left eye by a Confederate sharpshooter.
25. Tennessean Felix Zollicoffer. The white raincoat made him an easy target for Union bullets.
26. The bloody Battle of Shiloh in April. It was bloodier than Napoleon's Battle of Waterloo.
27. He was 11 years old, the "Drummer Boy of Chickamauga," Johnny Clem.
28. Lawrence O'Bryan Branch.
29. Patrick Cleburne, one of several Confederate generals killed at the Battle of Franklin.
30. Only 17 days—after his unprecedented promotion from captain to brigadier general.
31. Archibald Gracie, Jr., a New York native who liked his adopted state of Alabama.
32. Micah Jenkins, widely mourned throughout the South.
33. William "Grumble" Jones, longtime antagonist of J. E. B. Stuart.
34. Ben McCulloch.
35. John S. Marmaduke, who had questioned Walker's courage.
36. He fired the shot that killed J. E. B. Stuart at Yellow Tavern.
37. His right foot, thanks to an artillery shell.
38. William Henry Forney, who received 13 wounds in the course of the war.

♫ Escapees, Refugees, and So Forth

1. What city's people started moving into caves to escape the Union siege?
2. What cheeky Confederate cavalryman escaped from a Columbus, Ohio, prison in 1863?
3. What Tennessee general defied a Tennessee state order and helped fleeing citizens load food supplies onto their wagons?
4. Who began looting Richmond at the time of evacuation?
5. What notorious outlaw was dressed as a woman as he escaped Union capture in Independence, Missouri?
6. What state's population was permanently increased by the Civil War?
7. When eight Confederate arsonists failed in their 1864 plot to set New York City ablaze, where did they flee?
8. What Southern association was formed to assist Union men escaping from Confederate prisons?
9. What Southern governor had to flee before Sherman's Union army and was imprisoned in Washington, D.C. after the war?
10. What governor served in three different state capitals during his term?
11. What governor fled to Cuba after the war but later returned home to rebuild his sugar plantation?
12. What two generals wrecked their military careers by their improper surrender of Fort Donelson?
13. What Kentuckian headed the Kentucky State Guard, refused a commission in the Union army, and fled south to avoid arrest as a suspected traitor?
14. What Missouri general fled his home in St. Louis because of local anti-Confederate feeling?
15. What Arkansas general fled North America after the war and lived on a small island in Brazil?
16. What caused Gen. John McCausland to flee to Europe after the war?
17. What noted naval man fled the South after the war, escaping to Cuba in a lifeboat?
18. What small town in Florida briefly became a refugee town for Confederates after the war?
19. Who published a well-received *History of the Mexican War*?
20. What acid-tongued general fled to Mexico after the war, swearing he would never live under the U.S. flag?
21. What cavalry wizard finally met his match in Selma, Alabama, in the war's closing days?

✎ Escapees, Refugees, and So Forth (answers)

1. Vicksburg, Mississippi.
2. John Hunt Morgan who had, according to one story, escaped through a tunnel.
3. Nathan Bedford Forrest. This occurred when Nashville was being evacuated.
4. Escapees from the state penitentiary (as if the poor city didn't have enough problems).
5. Cole Younger, of the infamous Younger gang, and a Confederate guerrilla.
6. Texas, which attracted many Confederate refugees fleeing Union occupation.
7. Toronto, Canada. They were wise to flee, since they would have been hanged if caught.
8. The Sons of America.
9. Joseph Brown of Georgia.
10. Thomas Moore. Fleeing the Union, the Louisiana capital moved from Baton Rouge to Opelousas to Shreveport.
11. Thomas Moore of Louisiana, whose plantation had been trashed by the Federals.
12. John Floyd and Gideon Pillow. Floyd, the commander, passed the command to Pillow, who passed it to Simon Bolivar Bucker. Floyd and Pillow then escaped before the surrender took place—a serious breach of military custom.
13. Simon Bolivar Buckner, one of Kentucky's finest Confederate generals.
14. Daniel Marsh Frost, who had hoped to see the whole state go Confederate.
15. Alexander Travis Hawthorne, who served as a missionary in Brazil.
16. He feared being arrested because of his role in the Confederates' burning of Chambersburg, Pennsylvania.
17. John Taylor Wood. Between Florida and Cuba he encountered pirates and a violent storm.
18. Madison.
19. Cadmus M. Wilcox, who, in addition to being a Confederate general, had served in the Mexican War and had fled there after the Civil War.
20. Jubal Early, who eventually did return to his native Virginia.
21. Nathan Bedford Forrest. Though his men lost in the skirmish, Forrest himself escaped.

22. What state saw many of its Confederate soldiers flee to Mexico when the war ended?
23. What special task did Douglas Cooper find that the Indians excelled at?
24. Where was Davis on the day of Lee's surrender to Grant?
25. What former U.S. vice-president and Confederate general fled to Cuba after the war and traveled there and in Europe for several years?
26. What governor fled to England after the war because he was charged with treason?

⏁ Immigrants, Foreigners, and Such

The Confederacy was more of an ethnic mix than is sometimes supposed. Though immigration in the 1840s and 1850s affected the Northeast and Midwest more than the South, the South had had, from its very beginnings, significant communities of Irish, Germans, French, and others. Some became sturdy soldiers of the Confederate rank and file, and a few went on to become generals.

1. What famous general was speaking French before he learned to speak English?
2. What ethnic group made up the renowned Texas unit called the Davis Guards?
3. What German was a member of Jefferson Davis's cabinet?
4. What Irish-born general had been a pharmacist, a lawyer, and a soldier in the British army?
5. Why did the Confederate draft bureau exempt foreigners from service as soldiers?
6. What did Englishman Harry McCarthy contribute to the Confederacy?
7. Who was the best-known foreign-born soldier of the Confederacy?
8. What Scottish-born nurse published *Hospital life in the Confederate Army of Tennessee*?
9. What Irish general graduated first in his class at the Virginia Military Institute and later taught math there?
10. What Frenchman served under French Creole P. G. T. Beauregard at the Battle of Shiloh?
11. Who was the only Jewish member of the Confederate Cabinet?
12. What redheaded Irishman achieved fame for beating back an attempted Union invasion of the Texas interior?
13. What much-loved substance caused a protest by some German soldiers when it was unobtainable?

22. Texas, naturally.
23. Tracking down escaped prisoners.
24. In Danville, Virginia. He departed the next day for Greensboro, North Carolina, hoping to escape the Union cavalry on his heels.
25. John C. Breckinridge.
26. Isham Harris of Tennessee.

🖋 Immigrants, Foreigners, and Such (answers)

1. P. G. T. Beauregard, "the Grand Creole," born to a French Creole family in Louisiana.
2. Irishmen.
3. Christopher Gustavus Memminger, Secretary of the Treasury.
4. Patrick Cleburne.
5. Many, especially Germans, were skilled at arms manufacture, and thus needed more in the iron works than in the army.
6. Its unofficial anthem, "The Bonnie Blue Flag."
7. Probably the dashing cavalryman Heros von Borcke, born in Germany, a close friend of Gen. J.E.B. Stuart.
8. The energetic Kate Cumming.
9. John McCausland.
10. The Prince de Polignac.
11. Judah Benjamin, who held three different positions.
12. Richard Dowling, who won the official Thanks of the Confederate Congress.
13. Coffee. Several German soldiers staged a mock funeral procession when they were told that coffee rations were suspended.

14. What English-born general was wounded and captured at Gettysburg, then imprisoned for nine months?
15. In what Florida battle did Irishman Joseph Finegan beat back the Union troops of Gen. Truman Seymour?
16. What was the ethnic background of the men of the Palmetto-Schutzen?
17. What Irish-born general distinguished himself as a cavalry commander in Texas and Louisiana?
18. What German unit of South Carolina cavalry was named for a famous Germany military unit?
19. What was the most pro-Confederate ethnic group in the South?
20. What noted French Creole general had once headed a *comité de vigilance* in his native Louisiana?
21. What unit, known as the "roughest battalion in the army," was composed largely of Irishmen and Frenchmen?
22. What name was given to the Macon German Artillery?
23. What large city had its own Irish brigade?
24. What now-common minority group served in a few regiments from Texas?
25. What nation was the birthplace of the only Confederate officer executed for war crimes?
26. What French official tried to settle Confederate veterans in Mexico after the war?

14. Collett Leventhorpe, who had married into a North Carolina family.
15. Olustee, the greatest Confederate victory in Florida.
16. German.
17. Walter P. Lane.
18. The Hussars.
19. Probably the Irish, many of whom saw soldiering as an exciting alternative to their usual work.
20. Alfred Mouton. A *comité de vigilance* is a band fighting against local outlaws and thieves.
21. The famous (or infamous) Louisiana Tigers.
22. The Jew Company—a respectful and accurate name, since most of its members were Jews.
23. New Orleans, with a large Irish population.
24. Mexican-Americans, naturally.
25. Switzerland, the homeland of Henry Wirz, commandant of Andersonville Prison. He was hanged for the horrible conditions at the prison.
26. Pierre Soulé, one of the Confederacy's more interesting immigrants.

⚐ Native Rebels: Confederate Indians

Indians in the Confederacy? Yes, indeed, and an important part of it, too. When the Civil War began, both South and North were eager for the Indians' aid. As the war progressed, both sides realized that Indian soldiers did not always follow established military procedures.

1. Who was the Confederacy's only Indian general?
2. What Indian nation declared itself for the Confederacy in February 1861?
3. What was the purpose of the Indian Grand Council on June 15, 1865?
4. What general was put in charge of making treaties with the Indians?
5. What Indian tribe sent a delegation to the Confederate Congress in Montgomery?
6. Who were the Five Civilized Tribes that signed treaties with the Confederacy?
7. What was the only major battle in which Confederate Indians fought?
8. What did Confederate Indian soldiers do that outraged public opinion in the North?
9. After the war, what fate befell Indians who had aided the Confederacy?
10. How did the Indian word "Tsikamagi" enter American history?
11. What were the Choctaw Resolutions?
12. Why did the Indians of the Five Civilized Tribes readily sign treaties with the Confederate government?
13. When the Confederate government tried to make Indian soldiers promise to engage in "civilized warfare," what practice were they trying to stop?
14. What famous frontiersman said he had joined the Union army to fight Confederates, when in fact he spent the war mostly fighting Indians?
15. What Confederate governor had to deal not only with Union armies but with Indian raids?
16. What noted Confederate general was uncle of Indian agent Elias Boudinot?
17. What tough Texan had launched his military career as an Indian fighter at age seventeen?
18. What sort of people did Douglas Cooper organize for the Confederate army?
19. What was the Confederacy's main reason for forming alliances with Indian tribes?

✎ Native Rebels: Confederate Indians (answers)

1. Stand Watie, a Cherokee born in Georgia.
2. The Choctaws.
3. Confederate Indians met to discuss making peace with the Federals.
4. Albert Pike.
5. The Choctaws.
6. Cherokees, Creeks, Choctaws, Chickasaws, and Seminoles.
7. Pea Ridge, Arkansas, March 1862, where they performed well.
8. Scalped defeated Union soldiers.
9. All treaties with them were declared void.
10. The name eventually became "Chickamauga," one of the great battles of the Civil War.
11. A declaration of the Choctaw nation that they sided with the Confederacy.
12. The Confederacy was willing to establish them as near-equals with white men, going far beyond the Union.
13. Scalping, which the Indians routinely performed on defeated foes.
14. Christopher Carson, better known as "Kit."
15. Edward Clark of Texas.
16. Stand Watie. Both were Cherokees.
17. John Robert Baylor.
18. Choctaw and Chickasaw Indians, which he commanded on the field.
19. Fear that the Indians would take advantage of the war and raid white settlements, especially in Texas.

20. What noted general had been wounded by a Florida Indian attack in 1838?
21. What leader of Confederate Indians avoided arrest and court-martial by hiding in the Arkansas hills?
22. What was the first Indian tribe to declare itself on the Confederate side?
23. Who was elected by the Cherokees to represent them in the Confederate Congress?
24. What rash act got John Robert Baylor removed from his post as Confederate governor of the New Mexico Territory?
25. Why did the Confederate government turn down Douglas Cooper's proposal to use Indians as guerrilla fighters in Missouri?
26. What famous American treaty had been signed by Stand Watie, who became the Confederacy's only Indian general?
27. How many Indian regiments served the Confederacy?
28. What role did George Washington play in the Confederate army?
29. What special weapons did the Indian fighters bring to the Confederate cause?
30. What noted general died, appropriately, in Oklahoma?
31. What Indian tribe rebelled during the Civil War, angered at not having citizenship rights?
32. Who led the Cherokee Mounted Rifles?
33. What Indian name was given to the Elijah White's wild band of guerrillas?
34. What conflict in the pre-war South led many Northern men to grow attached to the South, a fact that greatly influenced the number of Confederate officers?
35. What general kept an Apache boy as his personal servant?
36. What general had just finished an expedition against the Navajos in New Mexico when the war began?
37. What general had been one of Texas' best-known fighters against Comanches?
38. What special task did Douglas Cooper find that the Indians excelled at?
39. Who was Da-ga-ta-ga?

20. Joseph E. Johnston.
21. Albert Pike, later a leader among the Freemasons.
22. The Choctaws, February 1861.
23. Elias Boudinot, who had a committee voice but no House vote.
24. Baylor announced plans to trap and exterminate the Apache Indians.
25. The government feared the Indians would scalp and mutilate people, something the Federals would publicize widely.
26. The 1835 treaty in which the Cherokees gave up all their Georgia land and moved to Oklahoma.
27. Eleven, plus seven independent battalions in the West.
28. He was a Caddo Indian chief on the Confederate side.
29. Bows and arrows, tomahawks, and war clubs, naturally.
30. Stand Watie, the Confederacy's only Indian general. Until it became a state, Oklahoma was the Indian Territory.
31. The Lumbees, from the area around Pembroke, North Carolina.
32. Stand Watie, the Confederacy's only Indian general.
33. Comanches.
34. The Seminole Wars in Florida, which gave many Northerners their first exposure to Southern charm.
35. Gen. Richard Ewell, "Old Baldy."
36. Lafayette McLaws, nicknamed "Make Laws."
37. Lawrence Sullivan Ross.
38. Tracking down escaped prisoners.
39. Gen. Stand Watie. This was his Cherokee name.

Part 2

Military Matters

⚑ Star Men: The Generals

Were the Confederate generals all noble, chivalrous men of Robert E. Lee's caliber? Many were, but then, quite a few could make up a regular rogues gallery. Whether gallant or scandalous, they were certainly one of the most fascinating group of men ever to take on the daunting task of fighting a more powerful foe.

1. What beloved general's body was taken to the Richmond Capitol for viewing on May 12, 1863?
2. What general's birthplace lies only a short distance from the birthplace of George Washington?
3. What Tennessean, with no military training whatever, went from the rank of private to lieutenant general in three years?
4. What odd item would elderly Gen. William "Extra Billy" Smith carry while he was riding?
5. What were there more of—Southern-born Union generals or Northern-born Confederate generals?
6. Who was Gen. Richard Taylor's famous father?
7. When Union Gen. Edward Ord and Confederate Gen. James Longstreet had a tête-à-tête near Petersburg, what plan did they hatch?
8. What general was noted for curling both his hair and beard in ringlets?
9. What extremely religious general informed a captured Federal officer that his men would be imprisoned while the officer would be castrated?
10. What general usually bears the brunt of the blame for the Confederate defeat at Gettysburg?
11. What distinction did 23-year-old Gen. William Paul Roberts hold?
12. What Rebel general was known as the leader of a band of "merry men"?
13. What was the home state of Gen. States Rights Gist?
14. What tough-fighting brigade was Gen. John Gregg privileged to command?
15. What dreadful mistake did Gen. Ben Hardin Helm make that affected the Battle of Shiloh?
16. What cantankerous general had the reputation of "always stopping to quarrel with his generals"?
17. What future Confederate general commanded the company of U.S. Marines who trapped murderous abolitionist John Brown at Harpers Ferry?
18. What Union general's daughter was married to a Confederate general?
19. What general's mid-war wedding was performed by another general?

✎ Star Men: The Generals (answers)

1. Thomas "Stonewall" Jackson.
2. Robert E. Lee's. The Lee home, Stratford Hall, is still standing.
3. The remarkable Nathan Bedford Forrest.
4. A blue parasol.
5. Northern-born Confederate generals.
6. President Zachary Taylor.
7. They planned for the generals to suspend all fighting and let the politicians work out the details of a settlement. The plan went nowhere.
8. George E. Pickett.
9. Daniel Harvey Hill, who never cursed.
10. James Longstreet, whose slowness at the battle has been a subject of controversy.
11. The youngest Confederate general.
12. Cavalry leader John Hunt Morgan, whose brassy men often entered a town with "a whoop and a holler."
13. Appropriately, South Carolina, the hot-bed of states rights agitation.
14. The fearless Texas Brigade, originally commanded by John B. Hood.
15. He sent word to the Confederates that Union Gen. Grant was *not* on his way to reinforce the Federals. Grant was.
16. Braxton Bragg.
17. Robert E. Lee.
18. Philip St. George Cooke, whose daughter married J. E. B. Stuart.
19. John Hunt Morgan, whose wedding was performed by Gen. (and Bishop) Leonidas Polk.

20. What general may have been responsible for the infamous Lost Order, which gave the Federals information on Lee's Antietam battle plan?
21. What was Gen. P. G. T. Beauregard's first major accomplishment in the Civil War?
22. What was the one food that hypochondriac Gen. Richard Ewell would eat?
23. What did Union infantry major Richard C. Gatlin do after being captured by Arkansas state troops?
24. What general had eleven children during eleven years of marriage?
25. What important items were Gen. Henry Heth's troops searching for when they made the first encounter with Federals at Gettysburg?
26. What did Gen. Edward Johnson use as a cane after he suffered a foot wound?
27. Gen. Joseph E. Johnston ordered Gen. John Pemberton to evacuate Vicksburg. Who ordered Pemberton to stay?
28. What physical feature of Gen. Mansfield Lovell is sneered at in the "New Ballad of Lord Lovell"?
29. What Confederate general had been a law partner with former president James K. Polk?
30. What general, a noted ladies' man, was killed by a jealous husband in 1863?
31. What Confederate general literally marched his troops in circles to fool Union general McClellan into thinking the forces were much larger?
32. What notable accomplishment did cavalry general J. E. B. Stuart pull off in June 1862?
33. What general who had fought at Chickamauga later became commissioner of the Chickamauga and Chattanooga National Military Park?
34. Where did Gen. Stephen Elliott lose 700 of his brigade's men?
35. What Confederate defeat clouded the reputation of Gen. Richard S. Ewell?
36. What Virginia general had the daunting assignment as Gen. Jackson's successor leading the Stonewall Brigade?
37. What did Robert E. Lee give to 23-year-old William Paul Roberts when Roberts became the Confederacy's youngest general?
38. What U.S. senator had the agony of seeing two sons as Civil War generals on opposing sides?
39. What future general was made a U.S. cavalry colonel after the Confederacy had already been formed?
40. What general was in charge of moving weapon-making machinery from Harpers Ferry to points farther south?
41. What portly general led a fruitless raid through his home state, hoping the citizens would rise up and join the Confederate cause?

20. Daniel Harvey Hill. The copy of the order, intended for Hill, had been found by a Union soldier. Most likely one of Hill's staff officers lost the order—much to the South's regret.
21. The capture of Fort Sumter.
22. Frementy, a rather bland wheat preparation.
23. Joined the Confederate army, eventually becoming a general.
24. John B. Hood.
25. Shoes, desperately needed for the poor Confederate troops.
26. A very large club, which doubled as a weapon.
27. President Jefferson Davis.
28. His red nose, the result of frequent drinking.
29. A fellow Tennessean, Gideon Pillow.
30. Earl Van Dorn.
31. "Prince John" Magruder. The ruse was effective.
32. His famous ride around the army of Union general George McClellan. It accomplished little from a military standpoint, but it was a great morale-booster for the South.
33. Alexander P. Stewart, "Old Straight."
34. In the Crater, Petersburg, where Elliott himself was wounded.
35. Gettysburg. Ewell was sometimes blamed for not capturing Cemetery Hill there.
36. Richard Garnett, who had a running battle with Jackson afterward.
37. Lee's gauntlets.
38. John J. Crittenden of Kentucky.
39. Robert E. Lee. His home state, Virginia, had not yet joined the Confederacy.
40. Thomas "Stonewall" Jackson.
41. Sterling Price, former governor of Missouri.

42. What victorious general announced that the people of Missouri would have to forsake neutrality and go for either South or North?
43. What was shocking about the Confederacy's appointment of five full generals in August 1861?
44. What young Tennessee general's body was retrieved after the Battle of Stone's River and given a hero's burial in Nashville?
45. What Tennessee lawyer gave himself the title "General" and led a wild band of guerrillas in west Tennessee?
46. What was the crime of the 22 men executed by Gen. George Pickett in Kinston, North Carolina?
47. What Kentucky general had been offered a Union army commission by his brother-in-law, Abraham Lincoln?
48. Which of Lee's generals did he have the longest-running feud with?
49. What chemistry wiz became, after the war, a professor of chemistry?
50. What explanation did Clement Stevens give for Gen. "Stonewall" Jackson's nickname?
51. What Confederate subversive called himself "General" though he had no real military background?
52. What caused Gen. Patrick Cleburne to relinquish command at the Battle of Richmond, Kentucky?
53. What rash act did Gen. Philip St. George Cocke do after eight months of Confederate service?
54. What key Tennessee fort was named for the sixty-year-old general who built it?
55. Who was Union Cmdr. Percival Drayton's opponent in the Port Royal expedition?
56. Who, in post-war days, had a sign outside his Georgia home that read "Good Homemade Wine, Sold Cheap"?
57. What general, dying in Washington, D.C. in 1890, had four Confederate generals and four Union generals as his pallbearers?
58. What Charleston-born cavalry general is honored by a monument in his hometown?
59. What North Carolina general had a total of 11 wounds, 5 of them from his fighting at Chancellorsville?
60. What general grieved over the loss of three children in a scarlet fever epidemic in Richmond?
61. What brother of a Union general was sent to lead a Confederate invasion of their native Kentucky?
62. What excellent general, noted for commanding the "Tramp Brigade," lost his command because of drunkenness?
63. What fugitive general was allowed to return to the U.S. through the good graces of U. S. Grant?
64. What did Gen. John Porter McCown threaten to do if his superior, Braxton Bragg, wasn't removed from command?

42. Ben McCulloch, who had just won the Battle of Wilson's Creek in Missouri.
43. America had never had so many four-star generals at one time.
44. James Rains. Most of the Confederate dead at Stone's River were buried in a mass grave at Evergreen Cemetery.
45. Robert Richardson, who finally did receive an official appointment as brigadier general.
46. They were former Confederate soldiers who had joined the Union army, an offense punishable by hanging. Pickett did this.
47. Ben Hardin Helm, married to Mrs. Lincoln's sister, Emily Todd.
48. Daniel Harvey Hill, who criticized Lee almost constantly.
49. Gen. George W. Rains, who headed the Confederacy's gunpowder production.
50. He claimed that Gen. Barnard Bee, who bestowed the nickname at First Manassas, was referring to Jackson's lethargy, not to his firmness.
51. George Bickley, founder of the subversive fraternity the Knights of the Golden Circle.
52. Shot through his left cheek, he was unable to speak.
53. Killed himself.
54. Fort Donelson, named for Gen. Daniel Smith Donelson.
55. His brother, Confederate Gen. Thomas Drayton.
56. Gen. James Longstreet. To be precise, the sign read "good home made wine sold cheap."
57. Cadmus M. Wilcox.
58. Wade Hampton.
59. William Ruffin Cox, who lived to be 87.
60. James Longstreet, "Old Pete."
61. George Crittenden.
62. Nathan George "Shanks" Evans.
63. George Pickett, who was on the lam because of his hanging of several Confederate deserters. Grant pleaded with President Andrew Johnson for mercy.
64. He would go home to raise potatoes on his 4-acre Tennessee farm.

65. What non-fighting general made his great contribution to the Confederacy as a factory manager?
66. What state capital was captured by Confederate general Edmund Kirby Smith?
67. What general issued a proclamation to the people of Maryland, offering protection to any who would side with the Confederacy?
68. What Virginia general, too sick to walk, rode out to cheer his men on at Gettysburg and was shot dead?
69. What elderly U.S. Army officer turned over all Texas troops, forts, and supplies to the Confederacy in February 1861?
70. What Virginia Military Institute professor did cadet James A. Walker challenge to a duel?
71. What noted cavalry general went on to become a major general in the Spanish-American War?

⚑ Dress Grays, and Other Uniforms

If you've ever seen a picture of Gen. Robert E. Lee in his dress grays, ornamented with stunning gold braid, you might think the Confederate soldier was a sharp-dressed man. The truth, alas, is a little less pretty. The Confederacy did have a standard uniform . . . but what Johnny Reb actually wore was often a far cry from the standard.

1. Though we think of the Confederate army uniform as gray, what color were the pants supposed to be?
2. What color uniform was worn by the Emerald Guards from Mobile?
3. When the Orleans Guard Battalion of New Orleans arrived at Shiloh in mid-battle, why were they fired on by their fellow Confederates?
4. What name do we give to the French-modeled Confederate cap?
5. What unit's uniforms allowed the display of chest hair?
6. What name was given to the dye color made from walnut hulls?
7. What state had the means (but not the will) to supply all the Confederacy's uniform needs?
8. When shoes and boots became scarce, where did Confederate soldiers find new ones?
9. When regulation blankets were scarce, what did soldiers use as substitutes?
10. What North Carolina unit sported flaming red shirts and black pants?
11. What name did the army give to overcoats?
12. What color uniform was worn by the Tennessean "Yellow Jacket" unit?
13. What was the most popular hat among Confederate soldiers (well-liked because it also made a good pillow)?

65. Joseph Reid Anderson, head of Richmond's Tredegar Iron Works.
66. Frankfort, Kentucky.
67. Robert E. Lee. There were not many takers, however.
68. Richard Garnett, one-time leader of the Stonewall Brigade.
69. David Twiggs, a Georgia native and later commissioned as a Confederate general.
70. Thomas "Stonewall" Jackson. In war days, Walker made such a good officer that Jackson requested his promotion to brigadier general.
71. Joseph "Fightin' Joe" Wheeler.

✎ Dress Grays, and Other Uniforms (answers)

1. Sky blue. Eventually, though, most soldiers ended up wearing gray trousers.
2. Green, of course, in honor of Ireland, the mother country of many of the unit's members.
3. The Battalion's uniforms were dress blue—just like the Yankees'.
4. The kepi.
5. The colorful Zouaves of Louisiana, with scarlet trousers, sashes, and open-necked blue shirts.
6. Butternut. It came to be widely used as dyes became scarce.
7. North Carolina, with over forty textile factories. Unfortunately, the state stubbornly reserved the fabrics for its own soldiers, not for the entire Confederacy.
8. From dead Yankees or dead Confederate comrades. A common remark among the Rebs was, "All a Yankee is worth is his shoes."
9. Carpet strips, which also sometimes doubled as overcoats.
10. The Granville Rifles. Doubtless the uniform made them an easy target.
11. "Great coats," which became increasingly uncommon as the war progressed.
12. Yellow. (Did anyone miss this question?)
13. The much-loved "slouch hat," which was one of dozens of hats worn, in addition to the "official" kepi.

14. What was distinctive about the headgear of the Tiger Rifles unit from New Orleans?
15. What was the greatest problem in the Confederacy's obtaining fresh uniforms?
16. What type of uniform had to be officially forbidden, for safety reasons?
17. What did Confederate soldiers call the little sewing kits they used to repair their uniforms?
18. What camp phenomenon served as a substitute for blankets at times?
19. What, in times of need, served as substitutes for shoes?
20. On the Confederate uniform, collar and cuffs of blue indicated which branch of the army?
21. What about yellow collar and cuffs?
22. And red?
23. Confederate troops dressed in blue and orange uniforms were from what state?
24. What item of the uniform was usually dispensed with?
25. When boots proved ill-suited for long marching, what replaced them?
26. Who was the great villain in the saga of the Confederacy's lack of adequate clothing?
27. What item's scarcity was the prime reason in Confederate uniforms wearing out so quickly?
28. What was done to dispose fairly of the clothes of Confederates who died in camp?
29. With a chronic lack of overcoats and blankets, what provided protection from the rain?
30. What was the (regulation) fabric for the Confederate uniform?
31. What Confederate unit was noted for wearing the north African fez hat?
32. What cash payment was given by the Confederate government to soldiers who supplied their own uniforms?
33. What color uniform was absolute anathema to the Confederate soldier?
34. Why would some Confederate officers require barefoot soldiers to continue marching and fighting?
35. Who were the only Confederates known to have shaved their heads?
36. What did an eagle signify on Confederate uniform buttons?
37. Who was entitled to wear gold braid on sleeves?
38. What would a single star on a collar have indicated?
39. Who would have worn chevrons on their sleeves?
40. What men would have had an ornate "E" on their uniform buttons?

14. Each man's hatband sported a slogan, such as "Tiger—Try Me" or "Tiger in Search of Abe."
15. The Union's blockade of Southern ports, which cut off large quantities of supplies from Europe.
16. A blue Yankee uniform, which many Confederates wore after stripping a downed Yankee. At certain times, Confederate regiments sported more Union blue than Confederate gray—which would obviously cause some confusion in the thick of fighting.
17. "Housewives."
18. The "warm earth" policy of shifting the campfire to another spot and then sleeping on the earth that had been warmed.
19. Rawhides, often obtained from butcher shops.
20. The infantry.
21. Cavalry.
22. Artillery.
23. Maryland (which, though it stayed in the Union, supplied many Confederate soldiers).
24. The cravat, or necktie, which many soldiers regarded as fussy or effeminate.
25. Brogans, when available.
26. North Carolina's Gov. Vance, who hoarded thousands of uniforms in his state's warehouses while many Confederates went barefoot and ragged.
27. Soap. Being in short supply, uniforms were washed infrequently, so they rotted more quickly.
28. They were auctioned off to the highest bidder.
29. Trees, when available.
30. Wool, in theory. But as supplies became limited, cotton often substituted. (The South had its own supplies of cotton, obviously.)
31. The Zouaves of Louisiana. Being of French origin, they borrowed some details from French-controlled north Africa.
32. Fifty dollars per year. The government later modified this policy, thinking (optimistically) that it could supply uniforms for every soldier.
33. White—or, more precisely, undyed wool, which was somewhat off-white. Such uniforms were sometimes issued when dye was in short supply. To the soldier of the 1860s, such a uniform looked too much like "burying clothes."
34. In spite of sympathy for the poor boys who lacked shoes, officers were aware that some lazy soldiers would inevitably hide or discard their shoes if they thought this would keep them from their duties.
35. Again, the Zouaves of Louisiana, in imitation of some of the French north African fighters.
36. The wearer was a general.
37. Officers.
38. The wearer was a major.
39. The enlisted men—same as today.
40. Engineers.

41. What general had the most famous hat of the Confederacy?
42. What colorful nickname did enlisted men give to the gold lace on the sleeves of officers?
43. What type of Confederate soldiers wore earrings?
44. What type of fruit seeds often had to serve as makeshift buttons?

🏳 Soldier's Mess

Blessed with a long growing season, the South should yield food aplenty. It does, and it did during the course of the Civil War. But war, being a wasteful activity, often snatches food from the mouths of people living in a rich land. Foodwise, the South suffered during the war, and this was especially true for the Southern soldier, who often had to eat on the march.

1. During hard times, what pork product was issued as a substitute for bacon?
2. What type of meat was, as of 1863, officially part of the Confederate soldier's diet?
3. What major Southern crop's production was curtailed during the war so as to free up more land for food production?
4. What was the most constant item in the soldier's diet?
5. What animal sometimes served as food and was referred to as the "iron-clad possum"?
6. What was "grabbling"?
7. What, in times of want, served as substitute for squirrel meat? (Hint: biologically, a relation of the squirrel)
8. What soldier's item was often used to make plates and frying pans?
9. What reptilian item often served as a bowl in camp?
10. What name was given to the common dish made of bacon grease, cold beef, water, and crumbled cornbread?
11. What was the Rebel soldier's favorite method of obtaining food?
12. What name was given to obtaining food by means other than purchase or requisition?
13. What type of tea often substituted for the real thing in the soldier's diet?
14. What much-loved substance caused a protest by some German soldiers when it was unobtainable?
15. What food was often prepared by cooking around a hot ramrod?
16. What led the soldier to cook potatoes in their skins?

41. Jeb Stuart, the dashing cavalryman, whose plume, sword, and long beard have made him an icon of the Confederacy.
42. "Chicken guts."
43. Indians.
44. Persimmon seeds.

🖊 Soldier's Mess (answers)

1. Lard (alas!).
2. Mule meat—something that, in normal times, was almost never eaten.
3. Cotton, of course.
4. Cornbread—which can become tiresome when there is nothing else.
5. The armadillo.
6. Using the hands to catch fish under roots and rocks—a common practice when food (and fishing tackle) was scarce.
7. Rats, which (like squirrels) are rodents. Soldiers had to be pretty hard up to feast on rat meat.
8. Canteens, cut in half.
9. A turtle shell.
10. Cush—although some soldiers preferred to call it "slosh."
11. Capturing it from Yankees, of course—and, truthfully, hunger was often a significant motive as Rebs charged into battle.
12. "Foraging," which often meant begging from door to door, but was often a polite term for stealing (from fellow Southerners, that is—no one would have objected to stealing from Yankees).
13. Sassafras tea, made from sassafras roots, and not an unpleasant beverage.
14. Coffee. Several German soldiers staged a mock funeral procession when told that coffee rations were suspended.
15. Bread.
16. A shortage of knives. (In this era, potatoes were almost never cooked unless they were peeled.)

17. Who, for the Confederate army, was the real villain in terms of food distribution?
18. What name was given to the traveling food vendors, noted for their price-gouging of hungry soldiers?
19. What staple item's scarcity led to a widespread shortage of food?
20. What made Confederate farmers reluctant to sell their crops to the military?
21. What served as the soldier's usual substitute for silverware?
22. What was the favored beverage of the Confederate soldier?
23. Why did Confederate generals sometimes forbid soldiers to buy food from civilians?
24. What was the Confederacy's biggest problem in food distribution?
25. What was the soldier's canteen made of?
26. What were "war bags"?
27. What was "salt horse"?
28. When salt was scarce, what could be used as substitute?
29. What was the "mud method" of cooking small game?
30. What cavalry general made a desperate raid on a Union camp, making off with 5,000 cattle?
31. What was "farinaceous food"?
32. What easy-to-obtain plant was suggested to soldiers who lacked fresh vegetables?
33. What kind of mill did soldiers use to grind their coffee?
34. Why was milk or cream seldom used in the soldier's coffee?
35. What day would the sutler try to arrive in the soldier's camp?
36. What did President Jefferson Davis ask the people to do to help the army's food shortage?
37. What was the purpose of the "two-bale laws" passed in some Confederate states?

17. The Confederacy's Commissary General, L. B. Northrop, who seemed more devoted to bureaucratic red tape than to delivering food to the armies. Northrop had a knack for antagonizing every Confederate general.
18. Sutlers, notorious not only for their mark-up but for peddling sweets that made the buyers even more dissatisfied with dismal camp grub.
19. Salt, which at the time was more valuable as a preservative than as seasoning. With salt scarce, meat (which required the preserving qualities of salt) was also in short supply.
20. Greed, mostly—they knew that the longer they held onto the produce, the higher prices would soar.
21. A pocketknife—although, in a pinch, forked sticks would do, and so would bare fingers.
22. Coffee, without a doubt. And the scarcer it became, the more desired it became.
23. This order was issued only in areas where there were numbers of Union sympathizers. There was a suspicion that the Unionists would poison the goods they sold the Confederates.
24. Probably the railroads, which were inadequate at the war's beginning and even worse by the end. With railways in poor condition, much of the South's ample food supplies simply rotted in the rail depots.
25. Fabric-covered tin, although when tin was hard to get anything else might suffice—clay jugs, leather bottles, etc.
26. Soldier slang for haversacks, the kits in which rations were carried. Mostly they were made of canvas, leather, or sometimes metal. (The store at the Museum of the Confederacy in Richmond is known as The Haversack.)
27. Pickled beef, preserved in brine. Apparently it wasn't too tasty, so soldiers sneeringly called it "salt horse."
28. Gunpowder. (No, I'm not making this up.)
29. Roll the catch—squirrel, possum, whatever—in mud more than an inch thick, bake it in the campfire's hot coals until the mud is very hard, then crack open the mud shell, which will peel off the fur and hide. Not recommended, but apparently it worked.
30. Gen. Wade Hampton. He and the 7th Virginia Cavalry were ecstatic at capturing so many cattle for the famished armies in Virginia.
31. Ground corn for making mush.
32. Wild onions.
33. They crushed the beans with rifle butts or pounded them between rocks.
34. Aside from scarcity of milk, there was a common belief that only black coffee would make a man tough.
35. Payday, naturally. The soldiers would be eager for non-military food items, and (briefly, anyway) they would be able to pay.
36. Grow vegetables in "truck gardens." People did respond.
37. They prohibited any farmer from planting more than two bales of cotton per field hand. This was to encourage farmers to plant more food crops instead of cotton.

⚑ Bang, Pow, Boom: Weaponry

Visiting any Confederate battlefield, we have to imagine what the site would look like thronged with scurrying soldiers. But, thanks to the durability of weapons, we don't have to imagine what they were like, since they are often mounted for all to see. Some are impressive, and some are downright elegant. Small wonder that students of the Civil War continue to be fascinated by the weaponry of the age.

1. What part of the standard issue rifle was most resented by the Confederate soldier?
2. What elegant weapon was carried by the cavalry but not the infantry?
3. What was the most famous cannon factory of the Confederacy?
4. When Gen. Beauregard asked for the South's help in obtaining metal for artillery, what did he suggest be donated to the cause?
5. What was the greatest source of arms for the Confederacy?
6. What bladed weapon was a favorite of the Confederate soldier?
7. According to a blowhard Southern orator (speaking before the war), what type of gun could defeat the Yankees?
8. What was the grand mission of Caleb Huse?
9. Why were Confederate civilians reluctant to contribute their private arms to the army?
10. What was the drawback of the much-used .69-caliber smoothbore musket?
11. What was the most popular gun in Confederate use?
12. What was the standard projectile for Confederate rifles?
13. What was distinctive about the Le Mat revolver, obtained from France?
14. What medieval weapon was revived for use among Confederates?
15. What was distinctive about the Nashville Plow Works?
16. When the Confederacy needed copper for arms manufacture, what (very non-military) item was ordered confiscated?
17. What was the distinction of the Confederacy's Williams repeating gun?
18. How many horses were required to pull the large artillery pieces?
19. What was "chamber lye"?
20. What were "canisters"?
21. What was the chief cause of the Confederacy's inferior artillery?
22. What important factory was located in Augusta, Georgia?
23. The basic artillery piece of the army was named for a French ruler. Who?
24. What very accurate English-made gun was widely used as a sniper's weapon?

✎ Bang, Pow, Boom: Weaponry (answers)

1. Probably the bayonet, which made muzzle loading a bit risky, plus the Rebel soldier (according to their officers) was more inclined to swing his rifle like a club than to use the bayonet on the enemy.
2. The saber.
3. The renowned Tredegar Iron Works of Richmond, Virginia.
4. Bells from churches, schools, and plantations.
5. The camps of the Union armies, naturally.
6. The Bowie knife, in various shapes and weights.
7. A popgun. (He was proved wrong, as it turned out.)
8. He was dispatched to Europe in 1861 to buy arms for the Confederacy, since Union officials had quickly nixed any plans to buy arms from the North.
9. Quite simply, many of them needed arms for protection of their own homes, particularly people living in remote areas, or areas near the Union border. (This was an age before gun control, obviously.)
10. It wasn't much help at a distance of more than 100 yards, something the Yankees quickly discovered.
11. Probably the English-made .577 caliber Enfield rifle musket. Over 100,000 of them were purchased abroad by Caleb Huse.
12. The minié ball (actually a bullet, not a ball), invented by a French captain.
13. It was a "nine-shooter," three shots more than the popular Colt "six-shooter."
14. The pike, or lance, a long staff with a sharpened steel tip. They were only used, obviously, when firearms were in short supply.
15. The company, a farm implements plant, literally turned plowshares into swords—reversing the Bible's admonition to do the opposite.
16. Copper whiskey stills. No one is sure how effective this order was, since the Confederacy also seemed to need whiskey.
17. It was reportedly the first type of machine gun, firing up to twenty balls per minute, accurate for a thousand yards.
18. Usually six.
19. A nice name for human urine, used (believe it or not) in the making of the niter needed for gunpowder. At times people were asked to contribute the "chamber lye" from their household chamber pots.
20. Exactly what they sound like: metal canisters. Specifically, they were filled with small explosive balls. Thrown from cannon, they could be quite deadly.
21. Not the weapons themselves, which were usually adequate, but the shortage of horses, which worsened as the war progressed. Artillery is useless unless it can be transported.
22. The Confederacy's premier gunpowder factory, which produced almost 3 million pounds of good quality powder.
23. Napoleon III, French emperor. The cannon went by the name of Napoleon, and was developed in France under Napoleon III's auspices.
24. The Whitworth rifle. Equipped with a 14-inch telescope, it had an effective range of 1,800 yards.

25. What were "wrist-breakers"?
26. What was the official name of the very popular Bowie knife?
27. Where did the ever popular Springfield rifle get its name?
28. What is the claim to fame of Robert Parker Parrott?
29. What $5 weapon is found in many museums but was never actually used in combat?
30. What common name do we now use for "case shot"?
31. What substance was combined with lead bullets to make shrapnel?
32. Before a battle, what was the customary allotment of ammo to each fighter?
33. What did the Confederates call a "fox hole"?
34. When a Confederate spoke of a "torpedo," what was he referring to?
35. What was "hot shot" used for?
36. What name do we call the complete set of equipment for one soldier?
37. What was probably the most famous gun of the Confederacy, used in the defense of Vicksburg?
38. What material did C. G. Birkbeck propose as a weapon to use against the South?
39. Why did the double-barreled cannon never work?
40. How many barrels did the original Gatling gun have?
41. What was the Requia battery?
42. What innovative weapons were first deployed in July 1861 in the Potomac River?
43. What did Aguider Dufilho of New Orleans contribute to the Confederate army?
44. What military units were supposed to arm their men with cutlasses?
45. What common bit of ammunition was so heavy that it usually shattered any bone it hit?
46. What U.S. Secretary of War had already prepared for war by shipping weapons and large guns to the South?
47. What name was given by Confederates to the guns Lincoln ordered to be given to Unionists in Kentucky and Tennessee?
48. What pro-Southern governor of a border state paid $60,000 for weapons that wouldn't fire?
49. What kind of weapon was a "coffee mill"?
50. What innovative weapon saw its first use in Middleburg, Virginia, in 1862?

25. Gigantic 42-inch sabers used by cavalry. They were so heavy and cumbersome that many were cut down to a more usable length.
26. The "side knife," though Confederates liked to call it a "Bowie" in honor of the renowned Mexican and Indian fighter Jim Bowie.
27. From the place of their manufacture, Springfield, Massachusetts. (There is a town named Springfield in almost every state in America, so don't feel bad about missing this question.)
28. He invented the widely used Parrott guns, cannons that could fire projectiles from 10 pounds to 250 pounds. Parrott guns, particularly the larger ones, were useful in battering masonry forts.
29. The infamous "Joe Brown Pike," a 12-inch, double-edged blade mounted on a six-foot pole. They were named after Gov. Joseph Brown of Georgia, who advocated their use and manufacture. (See Answer 14, above.) They are interesting museum pieces, but, apparently, soldiers found them impractical.
30. Shrapnel, which was widely used by the Confederates.
31. Sulfur, with the addition of a fuse to set off the charge and scatter the lead in a deadly fashion.
32. From 40 to 60 rounds—each round consisting of a lead ball and enough powder for a single shot.
33. A "rifle pit." The modern term "fox hole" had not come into use at that time.
34. Probably a land mine, not a missile fired from a ship. Land mines were developed at the start of the war, but were considered unsportsmanlike. They were, however, used later in the war.
35. Setting fire to buildings or other objects. The shot would be heated in a special furnace about half an hour, then fired at the target, where the intention was incendiary, not explosive.
36. "Stand of arms," consisting of the rifle, bayonet, cartridge belt, and ammo box.
37. "Whistling Dick," an 18-pounder that gave its projectiles a peculiar spin (resulting in a distinctive whistle). Among Dick's accomplishments were sinking the Union gunboat *Cincinnati* in May 1863.
38. Cayenne pepper, which would be loaded in artillery shells, reducing the Confederates to sneezing. The proposal was never acted upon.
39. In theory, the cannon's two barrels would fire two balls joined together by a chain, but this required that the two would fire at precisely the same second, which never happened.
40. Six.
41. A wheel-mounted set of 25 rifle barrels, fired in succession. It was used in the Union's siege of Charleston.
42. Mines, at that time called "torpedoes." The Confederates were first to use them.
43. Some elegant swords, some inscribed with Louisiana's state symbol, the pelican.
44. The Confederate River Defense Fleet, which was never terribly effective.
45. The .58-caliber minié ball.
46. John Floyd of Virginia.
47. "Lincoln guns," appropriately enough.
48. Beriah Magoffin, who planned to give the guns to secessionists.
49. Lincoln bestowed this name on the early form of machine gun, first used against Confederates at Middleburg, Virginia, in March 1862.
50. The early form of machine gun, used by the Union against Confederate troops.

51. What weapon sometimes served as a spit for roasting meat?
52. What portly general's elegant sword was engraved with the coat of arms of Missouri?
53. What was the chief target of chain shot and bar shot?
54. What kind of weapon did the Nashville Plow Works produce?
55. What North Carolina city had a noted bayonet factory?
56. What unusual weapon was left behind when Federals evacuated the navy yard in Norfolk, Virginia?
57. What formidable weapon was used by naval men to repel boarders?
58. What was the pre-war profession of sword-maker James Conning?
59. When the Confederate navy ran short of cutlasses, what type of tool was used as a substitute?
60. What type of leaves were etched into the blades of Confederate naval cutlasses?
61. What other name were land mines called?
62. What artillery piece was the mainstay of coastal defense during the war?
63. What state supplied most of the iron used by the Confederacy?

Fun and Games and Soldier's Play

A soldier's life—today and in the past—is most often not spent in combat. Putting aside time for marching, drilling, cooking, and engineering, that still leaves many hours of idleness. So what's a soldier to do? The boys in gray proved they had imagination for recreation.

1. What were "musical sprees"?
2. Which much-loved camp song began "We are a band of brothers, and native to the soil"?
3. What patriotic song was sung to the tune we now know as "O Christmas Tree"?
4. What revered leader was quoted as saying, "I don't believe we can have an army without music"?
5. What were the two most popular instruments among the soldiers?
6. What was "townball"?
7. When Rebel soldiers bowled, what did they use for the ball?
8. What camp problem made swimming one of the most popular soldier recreations?
9. What name was given to the sport of riding a horse full tilt and attempting to grab the head of a goose hung by its feet?

51. The bayonet.
52. Sterling Price's. The gilded sword also has its grip in the shape of an ear of corn.
53. The masts and riggings of ships, which were difficult to hit with standard shot.
54. Swords, believe it or not.
55. Raleigh.
56. Battle axes, 411 of them.
57. The boarding pike, a seven-inch point attached to an eight-foot wooden pole.
58. Jeweler. Some of his swords indicate his love of fine handiwork.
59. Machetes.
60. Cotton and tobacco, naturally.
61. "Subterra shells"—that is, underground shells.
62. The Columbiad.
63. Alabama, which supplied about 40,000 tons

✎ Fun and Games and Soldier's Play (answers)

1. Mass singings of soldiers, more planned and organized than the impromptu small group singing around the campfires. Musical sprees were also called "jubilees."
2. "The Bonnie Blue Flag," which referred to the single-starred first flag of the Confederacy.
3. "Maryland, My Maryland." The tune, by the way, is called "Tannenbaum."
4. Gen. Robert E. Lee, who was impressed with a brass concert in 1864.
5. Probably the violin and banjo. (The guitar was still relatively new in America, and not widely used.)
6. A two-base version of baseball. The regular four-base version was also popular among the soldiers.
7. A cannonball, naturally. Pins being in short supply, they sometimes rolled the ball at a hole in the ground.
8. The recurring problem of "graybacks"—body lice, that is. Swimming was a way of relaxing *and* getting rid of some of the lice.
9. "Gander-pulling," one of the camp favorites. (The poor gander, hanging just within the rider's reach, probably didn't enjoy it.)

10. Who was the most widely read author among the soldiers?
11. What type of show (associated with songwriter Stephen Foster) was popular among the Rebs?
12. Who were the "Ethiopians"?
13. Without women as dance partners, how did the Confederate soldiers stage dances?
14. What holiday usually called for a ration of whiskey from the Confederate commissary?
15. What was "the delightful weed" so loved by the soldiers?
16. What type of soldier engaged in "brass ring" contests?
17. What served as the curtain in camp theatricals?
18. What was the favorite "table" game of the soldiers?
19. What was the most useful recreation for the Rebel soldier?
20. What was the usual reading matter for the Confederate?
21. What name was given to soldiers who went from camp to camp after battles, exchanging news?
22. What popular game for soldiers was invented by a Union man who had defended Fort Sumter?
23. What was a soldier's "horizontal refreshment"?
24. What did army sutlers do to ensure a captive clientele?
25. What cavalry general's brigade printed a satirical magazine called the *Vidette*?
26. What food item often had to substitute for a baseball?
27. What sort of dance was the "Virginia quickstep"?

⚑ The Military Manual

1. What European language was the main source of military terms for both Confederacy and Union?
2. What was a vidette?
3. What name is given a general's officer who took orders only from the general?
4. What name is given to the practice of cutting down trees and placing them in the path of the enemy?
5. How many men composed a company?
6. What name is given to the phenomenon of battle sounds being heard twenty miles away, while people nearby do not hear the sounds?

10. Probably Sir Walter Scott, author of dozens of British historical romances. Southerners enjoyed comparing themselves to the noble knights in Scott's fictional world.
11. The minstrel show, with participants in blackface. At times, soldier-actors charged admission, using the proceeds to buy provisions or help wounded friends.
12. The black (mock-black, rather) actors in the minstrel shows. For many years after the war, "Ethiopian" was a polite term for a black person.
13. By just pairing off, which sometimes involved one dance partner donning a bonnet or some other article of women's clothing. Occasionally, of course, women were allowed to visit the camps, and dances involved the usual male-female couples.
14. Christmas. New Year's was also a popular drinking day (nothing new, is there?).
15. Tobacco, not that other (illegal) weed. Soldiers chronically complained about the scarcity of tobacco, which was rationed by the army. (This was rather ironic, considering that almost all American tobacco was grown in the South.)
16. Cavalrymen—that is, soldiers with horses. Riding full tilt, the horseman would attempt to snatch with their hand, or a lance, a ring suspended from a post.
17. Whatever was available—usually a blanket or a tent fly.
18. Cards, naturally—as has been true for soldiers for decades. Cards were always more popular than chess or checkers.
19. Hunting, no doubt, since the soldiers were chronically short on food rations. When ammo was in short supply, soldiers became inventive about catching their prey without shooting.
20. Newspapers, which were much more widely read than periodicals or books, and more widely available (not to mention cheaper).
21. "News walkers." These unofficial reporters were a great source of entertainment as well as information.
22. Baseball, supposedly invented by Abner Doubleday, who (according to tradition) fired the first shot in defense of Fort Sumter.
23. Visiting a prostitute.
24. They issued change in tickets instead of money—tickets printed with their own name, redeemable only with them.
25. John Hunt Morgan.
26. A large nut, usually a walnut, wrapped in yarn or string.
27. It wasn't. It was one of many names for a common camp complaint, diarrhea.

✎ The Military Manual (answers)

1. French, which in those days was the language of war, not love.
2. A mounted sentry on guard duty.
3. Aide-de-camp.
4. Abatis. To make the defense even more effective, the branches are facing the enemy.
5. From 50 to 100, normally.
6. Acoustic shadow, probably caused by atmospheric conditions that affect the normal transmission of sound. This was noticed at several battles, such as Port Royal.

7. Roughly how many men served in the Confederate army?
8. What military articles required over a thousand yards of silk to make?
9. What was a two-man tent called?
10. What term means sleeping in the open, without shelter?
11. What rank was the commander of a corps?
12. What French term referred to a swift, vigorous attack that surprised the enemy?
13. How many aides-de-camp could each general have on his staff?
14. What were military observation balloons made of?
15. Who assigned the numbers to the Confederate army regiments?
16. What term refers to troops marching in advance or on the flanks of the main body?
17. How many men composed an artillery field battery?
18. How many regiments composed a brigade?
19. What name was given to a mine planted in the soil in front of fortifications, designed to explode if the enemy attempted to tunnel underneath?
20. How many divisions composed a corps?
21. What term referred to defeating an army unit by unit?
22. What name was given to a distracting maneuver designed to divert the enemy from an attack made elsewhere?
23. What name was applied to civilians following an army for either profit or employment?
24. How was telegraph wire used against the enemy?
25. What French name was given to obstructions made of long pointed stakes of iron or wood?
26. What rank of officer commanded a company?
27. What general's *Tactics* manual was used for drill discipline?
28. What type of voting was approved for all Confederate soldiers in 1863?
29. How many squads composed a company?
30. What term refers to a fight fought on a smaller scale than a battle?
31. What was the period of enlistment for a Confederate when the war first began?
32. How many companies composed a regiment?
33. What term refers to bundles of sticks used in reinforcing earthworks?
34. What remained with a soldier's unit when he went on furlough?
35. What type of fort is open on one side?
36. When a soldier was captured, how soon was he supposed to be paroled?

7. Between 600,000 and 900,000.
8. Observation balloons.
9. A dog tent (same as a pup tent, of course).
10. Bivouac.
11. A lieutenant general.
12. *Coup de main.*
13. A brigadier general had one, a major general two, and a lieutenant general four.
14. Silk.
15. The state governments.
16. Skirmish lines.
17. About 150.
18. From 4 to 6, normally.
19. A camouflet. It would explode if hit with a pick or shovel, causing the tunnel to collapse.
20. Two or more.
21. Defeat in detail.
22. Demonstration.
23. Camp followers.
24. Stretched between trees and stumps, it could trip or entangle the enemy.
25. *Chevaux-de-frise*, a sort of forerunner of barbed wire. They were placed around defensive fortifications.
26. Captain.
27. William Hardee's.
28. Absentee.
29. Four, normally.
30. Engagement.
31. One year or six months.
32. Ten, normally.
33. Fascines. Sand bags and cotton bales were preferred to them.
34. His arms and equipment.
35. A lunette.
36. Within 10 days.

37. What name is given to an outpost or guard duty for a larger post?
38. What term refers to a large, cylinder-shaped wicker basket filled with rocks or soil and used to brace earthworks?
39. What name was given to a cloth draped from the back of a cap over the man's neck and shoulders?
40. What name was given to soldiers who built bridges, dug trenches, and put up fortifications in advance of the infantry?
41. What was laid over the wooden flooring on pontoon bridges to muffle the sounds?
42. According to army regulations, how often was cavalry supposed to conduct reconnaissance?
43. What rank was the commander of a regiment?
44. What French term referred to a wounded soldier being out of combat?
45. What was the practice of confiscating private property for government use called?
46. What piece of soldier's equipment was seldom used in the war?
47. According to the records of Confederate Adjutant General Samuel Cooper, how many Confederate soldiers were killed in battle?
48. What rank was the commander of a division?
49. What was the responsibility of men in army observation balloons?
50. What name is given to a battle that is decided by the soldiers' determination, not the strategies and tactics of the commanders?
51. How many infantry regiments were in the Confederate army?
52. What name was given to the officially appointed peddlers who sold small items to soldiers?
53. What was regulated by Article 47 of the Confederacy's *Regulations for the Army?*
54. What was the most dangerous duty in an infantry regiment?
55. How many men did the U.S. army have at the beginning of the war?
56. Before the war, what were men between 18 and 45 required to do in most states?
57. Approximately what proportion of Confederate recruits had been farmers?
58. Why did the Union army have so few men when the war began?
59. What non-working occupation was sometimes listed in Confederate recruit applications?
60. What was the average height of the Confederate soldiers?
61. Roughly, what percentage of the Confederate army were foreign born?
62. What type of captured Union soldier could be executed immediately?

37. Pickets.
38. Gabion. They had the advantage of being light and easy to transport.
39. Havelock. The purpose was to ward off sunstroke on hot days.
40. Pioneers.
41. Dirt, naturally.
42. Daily.
43. Colonel.
44. *Hors de combat.*
45. Impressment.
46. The backpack, or knapsack, which proved to cumbersome on long campaigns.
47. According to Cooper, 53,973. The figure is probably fairly accurate.
48. Major general.
49. Sketching quick and accurate maps showing the locations of troops.
50. Soldiers' battles.
51. According to the records, 642.
52. Sutlers.
53. Uniforms.
54. Picket duty, since pickets were the first to be shot at by the enemy.
55. About 16,000.
56. Muster for militia drill once or twice a year.
57. Probably about two-thirds.
58. An American tradition: patriotic amateurs make better soldiers than paid professionals.
59. "Gentleman."
60. Between 5-foot-5 and 5-foot-9.
61. About 9 percent.
62. Blacks, who were considered guilty of leading "servile insurrection."

63. In the cone-shaped Sibley tent, in what position were men required to sleep?
64. What non-commissioned officer dominated the average soldier's life?
65. In what wartime locations would you have found Lee Boulevard and Jackson Alley?
66. What type of fluid was used as substitute for ink by the soldiers?
67. What type of fabric was used for the groundsheets that went under the soldier's blanket?
68. Why would underage recruits write "18" on a slip of paper and put it in their shoe?

⚐ The Seamy Side of Soldiering

Was the Confederate soldier really noble, clean, and brave? Many were, and the soldiers of the South certainly compare well with soldiers of other times and places. Still, the monotony of camp life can lead to some not-so-innocent forms of diversion.

1. What was "pop-skull"?
2. What object was probably the one most commonly stolen from civilians?
3. What was the commonest form of gambling game?
4. What disguise would camp prostitutes often wear?
5. What loathsome pest was often used in gambling races?
6. What were *nymphs du monde*?
7. What slang term was usually used by the Rebel soldier to mean "drunk"?
8. Which Southern city had the worst problem with prostitution?
9. What fruit, hollowed out, was often used to conceal liquor?
10. What was sometimes added to cheap liquor to give it an old, "mellowed" taste?
11. Whose faces graced the face cards of some Confederate playing decks?
12. What noble general issued an 1862 order stating that he was "pained to learn that the vice of gambling exists"?
13. Which branch of the service was most prone to pilfering from civilians?
14. What two vices were particularly offensive to religious men in the troops?

63. In a wheel formation, their feet toward the center.
64. The company's first sergeant.
65. In the soldier's camps. These were unofficial names given to the regulated passageways between lines of tents.
66. Juice from pokeberries.
67. Oilcloth. Too often, the poor soldier had no groundsheet.
68. When asked their age by a recruiting officer, they could truthfully say, "I'm over 18."

✎ The Seamy Side of Soldiering (answers)

1. One of many slang terms for whiskey, particularly bad whiskey.
2. Fence rails, which would be used for campfires. President Davis issued an order that this widespread practice had to be stopped.
3. Card playing, naturally.
4. Soldier's clothing, which gained them easy access to the men.
5. Body lice, which were certainly easy to find among the soldiers.
6. Prostitutes. The French term literally means "worldly nymphs."
7. "Tight," although there were (then as now) many other colorful terms.
8. Probably Richmond, since it was a good-sized city, the center of government, and the focus of large-scale military activities.
9. A watermelon.
10. Raw meat from wild game, which was soaked in the whiskey for a few weeks.
11. President Jefferson Davis and some of the high-ranking generals.
12. Robert E. Lee.
13. The cavalry, since they moved faster and were harder for headquarters to keep track of.
14. Cursing and Sabbath-breaking.

15. What type of "camp servant" was often just a camp prostitute?
16. Which form of gambling was particularly common with cavalry units?
17. Besides the problem of venereal disease, what was the biggest camp problem caused by prostitution?
18. In times of hard campaigning, what substance was often officially rationed to the soldiers?
19. What day was usually the most notorious day for gambling?
20. What Union-occupied city had so many prostitutes that they had their own hospital, plus a hospital for soldiers with syphilis?
21. What was "chuck-a-luck"?
22. What was the "Devil's Half-Acre"?
23. What was "Oil of Gladness"?
24. What was the real identify of soldiers Tom Parker and Bob Morgan?
25. What general claimed that the Confederate army had lost more men to drunkenness than to Union bullets?
26. What type of military men were allowed to buy whiskey?
27. When prostitutes advertised themselves in magazines, what would they claim to be seeking?
28. What were women required to carry to show they were not prostitutes?
29. What devout Union general rounded up 111 prostitutes in Nashville and shipped them off to Louisville?
30. What part of a civilian home was most likely to be robbed by soldiers?
31. What kind of birds did a Richmond newspaper compare prostitutes to?
32. What well-known Virginia general suffered ill health throughout his life because of contracting gonorrhea in his teens?

15. A laundry woman. An order was issued to the effect that laundresses not actually doing laundry must be discharged.
16. Horse racing—since the cavalrymen had access to horses, of course.
17. The soldiers often resorted to stealing in order to pay prostitutes.
18. Whiskey.
19. The soldiers' pay day—which could result in a total loss of the pay, alas.
20. Nashville.
21. The preferred form of dice gambling among soldiers.
22. An infamous gambling den close to Fredericksburg, Virginia.
23. One of many names for bootleg whiskey.
24. They were two prostitutes, Mary and Mollie Bell, dressed as soldiers.
25. Braxton Bragg.
26. Only officers. Enlisted men could not (theoretically, anyway).
27. A "soldier correspondent."
28. "Proof of respectability," whatever that meant.
29. William Rosecrans. In Louisville they were not given permission to disembark.
30. The smokehouse, of course, since soldiers were always desperate for food better than the usual camp rations.
31. Buzzards and vultures, which always follow an army around.
32. A. P. Hill.

⚑ A Battle By Any Other Name . . .

The Battle of Gettysburg is always called the Battle of Gettysburg. But what about Manassas, Stone's River, and so many other battles that have more than one name? Often the Southerners gave one name to a battle while the Yanks gave another. For each battle listed here, give the alternate name. (If you're really sharp, you'll know why there are alternate names for each battle.)

1. Bull Run.
2. Stone's River.
3. Sharpsburg.
4. Big Bethel.
5. Wilson's Creek.
6. Shiloh.
7. Malvern Hill.
8. Beaver Dam Creek.
9. Mill Springs.
10. Ball's Bluff.
11. Honey Springs.
12. Fort Darling.
13. Brice's Cross Roads.
14. Darbytown.
15. Mansfield.
16. Oak Grove.
17. Olustee.
18. Chantilly.
19. Elkhorn Tavern.
20. Perryville.
21. White Sulphur Springs.
22. Salem Church.
23. Fair Oaks.
24. Buzzard's Roost.
25. Tupelo.
26. White Oak Swamp.
27. Franklin's Crossing.
28. Hatcher's Run.

✎ A Battle By Any Other Name . . . (answers)

1. Manassas. (Bull Run is the stream near Manassas, Virginia.)
2. Murfreesboro. (Stone's River is near the town of Murfreesboro, Tennessee.)
3. Antietam. (Antietam was the creek near Sharpsburg, Maryland.)
4. Great Bethel, or Bethel Church (a case where the alternative names are at least similar).
5. Oak Hills, or Springfield (Springfield being the nearby Missouri town, though the battle is most commonly known by its Creek name).
6. Pittsburg Landing (Shiloh being the name of the church at the site in Tennessee).
7. Crew's Farm, or Poindexter's Farm (Virginia).
8. Mechanicsville, or Ellerson's Mill (Mechanicsville being the Virginia town, the Mill and the Creek being nearby).
9. Beech Grove, or Fishing Creek, or Logan's Cross Roads (all near the same location in Kentucky).
10. Conrad's Ferry, or Harrison's Island, or Leesburg. (Leesburg is the nearby town in Virginia.)
11. Elk Creek (both names refer to the battle site in what was then known as the Indian Territory).
12. Drewry's Bluff (Fort Darling being the official name of the location in Virginia).
13. Guntown, or Tishomingo Creek (the creek was, obviously, near Brice's Cross Roads in Mississippi).
14. Deep Bottom, or New Market Road, or Strawberry Plains (all of these are features near Darbytown, Virginia, of course). To confuse the names further, there was also a later battle called Darbytown Road.
15. Pleasant Grove, or Sabine Cross Roads (Mansfield being the Louisiana town).
16. French's Field, or King's School House, or the Orchard (Virginia).
17. Ocean Pond (Olustee being the nearby depot at the Florida site).
18. Ox Hill (Chantilly being the country mansion near the Virginia site).
19. Pea Ridge (Arkansas).
20. Chaplin Hills (Perryville is the town in Kentucky).
21. Rocky Gap (White Sulphur Springs being the name of the West Virginia town).
22. Salem Heights (a case where the two names are too similar to warrant any confusion; the site is in Virginia).
23. Seven Pines ("Oaks" and "Pines" for the same Virginia battle site? Curious, isn't it?)
24. Tunnel Hill (a case where the battle site, in Georgia, has one name clearly more attractive than the other).
25. Harrisburg (both are names of Mississippi towns).
26. Frayser's Farm, or Turkey Bridge, or Willis' Church, or four other names. This Virginia battle holds the record for alternate names.
27. Deep Run (the place on the Rappahannock River near Franklin's Crossing, Virginia).
28. Armstrong's Hill, or Boydton Plank Road, or Dabney's Mill, or Vaughan Road (all in Virginia, and all referring to one battle).

⚑ The Dreaded Draft

When the Civil War began, the Confederacy had more than enough eager young men willing to fight for the dear old South. Of course, they expected the war would end in about three months. It didn't, so the Confederacy hit upon a novel way of getting men for its army. Some of the men, in turn, hit upon ways to avoid the dreaded draft.

1. About what proportion of the Confederate army were drafted men?
2. What Confederate Cabinet member convinced Jefferson Davis to institute a draft?
3. After the Confederate draft was instituted, why did many Southern men rush to enlist?
4. What grumpy general claimed that the Confederacy's draft bureau was corrupt and incompetent?
5. What infamous law passed the Confederate Congress in April 1862?
6. What sort of people did Robert E. Lee propose drafting into the Confederate army?
7. How did many Southern men avoid the "enrollment" that preceded being drafted?
8. What was added to the Confederate draft bill on April 21, 1862—much to the relief of many men?
9. When the Confederate draft bill was signed in 1862, what age men were to be drafted?
10. When Southerners departed for the North for reasons of "liberty infringement," what were they running away from?
11. What new age limit was set for the Confederate draft in September 1862?
12. Why did the Confederate draft bureau exempt foreigners from service as soldiers?
13. How was the draft age extended in the last months of the war?
14. What type of people could exempt themselves from the Confederate draft by paying a $500 fee?
15. The Twenty-Negro Law allowed a draft exemption for planters or overseers with twenty or more slaves. What change was made in the law in February 1864?
16. What did Texas Gov. Francis Lubbock do to appease German Texans after several were massacred in 1862?
17. What unpleasant job did John Smith Preston hold in the Confederacy?
18. What radical idea was proposed for drafting more soldiers for the Confederate army?

✎ The Dreaded Draft (answers)

1. From one-fourth to one-third.
2. Secretary of War George W. Randolph.
3. Enlisting, as opposed to being drafted, might give them a choice of which regiment to serve in.
4. Braxton Bragg. He was correct.
5. The conscription (draft) bill.
6. Blacks. This shocking proposal was made in March 1865, when the army had dwindled away alarmingly.
7. They would visit relatives in other areas. The enrollment involved a local official taking a survey of an area, listing men of draft age.
8. A list of occupations that exempted men from the draft. It was a *long* list.
9. Those between 18 and 35.
10. The Confederacy's draft law, enacted April 1862.
11. Forty-five. The original limit was thirty-five.
12. Many, especially Germans, were skilled at arms manufacture, and thus needed more in the ironworks than in the army.
13. Boys 14 to 18 were drafted for the "junior reserve," and men 45 to 60 were the "senior reserve."
14. Men of pacifist Christian sects—Quakers, Mennonites, etc.
15. The number was reduced from 20 to 15.
16. Exempted them from the draft.
17. Head of the Bureau of Conscription (i.e., the Draft Board).
18. Drafting slaves. First proposed by Gen. Patrick Cleburne, the plan was adopted by the Confederate Congress in 1864. It was assumed that slaves who fought would eventually be given their freedom.

♭ Just Deserts

Every army has soldiers who are, well, less than devoted. As a rule, when the army is winning, morale is high and desertions are few. But when things go bad, as they often did in the Confederate army . . .

1. Approximately how many desertions occurred from the Confederate army?
2. What warning was included in a soldier's furlough papers?
3. What generous offer did President Jefferson Davis make to deserters in August 1863?
4. In the Confederacy's last proclamation of amnesty for deserters, what type of deserters were not included?
5. What did President Jefferson Davis do with every Confederate deserter condemned to death?
6. When President Jefferson Davis issued his general amnesty for deserters in August 1863, who many days did deserters have to return to their units?
7. What kind of deserters were exempted from President Jefferson Davis's general amnesty in August 1863?
8. Where was a soldier when he was "running the guard"?
9. What state had more deserters than any other?
10. What was the purpose of the Peace and Constitutional Society?
11. What former U.S. cabinet member lost his Confederate army post for deserting his command?
12. What partisan fighter was court-martialed for taking Confederate deserters into his unit?
13. What was sometimes done as a final disgrace to executed deserters?
14. What Southern fort, captured by the Union, became a prison for army deserters?

🐾 Just Deserts (answers)

1. More than 100,000.
2. A warning to return to his unit by a specified time, "or be considered a deserter."
3. He requested that all "absentees" return their regiments, with no fear of punishment.
4. Those who had deserted to the enemy.
5. Commuted his sentence. Davis had a compassionate streak.
6. Twenty.
7. Those who had already been convicted twice of desertion.
8. Deserting, or, at least, on authorized leave.
9. North Carolina.
10. Encouraging Confederate soldiers to desert and encouraging civilians to support the Federal army.
11. Gen. John Floyd, former Secretary of War.
12. Hanse McNeill, who was acquitted.
13. They were buried face down.
14. Fort Jefferson, on Florida's Tortugas Keys in the Gulf.

⚑ Soldier Talk

Military men seem to have incredible imaginations, particularly in the area of vocabulary. The expressions and phrases in this section are only a sampling of the Confederate soldier's rich and fascinating parlance.

1. What kind of weapon was a "coffee mill"?
2. What battle was the "Picnic Battle"?
3. What were "Lincoln's hirelings"?
4. Who were the "pressmen" of the Confederacy?
5. Who were "P'inters"?
6. Who were "feather-bed soldiers"?
7. What general was called the "Great Retreater" for failing to defend Atlanta?
8. What were "white-washed Rebels"?
9. Who was "Whistling Dick"?
10. What sort of men comprised the "government reserves" called in to defend Richmond in December 1863?
11. What Kentucky battle site was known as the "Gibraltar of the West"?
12. What was the "Battle for Kilpatrick's Pants"?
13. What was the "Battle of the Generals"?
14. At what battle site was the "Hornet's Nest"?
15. What were the "dog-catchers" of Richmond?
16. Who was the "Hero of Manassas"?
17. What were "bombproofs"?
18. What infamous area of Appalachia, often called the "Bloody Ground," was the scene of an 1862 Civil War battle?
19. In what Southern state did the Union army's famous "Mud March" take place?
20. What gallant young Alabama hero was killed at Kelly's Ford, Virginia, in March 1863?
21. How was the draft age extended in the last months of the war?
22. What Union general moved so cautiously in the Peninsula Campaign that he was called the "Virginia creeper"?
23. What were "silent battles"?
24. What was the "danger zone" for army observation balloons?
25. What are "balks" and "chess"?
26. What name did the Confederate soldier use for a "foxhole"?
27. Where was a soldier when he was "running the guard"?
28. What name was given to the beef preserved in brine that was part of military rations?
29. What were the Union's "stone fleets"?

🖎 Soldier Talk (answers)

1. Lincoln bestowed this name on the early form of machine gun, first used against Confederates at Middleburg, Virginia, in March 1862.
2. First Manassas, July 1861. In a somewhat festive atmosphere, several U.S. congressmen and their wives watched the battle, bringing wine and picnic fixings, and actually getting in the way of the troops.
3. A nickname Southerners gave to Federal soldiers.
4. Government agents who had authority to seize—"impress"—wagons and livestock for government use.
5. West Point graduates—as in, "West P'inters."
6. This was a nickname given by infantrymen to partisan fighters, who, in the infantry's view, led an easy life.
7. Joseph E. Johnston, who was then replaced by the more aggressive John Hood.
8. Confederate prisoners of war who took a loyalty oath to the Union and became Union soldiers.
9. Not a who, but a what. It was a large cannon used by the Confederates at Vicksburg. It gave its shells a spin, which produced a whistling sound.
10. Government clerks. They functioned for only a week and went home.
11. Belmont, commemorated at the Columbus Belmont Battlefield State Park.
12. A cavalry skirmish at Monroe's Crossroads, North Carolina. Confederate Generals Wade Hampton and Joe Wheeler surprised Judson Kilpatrick's Union cavalry. Kilpatrick fled without his pants on.
13. The Battle of Franklin, November 30, 1864. Six Confederate generals died in the battle.
14. Shiloh, Tennessee. So called because of the intensity of the fighting.
15. Confederate agents sent to capture any soldier who didn't have a valid pass. Without a pass, the soldier was shipped back to the battle lines.
16. General Pierre G. T. Beauregard.
17. Underground shelters that were, theoretically, bombproof. It was also a name applied to generals.
18. The Cumberland Gap, the famous pass through the mountains.
19. Virginia, near the Rappahannock River, where Union general Burnside's army waded knee-deep through mud for miles.
20. Blond and blue-eyed John Pelham, known as "the gallant Pelham."
21. Boys 14 to 18 were drafted for the "junior reserve," and men 45 to 60 were the "senior reserve."
22. George McClellan, whose caution was his downfall.
23. Battles involving *acoustic shadow*, the phenomenon of people near a battle not hearing the sounds, while people several miles away could hear it. Port Royal was one such battle.
24. The height at which they could be hit by artillery fire.
25. The crossties and flooring used on pontoon bridges.
26. "Rifle-pit."
27. Deserting, or, at least, on authorized leave.
28. "Salt beef," sometimes called "salt horse."
29. Old ships that were loaded with stones and sunk in Southern harbors to serve as obstructions.

30. What Confederate prison was called the "Hotel de Zouave"?
31. What name was given to iron shot that was heated in a furnace and fired at wooden ships?
32. What name would we use for what Confederate soldiers called a "horological torpedo"?
33. What name was given to the Union supply line set up in Alabama and Tennessee to get food to Grant's troops?
34. What general's stalwart foot soldiers were called "foot cavalry"?
35. What is the military term meaning "living off the land"?
36. What was the "Pemberton oak"?
37. What prison was widely known as the "Georgia Hell"?
38. What was "Old Bogey"?
39. What was the "Mother Arsenal" of the Confederacy?
40. What were the Confederacy's "silk dress balloons"?
41. What was *guerre de corse*?

☈ Star Men: The Generals (Part 2)

1. What phrase did Robert E. Lee always use to refer to Yankees?
2. What famous general did William L. Jackson serve as staff officer?
3. What noted general was wounded by his own troops at the Wilderness, 1864?
4. When Ellen Marcy rejected the marriage proposal of future Gen. Ambrose Powell Hill, who did she marry?
5. What general jumped the gun by wiring the Richmond authorities that the Confederates had won at Shiloh?
6. What general almost resigned his command in mid-war to become a minister?
7. What distinction is held by Felix Robertson, who died in 1928?
8. What South Carolina officer with an improbable name assumed Gen. Barnard Bee's command when Bee fell at First Manassas?
9. What future general did Robert E. Lee request as his aide when Lee went to Harpers Ferry to subdue John Brown?
10. What Rebel generals left letters in Savannah, personally asking William T. Sherman to protect their families?
11. What did the pitiful Confederate army have way too many of in spring 1865?
12. What two generals met at the Bennett House in North Carolina to discuss terms of surrender?
13. What Confederate general refused to surrender in 1865 and instead headed for Mexico?

30. Charleston's Castle Pinckney, which was run by the colorfully dressed Charleston Zouaves.
31. "Hot shot," appropriately enough. It was widely used at coastal forts.
32. A time-bomb.
33. The "Cracker Line," so named for the bland-tasting hardtack crackers that were a staple food of soldiers.
34. Thomas "Stonewall" Jackson's. They were known to cover 50 miles in 2 days, and over 500 miles in 5 weeks.
35. "Foraging."
36. An oak tree at Vicksburg, under which Confederate General Pemberton and Union General Grant discussed terms of surrender.
37. The crowded, unsanitary prison of Andersonville.
38. A fake ironclad ship, used by Federals to spook Confederates. It was basically timber, canvas, and skillfully applied black paint.
39. The highly productive Tredegar Iron Works in Richmond, which ran night and day.
40. Observation balloons made of colorful dress silk. (Contrary to a common belief, the balloons weren't actually made of women's dresses.)
41. The French term that referred to commerce raiding—Confederate warships preying on Union merchant ships.

✎ Star Men: The Generals (Part 2) (answers)

1. "Those people."
2. His cousin, Thomas "Stonewall" Jackson. William had the nickname "Mudwall."
3. James Longstreet, who recovered.
4. Future Union Gen. George McClellan.
5. P. G. T. Beauregard. He was mistaken.
6. Edmund Kirby Smith.
7. He was the last surviving Confederate general.
8. States Rights Gist.
9. J. E. B. Stuart.
10. William Hardee and Lafayette McLaws.
11. Generals. With the army dwindled down to a fraction of its former strength, plenty of generals had survived—too many chiefs, not enough Indians.
12. Confederate Joseph Johnston and Union William T. Sherman.
13. Jo Shelby.

14. How did the Confederate administration deal with Gen. P. G. T. Beauregard's ego problem after he won the First Battle of Manassas?
15. In the fierce fighting at Seven Pines, what did Gen. Daniel Harvey Hill do to boost his troops' morale?
16. What illiterate Mississippi bricklayer went on to become a Baptist pastor, a Confederate general, and a major force in the Confederate army revival in 1864?
17. At Antietam, where was Gen. James Jay Archer as he directed his brigade?
18. When Gen. Joseph Johnston was wounded in the right shoulder, what was his biggest concern?
19. What vain general considered himself slighted when given the post of defending Charleston?
20. What name did Gen. "Stonewall" Jackson's men receive because of their ability to march amazing distances?
21. Who was the last Confederate general to surrender?
22. What general's approval was necessary before the Confederacy would accept the notion of having blacks serve in the army?
23. What was the name of the fraternal Confederate soldiers' organization conceived by Gen. Patrick Cleburne?
24. What Confederate general kept the Union forces of Benjamin Butler confined to the New Orleans area?
25. What general's 1865 marriage to Hetty Cary was the social event of the year?
26. What was Gen. Samuel Cooper's great contribution to history?
27. What is the key claim to fame of Union cavalry general Andrew Jackson Smith?
28. What Confederate general ordered the September 1861 invasion of Kentucky?
29. What did Union private Billy Mitchell find in Maryland, wrapped around three cigars?
30. Who was the Confederacy's most famous self-appointed "general"?
31. What Philadelphia-born Confederate general had the humiliation of ending the war with the rank of colonel?
32. What handsome Confederate cavalry general, operating in Kentucky, struck terror into the people of southern Ohio and Indiana?
33. What braggart Union general had his personal belongings captured (right under his nose) by Confederate cavalry general J.E.B. Stuart?
34. What testy general was court-martialed by his longtime adversary, J.E.B. Stuart?
35. How was surly Gen. George Steuart punished for his ill-will toward his Union captors?

14. Sent him west to serve under Gen. Albert Sidney Johnston.
15. Rode slowly through enemy fire while smoking his cigar nonchalantly.
16. Mark Perrin Lowrey, who returned to ministry after the war.
17. In an ambulance, recovering from illness.
18. His sword, which his father had used in the Revolutionary War. He begged his aides to return to the field to fetch the sword.
19. P. G. T. Beauregard, who would have preferred a field command.
20. "Foot cavalry."
21. Gen. (and Cherokee chief) Stand Watie, who surrendered on June 23, 1865.
22. Robert E. Lee's. Prior to Lee's approval, almost everyone in the South had called the policy "suicidal."
23. Comrades of the Southern Cross. It was organized to bind Confederate soldiers together in "exalted oneness of action."
24. Richard Taylor, son of President Zachary Taylor.
25. Gen. John Pegram of Virginia. Three weeks later, he died in battle.
26. Record keeping. As the Confederacy's adjutant general, he kept good records on the Confederate military, and at the war's end, he gave the records to the Federal government. This has been a blessing to historians.
27. He was one of only two generals to ever defeat Nathan Bedford Forrest in battle. This was in July 1864 in Mississippi.
28. Leonidas Polk. The invasion was unauthorized, since Kentucky was officially neutral.
29. Gen. Lee's Special Order 191, outlining his Maryland campaign strategy.
30. Jeff Thompson of Missouri, who became the "Swamp Fox of the Confederacy."
31. John Pemberton, who lost his rank as lieutenant general after he surrendered to Grant at Vicksburg in 1863.
32. The bold John Hunt Morgan, Alabama-born but Kentucky-bred.
33. John Pope. The incident was, needless to say, embarrassing.
34. William "Grumble" Jones, one of the few generals court-martialed during the war.
35. They sent him back to his camp via a waist-deep creek and deep mud.

36. What future general left the Pacific Northwest when war broke out and sailed all the way around South America before reaching Virginia?
37. What general, wounded seven times in the war, helped establish the Confederate Soldiers' Home in Richmond?
38. What general had a price placed on his head by a Northern newspaper publisher?
39. What former general was elected first head of the United Confederate Veterans?
40. What U.S. senator and future general joined up with the Confederacy but confided that he knew the South could not win its independence?
41. What Tennessee general was removed from command after being charged with incompetence and drunkenness by Braxton Bragg?
42. What general almost bled to death from the friendly fire he took at the Wilderness?
43. What general's family home became the official residence of New York City's mayors?
44. What inept professor at the Virginia Military Institute became one of the Confederacy's greatest generals?
45. What cheeky cavalry general charged into Memphis and captured two Union generals in their beds?
46. Who offered to resign because of the defeat at Gettysburg?
47. Gen. Daniel Harvey Hill was notorious for criticizing his superiors. What resulted from his criticism of Robert E. Lee and Braxton Bragg?
48. What Confederate defeat so humiliated Gen. Braxton Bragg that he asked to be relieved of command?
49. Of all the Confederate generals, which one spent the most time in the North during the war?
50. What was the purpose of cavalry general Nathan Bedford Forest's raids in the fall of 1864?
51. In what Tennessee battle were six Confederate generals killed?
52. What Rebel general, with 9,000 men under him, refused to surrender to a Union general with 62,000 men?
53. What noted Texas politician was made a brigadier general in the Confederate army, having no military experience whatever?
54. In what Virginia battle did Confederate general John Breckinridge make use of local manpower, including military school cadets?
55. In the battle at Brice's Cross Roads, Mississippi, in 1864, what Rebel general did the Union hope to capture?
56. What Confederate general was considered the "Savior of the Valley"?

36. George E. Pickett, stationed in the Washington Territory when war erupted.
37. John Rogers Cooke, brother-in-law of J. E. B. Stuart.
38. P. G. T. Beauregard. This occurred after "Old Borey's" rush of fame after Fort Sumter.
39. John B. Gordon.
40. John C. Breckinridge.
41. William Henry Carroll, one of many generals who ran afoul of Bragg.
42. James Longstreet, "Old Pete."
43. Archibald Gracie, of the Gracie Mansion in Manhattan.
44. Thomas "Stonewall" Jackson.
45. Nathan Bedford Forrest.
46. Gen. Robert E. Lee.
47. Hill was removed from command by President Jefferson Davis.
48. Chattanooga, November 1863.
49. John Hunt Morgan, the Alabama-born cavalry leader who made frequent raids into Kentucky, Ohio, and Indiana.
50. Getting Union Gen. Sherman's attention enough to draw him out of Georgia.
51. Franklin, November 1864. The generals were Cleburne, Gist, Granbury, John Adams, Carter, and Strahl.
52. William Hardee who, at Savannah, faced the army of William T. Sherman. Hardee wisely chose to evacuate rather than fight or surrender.
53. The imposing Louis Wigfall who, fortunately, did not serve long as a general.
54. The Battle of New Market, May 15, 1864. The cadets from the nearby Virginia Military Institute played a prominent role in the battle.
55. The elusive Nathan Bedford Forrest. The Union failed.
56. Thomas "Stonewall" Jackson, whose many victories in the Shenandoah Valley endeared him to the people.

57. What did an optimistic Gen. Braxton Bragg carry with him to Kentucky on his Confederate recruiting mission?
58. What ousted Confederate general became notorious for harassing Confederate recruiting officers?
59. What was Gen. Jubal Early's goal in menacing Washington in July 1864?
60. What did Gen. Wade Hampton's cavalry go out seeking in September 1864?
61. What armies was Gen. Joseph Johnston authorized to surrender in 1865?
62. Who threatened Gen. Edward Kirby Smith with arrest if he dared to suggest surrendering his army to the Federals?
63. What quarrelsome general was given the office job of Confederate Chief of Staff after he resigned his field command?
64. What was so controversial about cavalry general Nathan Bedford Forrest's killing of black soldiers at Fort Pillow, Tennessee?
65. What peacetime enemy of Thomas "Stonewall" Jackson became a Union general during the war?
66. What Confederate cavalry general became noted for his raids on Southern civilians?
67. Who was the South's most famous non-fighting general?
68. In what classic cavalry battle did Rebel cavalry general Nathan Bedford Forrest prevail with 3,500 men against the Union's 8,000?
69. What was Thomas "Stonewall" Jackson's middle name? (No, it wasn't "Stonewall.")

⚑ Dating the Battles

Dates have a way of sticking in the mind. What was significant about July 4, 1776? How about October 12, 1492? If you were given the date for a specific Civil War battle, could you name the battle? Perhaps—if given a hint in each case.

1. July 1–3, 1863. (Still the most talked-about battle of the Civil War.)
2. May 1–4, 1863. (Resulted in the death of Stonewall Jackson.)
3. May 12–13, 1865. (The last Confederate victory in the war, occurring after the Appomattox surrender.)
4. July 21, 1861. (A Confederate victory, and the first major engagement of the war.)
5. March 9, 1862. (A world-famous naval battle.)

57. Wagonloads of muskets. There were few recruits, and most of the muskets were carried back to Tennessee.
58. John Floyd, who had been removed from command by President Jefferson Davis.
59. He hoped that by threatening it, Union troops would leave the Richmond area to defend it.
60. Cattle, which they captured from Federal troops. This was the famous "Beef-steak Raid."
61. The Confederate armies east of the Mississippi River. This was still not a full surrender of the Confederacy.
62. The governors of Arkansas, Louisiana, and Mississippi—the area Smith was helping to defend.
63. Braxton Bragg, a close friend of President Jefferson Davis, but a poor general in the field.
64. The killing was supposedly done after the men had already surrendered.
65. William French, who had served with Jackson in Florida and was in several Civil War battles against Jackson. The two detested each other.
66. Joe Wheeler, who justified the raids by pleading the need for horses and food.
67. Samuel Cooper, who, as adjutant general, was mostly a desk man.
68. Brice's Cross Roads, Mississippi, an example of Forrest's abilities.
60. He didn't have one. He used the initial "J," and some people have assumed it was Jonathan, since that was his father's name. In fact, his full legal name was Thomas J. Jackson.

✎ Dating the Battles (answers)

1. Gettysburg, in Pennsylvania, of course.
2. Chancellorsville, in Virginia.
3. Palmito Ranch, in Texas.
4. First Bull Run, or First Manassas, in Virginia.
5. The battle of the *Monitor* and the *Virginia/Merrimack* near Hampton Roads, Virginia.

6. April 6-7, 1862. (Resulted in the death of Confederate general Albert Sidney Johnston.)
7. September 19-20, 1863. (A major Confederate victory in Georgia, and Gen. Bragg's greatest victory.)
8. May 15, 1864. (Noted for the involvement of the nearby VMI cadets.)
9. July 30, 1864. (The "holey" battle.)
10. April 6, 1865. (The last major battle in Virginia.)
11. June 3, 1861. (The first real battle in what became West Virginia.)
12. December 31, 1862-January 2, 1863. (A very bloody Tennessee battle.)
13. March 28, 1862. (One of the few battles associated with New Mexico.)
14. August 10, 1861. (Probably the most famous battle in Missouri.)
15. March 19, 1865. (The last major battle in North Carolina.)
16. March 23, 1862. (The beginning of Stonewall Jackson's famous Valley Campaign.)
17. August 29-30, 1862. (Not the first battle at this site.)
18. September 17, 1862. (The battle that made the Confederates eager to leave Maryland.)
19. September 8, 1863. (A Confederate victory, and a major battle in Texas.)
20. April 12, 1861. (The beginning of it all.)
21. June 25-July 1, 1862. (A remarkable series of Confederate victories.)
23. November 29, 1863. (Resulted in Confederate forces being driven from Tennessee.)
24. November 23-25, 1863. (A stunning blow for Gen. Bragg.)
25. August 5, 1864. (The key naval battle on the Gulf coast.)
26. May 5, 1862. (A colonial capital.)
27. February 15, 1862. (A major Confederate loss in Tennessee.)
28. October 8, 1862. (Repelling a Confederate invasion of Kentucky.)
29. May 5-7, 1864. (A dense growth of Virginia woods.)
30. December 13, 1862. (Pontoon bridges on Virginia's Rappahannock River.)
31. July 18, 1863. (A South Carolina battle involving the Union's Colored Infantry.)
32. November 24, 1863. ("Above the clouds.")
33. May 11, 1864. (A small battle, but one that resulted in the death of J. E. B. Stuart.)
34. July 22, 1864. (Scarlett O'Hara.)
35. June 1-3, 1864. (A major Union loss, 12,000 casualties in three days.)

6. Shiloh, in Tennessee.
7. Chickamauga.
8. New Market, in Virginia.
9. The Crater, in Virginia.
10. Sayler's Creek.
11. Philippi.
12. Stone's River, or Murfreesboro.
13. La Glorieta Pass.
14. Wilson's Creek.
15. Bentonville.
16. Kernstown, in Virginia.
17. Second Bull Run, or Second Manassas, in Virginia.
18. Antietam, or Sharpsburg.
19. Sabine Pass.
20. The firing on Fort Sumter, South Carolina.
22. The Seven Days Campaign, in Virginia.
23. Fort Sanders, in Tennessee.
24. Chattanooga.
25. Mobile Bay, Alabama.
26. Williamsburg, Virginia.
27. Fort Donelson.
28. Perryville.
29. The Wilderness.
30. Fredericksburg.
31. Fort Wagner.
32. Lookout Mountain, Tennessee.
33. Yellow Tavern, Virginia.
34. Atlanta.
35. Cold Harbor, Virginia.

36. November 30, 1864. (A Tennessee battle that resulted in the death of six Confederate generals.)
37. May 25, 1862. (A Virginia town that constantly changed hands during the war.)
38. July 9, 1864. (It delayed a Confederate raid on Washington.)
39. July 20, 1864. (A major loss in Georgia for Gen. Hood.)
40. June 9, 1862. (One of Stonewall Jackson's greatest victories in the Shenandoah Valley.)

⚑ Irregulars: Partisans, Bushwhackers, Etc.

Anyone who knows the Confederacy's story well is aware of how unromantic and unglamorous the soldier's life was. Long marches, bad food, bad shelter, camp sicknesses, and hours of boredom were the typical fare of Johnny Reb. Far more romantic and exciting was the life of the irregulars— the authorized (but more often unauthorized) fighters dedicated to harassing and capturing Union troops and supplies. Usually called partisan rangers, these mounted men moved in small bands, covering ground much more swiftly than the regular armies. Some of these men were the Confederacy's bravest of the brave—and some were the most unsavory characters the Confederacy ever blushed over. The border states of Missouri (a slave state) and Kansas (a free state) had more than their share of guerrilla brutality.

1. What four notorious outlaws were members of William Quantrill's gang of Confederate guerrillas?
2. What name was given to the guerrilla fighters who brutalized pro-Union citizens of Missouri and Kansas?
3. What Union guerrilla was so unscrupulous that his gang even stole Bibles?
4. What was "Mosby's Confederacy"?
5. What official issued a declaration that guerrillas were *not* a part of the Confederate military?
6. What was the preferred weapon of Confederate raider Hanse McNeill?
7. What act had gotten partisan fighter John S. Mosby expelled from the University of Virginia?
8. What act of Congress provided for organizing companies of partisan fighters?

36. Franklin.
37. Winchester, Virginia.
38. Monocacy, Maryland.
39. Peachtree Creek.
40. Port Republic, Virginia.

🖎 Irregulars: Partisans, Bushwhackers, Etc. (answers)

1. Jesse and Frank James, Cole and Jim Younger.
2. Bushwhackers.
3. Charles Jenison, leader of the notorious regiment that raided and robbed the pro-South people of Missouri.
4. The area in Virginia between the Potomac and Rappahannock, named for partisan ranger John S. Mosby who made this area his theatre of operations.
5. Secretary of War Judah P. Benjamin.
6. A double-barreled shotgun.
7. Shooting a fellow student who had made a "disagreeable allegation."
8. The Partisan Ranger Act of 1862.

9. Who was the most famous (and infamous) of the bloodthirsty bushwhacker leaders?
10. Why was service in a Confederate partisan unit so attractive for young men?
11. What noted guerrilla fighter had his unit absorbed into Stonewall Jackson's Army of the Valley?
12. What did partisan fighter John Mosby do while imprisoned for shooting a fellow student?
13. How could partisan fighters disable a train by firing only one shot?
14. What partisan activity did Robert E. Lee call "unauthorized and discreditable"?
15. What noted partisan fighter carried poetry books by Byron and Shakespeare in his saddlebags?
16. What daring feat was accomplished by fighter Jesse McNeill in January 1865?
17. How would partisan rangers practice their marksmanship?
18. What famous cavalry general did partisan John S. Mosby scout for?
19. What Confederate guerrilla had also been a Union guerrilla?
20. What British-born Union commander was the object of partisan fighter John Mosby's grudge?
21. How did the Confederate Congress respond to repeated stories of theft by partisan fighters?
22. Which two partisan fighters were permitted to continue after the Confederate Congress had made their activities illegal?
23. What gory items did bushwhacker leader Bill Anderson carry on his horse's bridle?
24. What was special about the woman guerrilla leader Sue Mundy?
25. What name was given to guerrillas who harassed pro-slavery citizens of Kansas?
26. When the Union's 6th West Virginia Cavalry was captured by the Confederacy's McNeill's Rangers, where were they?
27. What guerrilla fighter of the American Revolution was the idol of Confederate partisans?
28. What Kansas town was the scene of the bushwhackers' most brutal massacre?
29. What was the nickname of the brutal bushwhacker Bill Anderson?
30. What egotistical (and drunk) Union general was captured while sleeping by partisan John Mosby?
31. What distinctive item of clothing was worn by many guerrilla fighters?
32. What did bushwhacker leader William Quantrill do just before he died from the wounds of Union soldiers?

9. William Quantrill.
10. The Confederate Congress paid the men for arms and ammo they captured.
11. Turner Ashby.
12. Studied to become a lawyer, which he became soon after his release.
13. Using a mountain howitzer, one shot through the train's boiler would disable it.
14. Robbing individuals. The partisans were supposed to confine themselves to capturing (or harassing) Union troops and supplies.
15. John S. Mosby.
16. His band captured two Union generals asleep in their hotels.
17. Firing bullets at a tree while riding past it at a gallop.
18. J. E. B. Stuart.
19. William Quantrill, who was a jayhawker before he became a bushwhacker.
20. Colonel Percy Wyndham, who made the mistake of calling Mosby "a common horse thief."
21. They repealed the Partisan Ranger Act in 1864, thus removing the official status of the partisans.
22. John Mosby and Hanse McNeill, along with their companies.
23. The scalps of his victims.
24. She was actually a petite, long-haired man, Marcellus Clark. A Louisville newspaper reported the Sue Mundy story to embarrass the Union army.
25. The Jayhawkers.
26. Bathing nude in a river.
27. Francis Marion, known as the "Swamp Fox."
28. Lawrence. William Quantrill's pro-Southern gang especially hated the town because it was home of the pro-Union jayhawker leader Jim Lane. Interestingly, Lane was not killed in the massacre.
29. "Bloody Bill," appropriately enough.
30. Gen. Edwin Stoughton. Mosby crept into Stoughton's room, lifted up his nightshirt, and awakened him with a slap on the bare behind.
31. "Guerrilla shirts," shirts with elaborate embroidery, usually sewn by wives or girlfriends.
32. He was baptized as a Roman Catholic.

33. When did partisan leader John Mosby surrender his command?
34. In what embarrassing position was guerrilla fighter Harry Gilmor when he was captured?
35. What would partisan leader Hanse McNeill give captured Union men in exchange for food supplies?
36. What railroad line was the special focus of Confederate partisans' attention?
37. What Indian name was given to the Elijah White's wild band of guerrillas?
38. How did the partisan bands usually obtain food?

♜ Bang, Pow, Boom: Weaponry (Part 2)

1. What item did Richmond's Second Baptist Church donate to the Confederacy to make cannons?
2. What was the colorful name of the mighty gun used in the siege of Charleston?
3. What did Union general Benjamin Butler do with the New Orleans church bells that the Confederates planned to turn into cannons?
4. How did Sherman's Union troops celebrate Lincoln's Inauguration Day in 1865?
5. What Southern port received a floating bomb with 350 tons of gunpowder?
6. What important machinery did the town of Fayetteville, North Carolina, receive (courtesy of "Stonewall" Jackson)?
7. What famous gun manufacturer in the North was eager to sell his goods to Confederates?
8. What deceptive objects did General Joseph Johnston leave behind when he evacuated an outpost near Washington?
9. What was the most important item brought in by the Confederate blockade runners?
10. What was the important role played by General Joseph Reid Anderson in the Confederacy?
11. What important product was made by Col. George Washington Rains' factory in Augusta, Georgia?
12. What type of weapon was classed as either *sword* or *angular*?
13. How many guns comprised an artillery battery?
14. What was a limber?
15. What use did soldiers find for bayonets (other than killing, that is)?

33. He didn't. When he learned of Lee's surrender at Appomattox, Mosby simply disbanded his gang.
34. In bed with a woman.
35. He would set them free if they wished to go home. Thus he increased the Confederacy's food supply and got Union soldiers out of the way.
36. The B & O (Baltimore and Ohio), which was crucial for transporting troops and supplies. Since much of it ran through Virginia, the Rebs frequently raided Union trains.
37. The Comanches.
38. They took it from captured Union supplies, or they were hosted by friendly farm families. (This last option showed the advantage of operating in small groups instead of regular regiments.)

✎ Bang, Pow, Boom: Weaponry (Part 2) (answers)

1. The church's bronze bell. The church also promised to donate money to buy artillery.
2. The "Swamp Angel," able to fire a 200-pound projectile.
3. Sold them at auction in Boston.
4. Firing off captured ammunition.
5. Wilmington, North Carolina. The bomb was actually the USS *Louisiana*, designed to destroy Fort Fisher near Wilmington.
6. The rifle-making machinery taken from the old Federal arsenal at Harpers Ferry, Virginia.
7. Col. Samuel Colt of the renowned Colt's Patent Fire Arms Company of Connecticut.
8. "Quaker guns," logs made to look (at a distance) like cannons, to fool the enemy.
9. Probably the British-made Enfield rifles, desperately needed by the common soldiers.
10. Managing the Tredegar Iron Works in Richmond, a prime source of artillery pieces.
11. Gunpowder, up to 5,000 pounds per day.
12. The bayonet.
13. Six, normally.
14. A two-wheeled ammunition chest in the artillery.
15. Candlesticks and tent pegs.

16. What rank was an artillery gunner?
17. The largest gun in use in the war was a Blakely seacoast rifle. How much did it weigh?
18. What was a popular shoulder arm for soldiers, though the army never issued them?
19. What name was given to the ammunition chests mounted on four-wheel carts?
20. What rank was the officer who headed an artillery battery?
21. What time-honored weapon became outmoded during the Civil War?
22. What types of fortifications were defended by Blakely, Armstrong, Whitworth, and Columbiad guns?
23. What was another name for sharpshooters?
24. What were most rifled cannons made of?
25. What term referred to horse-drawn cannon firing from different positions as they moved about a battlefield?
26. What name did the Confederate soldier use for a "foxhole"?
27. What type of cannon was little used in the Civil War, even though it became the world standard afterward?
28. What name was given to the flammable solution of phosphorus in bisulfide of carbon?
29. What metal were smoothbore cannons made of?
30. What did the Georgia firm of Griswold & Gunnison produce for the Confederacy?
31. What type of rifle bore the name of a Virginia town that played a major role in the Civil War?
32. What noted Confederate munitions factory was completely destroyed by the Union in April 1865?
33. What famous artillery unit had guns named Matthew, Mark, Luke, and John?
34. What famous Georgia factory contributed 5,000 pounds of gunpowder per day to the Confederacy?
35. What contribution did Capt. Alexander Blakely make to the Confederate army?
36. Why was the artillery piece called the Brooke rifle so highly regarded in the Confederacy?
37. What type of rifle was called by Confederates "that damn Yankee rifle they load up on Sunday and fire all week"?
38. Which state had sixteen ironworks producing shot and shell for the Confederate army?
39. What nine-shot revolver was sometimes given to high-ranking Confederates as gifts at promotion?

16. A corporal, usually.
17. About 54,000 pounds.
18. Shotguns, particularly the sawed-off type. Many soldiers happily supplied their own.
19. Caissons.
20. Captain.
21. The bayonet. As hand-to-hand combat became less frequent, bayonets were less in demand.
22. Seacoast forts, where the heaviest guns were used.
23. Snipers.
24. Iron.
25. A flying battery.
26. "Rifle-pit."
27. Breech-loaded.
28. Greek fire, an ancient weapon used in the Union bombardment of Charleston in 1863.
29. Bronze.
30. About 100 revolvers per month, copies of the 1851 Colt revolver.
31. The Harpers Ferry rifle, named for the Harpers Ferry Arsenal which produced it.
32. The Columbus Iron Works, chief supplier of ammo to the navy.
33. The Rockbridge Artillery of Virginia.
34. The Augusta Powder Works.
35. Lots of cannons. Blakely was one of the chief British gun makers.
36. It had been designed and built by a Confederate, John M. Brooke. Most artillery was of U.S. or British design.
37. The popular Henry rifle, loved by the Federals but little used in the Confederacy.
38. Alabama.
39. The famous LeMat revolver, which could not only fire standard rounds but also "grapeshot."

40. What type of ammo, used in the famous Springfield rifle, made older rifle ammo obsolete by the war's end?
41. What was the purpose of the Confederacy's Niter and Mining Bureau?
42. What were "niter beds"?
43. What product, much used by both Confederacy and Union, was produced by the West Point Foundry in New York?
44. What Confederate invention was able to fire about 20 rounds per minute at a maximum range of 2,000 yards?
45. What famous rifle was used in every major battle of the Civil War?
46. What much-loved English-made rifle was often issued to men on sniper duty?
47. What famous artillery unit had served in the Mexican War and went on to serve in the Spanish-American War and both World Wars?
48. What governor was kind enough to share the guns he captured from Federal arsenals with another state?
49. What type of new weapons did Stephen Elliott experiment with in Charleston harbor?
50. What Pennsylvania-born ordnance wizard dazzled everyone with his abilities at procuring arms and ammo for the Confederacy?
51. What gift did Col. Zachariah Deas give to his regiment, the 22nd Alabama?
52. What one man was largely responsible for keeping the Confederate army supplied with guns and equipment?
53. What general used his background as a chemist to improve the processing of gunpowder?
54. What new use did Gabriel Rains find for 10-inch Columbiad artillery shells?
55. What special weapons did the Indian fighters bring to the Confederate cause?

40. Conical, or, in common terms, a normal bullet-shaped bullet.
41. Mining nitrates, saltpeter, lead, and iron for the South's gunpowder and armaments.
42. Trenches and holes outside communities where people could dump urine, used in the making of niter needed for gunpowder.
43. The famous Parrott guns, some of the most widely used artillery in the war.
44. The Williams rapid-fire gun. They fell out of use after the war.
45. The Springfield rifle.
46. The Whitworth, with a range of over a mile.
47. The Washington Artillery of New Orleans. (The same men did not serve in all those wars, needless to say.)
48. Louisiana's Thomas Moore, who shared the loot with Mississippi's John Pettus.
49. Mines (or, as they were called then, torpedoes).
50. Josiah Gorgas, whose *Civil War Diary* is interesting reading.
51. Enfield rifles, costing $28,000 out of his own pocket.
52. Caleb Huse, the army's European purchasing agent.
53. George W. Rains, head of the Confederacy's Niter and Mining Bureau.
54. Buried under ground level, they became land mines (or "torpedoes," as they were called in the 1860s).
55. Bows and arrows, tomahawks, and war clubs, naturally.

⚐ A War by Any Other Name . . .

Is it "the Civil War," or is there some other name that describes the conflict more accurately? People in both South and North (and abroad as well) have shown great imagination in naming the war. While "Civil War" is short and easy, some of the other names are quite interesting.

1. What popular name for the war was coined by Vice-president Alexander Stephens?
2. During the war, what was it usually called by the Northern press?
3. What name, harking back to 1776, was popular among Confederates?
4. What name was commonly used by foreign writers to describe the war?
5. What name was popular among Northern (and Southern) abolitionists?
6. What name, with a "family" connotation, is sometimes used for the war?
7. What name takes its name from a key political figure?
8. What charming name, which doesn't use "war" at all, was popular after the war (and still is)?
9. What popular name in the South suggested that the American Revolution was being fought over again?
10. What is the shortest name ever used for the Civil War?
11. What name, little used now, harks back to the way the Confederacy began?
12. What joking name accurately describes the conflict?

⚐ The West Point Gang

The Civil War was fought between South and North. It was also fought between members of a nationwide "good ole boys" network, since many of the officers on both sides were "P'inters," graduates of the United States Military Academy. Many had fond memories of each other from the pre-war days. Some memories were less than fond, and more than a few personal grudges were carried into the fighting that began in 1861.

1. Of the Confederacy's 425 generals, how many were West Point graduates?
2. Who was superintendent of the U.S. Military Academy at West Point just before the Civil War?
3. Who was superintendent of West Point in the 1850s?

✎ A War by Any Other Name . . . (answers)

1. "The War Between the States." If Stephens did not invent the name, he did popularize it—*after* the war, by the way.
2. "The War of the Rebellion," since (in Northern eyes) the South was rebelling against the U.S.
3. "The Second American Revolution."
4. "The Confederate War."
5. "The War Against Slavery."
6. "The Brothers' War"—as in "brother against brother."
7. "Mr. Lincoln's War."
8. "The Late Unpleasantness."
9. "The War for Southern Independence."
10. "The War," which, in many parts of the South today, needs no further explanation.
11. "The War of Secession."
12. "The Uncivil War."

✎ The West Point Gang (answers)

1. A grand total of 146.
2. P. G. T. Beauregard, who held the position only a short time before entering the Confederate army as a general.
3. The beloved Gen. Robert E. Lee, who greatly improved the academy during his time there.

4. What West Point graduate was so fond of the place that he took his wife there on their honeymoon?
5. Why were Federal authorities angry about West Point graduates joining the Confederate army?
6. What future general had almost been expelled from West Point by his uncle, the superintendent?
7. What future general was dismissed from West Point for breaking a mess-hall plate over the head of future general Jubal Early?
8. What statesman referred to West Point graduates who joined the Confederacy as men who "proved false to the land which had pampered them"?
9. What title would Gen. William "Extra Billy" Smith call West Point graduates?
10. What Union general apologized to the Confederate officers for attacking Fredericksburg?
11. What future leader graduated second in his West Point class of 1829?
12. What dubious distinction did George E. Pickett hold in his 1846 West Point class?
13. What future general gave up his army commission after leaving West Point to study for the ministry?
14. What West Point classmate of Thomas "Stonewall" Jackson later taught at the academy and wrote a textbook on rifle practice?
15. What familiar name was Union Gen. U. S. Grant called by Confederates who knew him at West Point?
16. What qualifications did President Jefferson Davis have to be the Confederacy's military commander-in-chief?
17. What role did Baron Antoine Henri Jomini play in the Civil War?
18. What was the source of the longstanding quarrel between President Jefferson Davis and General Joseph E. Johnston?
19. What West Point classmate was defeated by Gen. P. G. T. Beauregard at First Manassas?
20. What Confederate leader was so frustrated in his attempts to get military training that he bestowed the title "general" on himself?
21. What Confederate general surrendered Fort Donelson to former West Point classmate U. S. Grant?
22. Who was removed from being head of West Point because of his blunt Southern sympathies?
23. What valiant Alabama soldier joined the Confederate army just a few weeks after his graduation from West Point?
24. Gen. Joseph Reid Anderson was a West Point graduate, but what notable non-combat contribution did he make to the Confederacy?

4. Thomas "Stonewall" Jackson. (It was not the *only* stop on their honeymoon trip.)
5. It seemed ungrateful, the men having been educated at taxpayers' expense, then heading south.
6. Fitzhugh Lee, nephew of Robert E. Lee.
7. Lewis Addison Armistead, who was killed at Gettysburg.
8. Lincoln.
9. "Mister," regardless of their rank. He liked to hassle the "West P'inters."
10. Ambrose Burnside, a West Point classmate and close friend of many Confederate generals.
11. Robert E. Lee.
12. He was last.
13. Leonidas Polk, who became both a bishop and a general.
14. Cadmus M. Wilcox, who also fought under Jackson in the war.
15. "Sam" (which is not what his initial "S" stands for).
16. Davis was a West Point graduate, a soldier in the Black Hawk War, a commandeer in the Mexican War, and a U.S. Secretary of War.
17. His *Treatise on Grand Military Operations* was much used at West Point and was a great influence on Lee, McClellan, and other generals.
18. According to rumor, they had a fight over a woman when both men were West Point cadets.
19. Union Gen. Irvin McDowell.
20. Jeff Thompson of Missouri, who was rejected by both West Point and the Virginia Military Institute.
21. Simon Bolivar Buckner.
22. P. G. T. Beauregard.
23. John Pelham, who became the legendary "Gallant Pelham."
24. He headed the Tredegar Iron Works in Richmond, the South's main source of armaments.

25. Who was the last Confederate West Point graduate to die during the war?
26. What member of the distinguished Lee family graduated first in his class at West Point?
27. What noted Union officer found himself fighting frequently with his old West Point friend, Thomas Lafayette Rosser?
28. Who was head of West Point while J.E.B. Stuart was a cadet there?
29. What quarrelsome Mississippi officer had ranked first in his class at West Point?
30. What Louisiana general had dropped out of West Point because of his bad grades?
31. What U.S. army post did P. G. T. Beauregard hold before his commission as brigadier general for the Confederacy?
32. What Alabama general taught tactics at West Point until the war began?
33. What relation were Gen. Robert Garnett and Gen. Richard Garnett?
34. What Louisiana general had graduated first in his class at West Point?
35. What courageous 27-year-old major general fell mortally wounded a Cedar Creek?
36. What renowned general, West Point class of 1826, died at the Battle of Shiloh?
37. What noted Confederate leader had graduated twenty-third in the West Point class of 1828?
38. Who had the nickname "Beaut" in his West Point days?
39. Of all the West Point grads among the Union generals, which one was most liked by the Confederate men?
40. What high-ranking general had graduated in the same class as Robert E. Lee?
41. What did Union Gen. U. S. Grant send across the Confederate line to Gen. George Pickett?

25. Ambrose Powell Hill.
26. Custis Lee, Robert E. Lee's eldest son.
27. George A. Custer.
28. Robert E. Lee.
29. William Whiting, class of 1845.
30. St. John Richardson Liddell.
31. Superintendent of West Point.
32. John Horace Forney, brother of Gen. William Henry Forney.
33. They were cousins, both in the same class at West Point. Both became Confederate generals.
34. Paul Hébert, a classmate of William T. Sherman and George Thomas.
35. Stephen Ramseur, who had graduated from West Point in 1860.
36. Albert Sidney Johnston.
37. Jefferson Davis.
38. J. E. B. Stuart, called "Beaut" or "Beauty" *not* because he was beautiful.
39. Probably Ambrose Burnside, an affable "good ole boy" that the Confederate generals almost hated to fight.
40. Joseph E. Johnston, class of 1829.
41. A silver service for Pickett's newborn son. Grant and Pickett were both West Point grads and old Mexican War comrades.

⚑ Soldier Talk (Part 2)

1. What was the "Yankee buzzard"?
2. What were "songsters"?
3. What was the medicinal food called "panada"?
4. Who was "Polecat"?
5. What were "white-washed Rebels"?
6. Who were "Joe Brown's Pets"?
7. What was the CSMC?
8. Where was the "Rat-Hell" in Richmond?
9. Who were the "Katydids" at the Battle of New Market, Virginia?
10. What Georgia city did Ordnance Chief Josiah Gorgas call "the nucleus of our Ordnance"?
11. What kind of man was a "butternut"?
12. What was the nickname of the renowned 1st Kentucky Brigade?
13. What Union prison was called "the rat-catcher's paradise"?
14. What name was given to the Union gunboats that wore only a light armor of iron?
15. What was the name of the communications system using Morse code adapted to flags and signal torches?
16. What far western battle was called the "Gettysburg of the West"?
17. Who was the "damned little Yankee" lauded for killing a Confederate officer at Chickamauga?
18. What Confederate general was almost always called "Tige"?
19. What nickname was given to Gen. Nathan George Evans' troops?
20. What diminutive professor was called "the Little General" by his troops?
21. What respected general was known as "the Tycoon" to his aides?
22. What North Carolina general led the brigade that became known as the "Star Brigade of Chickamauga"?
23. What Philadelphia-born general was known as the "Defender of Vicksburg"?
24. What dashing cavalry officer led the band called the "Iron Brigade of the West"?
25. Who did Robert E. Lee refer to as "the eyes of the army"?
26. What Confederate general was considered the "Savior of the Valley"?
27. What did "playing old soldier" mean?
28. What name was given to Jeff Thompson's band of Confederate raiders in Missouri?
29. What name was given to John Baylor's Confederate invasion of the New Mexico Territory?

✎ Soldier Talk (Part 2) (answers)

1. Old Abe, an eagle that was the mascot of the 8th Wisconsin Regiment. Being a morale booster for the Union, he was constantly shot at by Confederate soldiers.
2. Small songbooks printed for soldiers' use.
3. Crumbled hardtack in whiskey.
4. Gen. Camille Armand Jules Marie de Polignac. Faced with such a mouthful, soldiers shortened it all to "Polecat."
5. Confederate prisoners of war who took a loyalty oath to the Union and became Union soldiers.
6. Georgia militiamen. Gov. Joe Brown worked to exempt them from Confederate service.
7. The Confederate States Marine Corps.
8. The east section of Libby Prison, which had more than a few rats.
9. The eager cadets from the nearby Virginia Military Institute, who helped win the battle. The older soldiers gave them this nickname.
10. Columbus, with its Columbus Iron Works.
11. Any Confederate soldier, but particularly one whose homemade brownish uniform had been dyed with walnut hulls.
12. "The Orphan Brigade," so called because they were not recognized by their own state of Kentucky and had to train in Tennessee.
13. Point Lookout in Maryland. It was not the only prison where desperate men were known to eat rats.
14. "Tin-clads," though tin was not actually used.
15. The "wig-wag" system, which was extremely slow but much more useful than telegraph lines in a war zone.
16. The Battle of La Glorieta Pass in New Mexico.
17. Johnny Clem, an 11-year-old, the "Drummer Boy of Chickamauga."
18. George Thomas Anderson. "Tige" was short for "Tiger."
19. The "Tramp Brigade."
20. James Henry Lane, who distinguished himself at Gettysburg.
21. Robert E. Lee.
22. Evander McNair.
23. John C. Pemberton. Ironically, Pemberton had to *surrender* Vicksburg to Grant.
24. Jo Shelby.
25. Cavalry Gen. J. E. B. Stuart, famous as a scout.
26. Thomas "Stonewall" Jackson, whose many victories in the Shenandoah Valley endeared him to the people.
27. Faking sickness at sick call.
28. The "Swamp Rats."
29. Baylor's "buffalo hunt," that being (in theory) Baylor's reason for being in that region.

30. What contribution did Samuel M. Pook make to the war against the Confederacy?
31. What was J. E. B. Stuart's nickname before the war?
32. What bloody battle is sometimes called the "High Tide of the Confederacy"?

🏳 Four-legged Friends: Horses

Here at the end of the twentieth century we still have a fascination with horses. Is it the idea of strength, grace, and beauty? Is it an age-old belief that riding a horse is the sign of an aristocrat? Who knows? We do know that some horses of the Confederacy are almost as famous as their riders.

1. What general's horse is stuffed and displayed at the Virginia Military Institute?
2. Who rode the renowned Traveler?
3. What general was riding the beautiful bay horse Fire-eater when he was mortally wounded at Shiloh?
4. What very Southern name was given to Gen. Patrick Cleburne's steed?
5. What dashing cavalryman rode Virginia and Highfly?
6. Who was originally supposed to own "Stonewall" Jackson's horse Little Sorrel?
7. Who rode Richmond, Brown Roan, Lucy Long, and Ajax?
8. What was Traveler's original (and very political) name?
9. What wild man of the Confederate cavalry rode a horse name King Philip?
10. What beautiful horse lies buried near his master's tomb in Lexington, Virginia?
11. What famous partisan ranger rode a beautiful thoroughbred named Coquette?
12. In what state did the largest cavalry battle in America take place?
13. What famous Virginia college had its main building used as a horse stable by Union troops?
14. At the war's beginning, who was supposed to supply the horse for a cavalryman?
15. If a Confederate cavalryman's horse was lost or disabled, what provision was made for getting a new one?
16. What amputee general had to be tied to his horse when he took to the field?

30. He designed ironclad gunboats, known as the "Pook turtles" from their shape.
31. "Beauty," or just "Beaut." It was a joke, since no one thought him beautiful.
32. Gettysburg.

✎ Four-legged Friends: Horses (answers)

1. Thomas "Stonewall" Jackson. His beloved Little Sorrel is preserved in VMI's Museum, as is the coat Jackson was wearing when he was mortally wounded.
2. Gen. Robert E. Lee. Traveler was not his only horse, but definitely his favorite, and surely the best-known horse of the Confederacy.
3. Albert S. Johnston. "Fire-eater," by the way, was a term used to describe zealous Southern secessionists.
4. Dixie, who was killed in action at Perryville.
5. Gen. Jeb Stuart. As a cavalryman, Stuart rode several fast horses, but these two were his favorite mounts.
6. It was to be a gift for his wife, Anna. Jackson took such a liking to the 11-year-old horse that he kept it for himself.
7. Robert E. Lee. As mentioned earlier, Traveler was his favorite.
8. Jeff Davis, in honor of the Confederacy's president.
9. Gen. Nathan Bedford Forrest.
10. Lee's Traveler. The beautiful pale gray animal died of lockjaw after Lee's death. Master and mount are both buried on the campus of Washington and Lee University.
11. John S. Mosby, the "Gray Ghost" of the Confederacy.
12. Virginia. The battle at Brandy Station involved about 20,000 horsemen.
13. Washington College in Lexington, later headed by Robert E. Lee, and finally named Washington and Lee University.
14. The man himself.
15. The man was given a 30-day furlough to go home and procure a new horse.
16. John Hood, who had lost a leg and the use of one arm.

17. What was done with horses that died in battle?
18. How many horses normally towed a cannon?
19. Who received breakfast first, men or horses?
20. What term referred to horse-drawn cannon firing from different positions as they moved about a battlefield?
21. What noted New York artist of Civil War battles was better known for his paintings of horses?
22. What brave general died in Alabama when he fell from his horse because of a broken stirrup?
23. Why did Gen. Patrick Cleburne lead his men on foot at the Battle of Franklin?
24. What noted cavalry general trained his men to fight on foot as horses became scarce?
25. What noted Tennessee cavalry general became a horse breeder after the war?
26. What two border states led the country in the raising of horses?
27. What animal often had to substitute for hauling as horses became scarce?
28. What gutsy cavalry general claimed he had had twenty-nine horses killed beneath him?
29. What made Union Gen. Philip Kearny such an easy target for the Rebel marksmen who killed him?
30. What North Carolina general had seven of his mounts killed during the war?

17. Usually they were burned, not buried.
18. Six, working in three pairs.
19. Horses. The bugle call for this was "Stable Call."
20. A flying battery.
21. Edwin Forbes. Naturally his skill in painting horses served him well in painting war pictures.
22. Mississippi Gen. William Edwin Baldwin.
23. He had had two horses shot from under him.
24. Wade Hampton.
25. William Hicks Jackson, whose Belle Meade stables near Nashville produced several champion thoroughbreds.
26. Missouri and Kentucky.
27. Mules, of course.
28. Nathan Bedford Forrest.
29. In a storm, Kearny's horse had shied and galloped right toward the Confederate lines.
30. Bryan Grimes.

Part 3

All Over
The Map

⚑ Cities Great and Small

1. What was the Confederacy's largest city?
2. What city was Union General Sherman's Christmas present to Lincoln on Christmas 1864?
3. In what city was the Confederacy's provisional government organized?
4. In the Confederate plot to burn New York City in 1864, what buildings were supposed to be torched?
5. What Shenandoah Valley town changed hands more than seventy times during the Civil War?
6. How old was the city of Richmond when it became the capital of the Confederacy?
7. What Maryland town saw a Union army entering as the Confederate army exited on the other side?
8. What Virginia city was the scene of a historic explosion of a 586-foot-long tunnel packed with gunpowder?
9. In what Virginia town did Confederate saboteurs plant a bomb that almost blew the wharf to smithereens?
10. What did Gen. Hardee do to delay Sherman's Union troops in entering Savannah?
11. What horrible act did Union general Benjamin Butler commit in the booze-loving city of New Orleans in 1862?
12. What unexpected form of recreation were Texas regiments allowed in Richmond in March 1863?
13. What besieged Southern city surrendered as the Battle of Gettysburg was being fought in Pennsylvania?
14. What was Nashville's "river of grease"?
15. What popular vice was outlawed by the Virginia legislature in December 1863?
16. What Georgia city's St. Stephen's Church had Union soldiers pouring sorghum syrup in the organ pipes so the organ couldn't be use to signal the Confederates?
17. What set the city of Columbia, South Carolina, ablaze at the time Sherman occupied it?
18. What did the mayor of Mobile do to prevent Union destruction in the city?
19. How did the town of Chambersburg, Pennsylvania, respond when General Jubal Early demanded $500,000 not to burn the town?
20. In what Virginia town was a salt manufacturing plant destroyed by Federals?
21. What were New Orleans citizens forced to do, under threat of being expelled from the city?

❧ Cities Great and Small (answers)

1. New Orleans.
2. Savannah, which was the end of Sherman's March to the Sea.
3. Montgomery, Alabama.
4. The hotels, with the hope that the fire would spread to other buildings.
5. Winchester, the "See-saw City" of the war.
6. The ripe age of 124, being founded in 1737.
7. Frederick.
8. Petersburg. The explosion resulted in the Crater, a hole 170 feet long.
9. City Point (now called Hopewell). The town and its wharf were in Union hands, so the saboteurs hoped to do some damage. They did.
10. Flooded the rice fields in the area, cutting off some roads into the city.
11. Butler, Federal governor of the occupied city, ordered all the breweries and distilleries closed. (New Orleans without liquor?)
12. Snowball fights following a rare eight-inch snow in the city.
13. Vicksburg, which surrendered after a 14-month siege.
14. The 30,000 pounds of bacon and ham that were set ablaze when the city was evacuated in February 1863. The grease and odor hung around for days.
15. Gambling, which was running rampant in the city of Richmond.
16. Milledgeville, Georgia's capital at that time.
17. Smoldering bales of cotton. No one is certain whether the Yankees or the evacuating Rebel cavalry set them on fire.
18. Politely surrendered, of course.
19. They couldn't come up with the money. Early burned the town.
20. Saltville, appropriately enough.
21. Swear allegiance to the U.S. This was common practice in Union-occupied areas.

22. What substance was destroyed by Richmond officials in order to avert total chaos in the city when it was occupied?
23. What Missouri city had a riot after the Federal capture of Camp Jackson?
24. What Southern city grew from 40,000 to 140,000 in about 18 months?
25. What was done to Austin, Mississippi, after Confederates fired on a Union quartermaster boat?
26. What city did Confederate General Jubal Early menace in order to draw Union troops away from Richmond?
27. What popular Southern tourist destination has Gen. William Sherman to thank for *not* entering the city?
28. In the Confederate plot to burn New York City, which notable public building caught on fire?
29. How many miles separated the Confederate capital from the Union capital?
30. What Kentucky town was occupied by Confederates and proclaimed the Confederate capital of Kentucky?
31. In what city were the Confederacy's observation balloons inflated?
32. What Georgia city was, in contrast to all others, treated well by Union General Sherman?
33. In what Tennessee town did the residents guide Nathan Bedford Forrest toward the Union hideout by silently waving their handkerchiefs?
34. What Georgia town was spared any destruction by Sherman's army because Joshua Hill, a noted antisecession senator, lived there?
35. What Georgia town has a marker on the spot where the Confederate government was officially dissolved on May 4, 1865?
36. What Mississippi city was occupied by the Union, evacuated, then occupied again, all in one summer?
37. What popular Richmond building celebrated its opening in 1863 with a performance of Shakespeare's *As You Like It*?
38. What Virginia town has Stonewall Jackson's home, his grave, and the church pew he normally occupied?
39. Who marched out to meet General Sherman and surrender the city of Columbia, South Carolina?
40. What key commodity was in short supply after the Federals' capture of Chattanooga?
41. What North Carolina city had one of the largest Confederate prison camps nearby?
42. What Virginia city has the Boyhood Home of Robert E. Lee, a 1795 house open for touring?

22. Whiskey—which wasn't actually destroyed, but poured into gutters.
23. St. Louis. The riot left 28 people dead.
24. Richmond.
25. The Federals burned the town.
26. Washington.
27. Charleston, South Carolina. The well-preserved historic buildings would not look as they now do if Sherman had marched there from Savannah, as people had expected.
28. The popular P. T. Barnum's Museum. It was not severely damaged.
29. Only 100.
30. Bowling Green.
31. Richmond, at the city's Gas Works.
32. Savannah, the end of his infamous "March to the Sea."
33. Trenton.
34. Madison.
35. Washington.
36. Natchez. The reoccupation occurred because the city fired on some Union boats on the river.
37. The New Richmond Theatre, a stunning success in a city that needed escapism.
38. Lexington, where he lived before the war.
39. The mayor (who was probably hoping that some politeness might keep the city from being torched).
40. Coal. The city was a key distribution center for it.
41. Salisbury.
42. Alexandria.

43. What city was the last capital of the Confederacy?
44. What city has a monument to the first Confederate officer killed in the war?
45. What Virginia city has the Old Blandford Church, with the graves of 30,000 Confederate soldiers?
46. What city invited the Confederate government to make it the capital of the Confederacy, due to limited facilities in Montgomery?
47. In what Tennessee city was there a riot between Union and Confederate sympathizers?
48. What leader installed his family in a red brick townhouse on Richmond's Franklin Street?
49. What major Tennessee city fell to Federals in 1862 and remained in Union hands for the rest of the war?
50. In what historic city would you find Signal Mountain, used as a signaling point for the Confederate army?
51. What Georgia city refused to bury the Confederate and Union dead together in a plot of donated land?
52. What was the main cause of the failure of the Confederate plot to burn all the hotels in New York City?
53. What Tennessee city's officials were suspended from office for refusing to take an oath of loyalty to the Union?
54. What city was the starting point for Union General William T. Sherman's March to the Sea?
55. What general was born in the nation's oldest city?
56. What Tennessee city has Confederate Park?
57. After the Union capture of Baton Rouge, what city was Louisiana's pro-Confederate capital?
58. What northern Virginia city was occupied by Federals throughout the war?
59. What Louisiana city was the main goal in the Union's Red River campaign?

43. Danville, where Jefferson Davis issued his last presidential proclamation.
44. Fairfax, Virginia.
45. Petersburg.
46. Richmond, of course.
47. Knoxville.
48. Robert E. Lee.
49. Nashville.
50. Chattanooga.
51. Marietta. The city used the donated land for Marietta National Cemetery, which has only Union graves. They buried the Confederate dead nearby in a separate cemetery.
52. They foolishly forgot to open the windows to ensure a draft, so the fires were easily put out.
53. Nashville, Tennessee's. This occurred after the Union had occupied the city.
54. Chattanooga.
55. Edmund Kirby Smith, born in St. Augustine, Florida.
56. Memphis.
57. Opelousas, then later Shreveport.
58. Alexandria, across the Potomac River from D.C.
59. Shreveport, the gateway to the western Confederacy and also a major supply depot.

⚑ A Path of Destruction

One of the most famous scenes in the film Gone With the Wind is the burning of Atlanta. That scene managed to convey some of the destructiveness of the Civil War. Gen. Sherman wasn't the only great destroyer in the war, and Atlanta wasn't the only place to suffer major devastation.

1. What leader's Mississippi plantation was burned by Federal troops on June 7, 1863?
2. What cavalry general entered Chambersburg, Pennsylvania, and pretty much carried off or destroyed everything in town?
3. What was the source of the many flames along the Georgia and South Carolina coasts in November 1861?
4. What explosion—the most famous "bang" of the Civil War— occurred on July 30, 1864?
5. What discovery in March 1864 temporarily rekindled the South's fighting spirit?
6. What branch of the Confederate military had its records destroyed by fire in its commandant's home?
7. What effect did Gen. Benjamin Huger have on the wartime service of the infamous CSS *Virginia*?
8. What is the claim to fame of Confederate saboteurs John Maxwell and R. K. Dillard?
9. What happened to the Union steamer *Greyhound* as it carried Union Gen. Benjamin Butler up the James River?
10. What was the loudest noise ever heard on Christmas Eve?
11. When the Union army menaced Richmond in May 1862, what did the panicked Virginia legislature vote to do with Richmond?
12. What general's ancestral home on Turkey Island was burned to the ground by Gen. Benjamin Butler?
13. What could Gov. Joseph Brown have done to stop the destruction of Sherman's troops in Georgia?
14. What Northern city was to be burned in retaliation for the Union atrocities in Georgia?
15. What role did Union general David Hunter play in the life of the Virginia Military Institute?
16. What product manufactured in Florida got a lot of attention from Union invaders?
17. What Mississippi town faced a five-day binge of destruction from Union Gen. Sherman's men in February 1864?
18. What important manufacturing facility in Fayetteville, North Carolina, was destroyed by Sherman's Union troops?
19. What major Richmond building exploded in 1863, killing 45 women and children?

✎ A Path of Destruction (answers)

1. President Jefferson Davis's.
2. J. E. B. Stuart.
3. Planters in the area were burning cotton to prevent it falling into Yankee hands.
4. The Crater incident of Petersburg, Virginia, in which Union men had dug a long tunnel under the city's siegeworks and packed it with gunpowder.
5. The discovery of papers on the body of Union Col. Ulric Dahlgren. The papers described a plot to burn Richmond and kill Jefferson Davis and his cabinet.
6. The Marines. Commandant Lloyd John Beall had kept all the Marine records in his own home, which burned.
7. He burned it, along with everything else at Norfolk, to keep it out of Union hands. The *Virginia* is better known by its former name, *Merrimack*.
8. They sneaked a timer bomb past Union sentries at the wharf at City Point, Virginia. When the bomb exploded, it set off a chain reaction that almost wrecked the Union-held wharf.
9. There was a major explosion, caused by a Confederate "coal torpedo," a bomb made to look like coal and placed on an enemy boat's fuelbox.
10. Possibly the deliberate explosion of the USS *Louisiana*. Loaded with 350 tons of gunpowder, it was set on fire with the aim of wrecking Fort Fisher in North Carolina. The explosion was heard for miles.
11. Burn it, rather than have it fall into Union hands. As it turned out, this rash step was unnecessary.
12. George Pickett's. Turkey Island is in the James River.
13. Withdrawn all of Georgia's forces from the Confederate armies, according to Sherman's offer. Brown didn't.
14. New York. In fact, the attempt was made, but only a few buildings burned.
15. He burned it in 1864.
16. Salt, always an essential product. Union men took great delight in destroying salt plants.
17. Meridian.
18. The rifle-making works, which had originally been at the Federal arsenal at Harpers Ferry, Virginia.
19. The Confederate State Laboratory, part of the Richmond arsenal.

20. What became of the Winston County, Alabama, men who formed the 1st Alabama Cavalry to serve the Union?

21. What Lee family home, destroyed by Union troops, was rebuilt after the war by "Rooney" Lee?

22. What future general burned bridges north of Baltimore to prevent Union troops passing through to Washington, D.C.?

23. What Pennsylvania town was burned because it couldn't meet Gen. Jubal Early's demand for $500,000?

24. What South Carolina general's mansion was burned in the Columbia fire?

25. What locally produced substance was used to burn the bridge on the Pee Dee River in South Carolina?

26. What Florida city was evacuated by the Union in March 1863, after the Federals had destroyed most of it?

27. What Union general tried to thwart Confederate raiders by making pre-cut bridges to replace supply bridges the raiders were burning in Tennessee?

28. What Union Cabinet member had his home burned by Gen. Jubal Early?

29. What city near Washington burned its bridges to prevent the passage of Union troops on their way to Washington, D.C.?

30. What old Virginia coastal town was burned in August 1861 to prevent it falling into Union hands?

31. What is the claim to fame of Confederate Col. Robert M. Martin?

32. After Nashville was occupied by the Union, what did Confederate raiders do to harass the Federals?

33. When the Union ship *Moose* send landing parties to the Tennessee River shores, what were they told to destroy?

34. What famous Georgia pistol-making firm was burned by Sherman's army in 1864?

35. What was the source of the columns of smoke along the Mississippi River in June 1862?

36. What elegant plantation house near Charleston was burned during the Civil War?

37. What important facility did the Federals destroy at New Topsail Inlet, North Carolina, in 1862?

38. What venerable James River plantation had its wood paneling used for firewood by Union soldiers?

20. While they were absent, their homes were burned and their families murdered.
21. White House.
22. Isaac Trimble, one of Maryland's finest generals.
23. Chambersburg.
24. Cavalry Gen. Wade Hampton's.
25. Turpentine, produced from the many pines in the area.
26. Jacksonville.
27. William T. Sherman.
28. Postmaster General Montgomery Blair.
29. Baltimore, which was strongly pro-Southern.
30. Hampton.
31. He headed the group of eight arsonists who hoped by burn New York City by starting fires in hotels. The plot failed.
32. Burned bridges between Nashville and Chattanooga.
33. Distilleries, mainly the property of Confederate guerrillas.
34. Griswold & Gunnison, who had produced over 3,000 revolvers for the South.
35. Bales of cotton being burned by Confederates to keep it from falling into Union hands.
36. Middleton Place.
37. A saltworks.
38. Brandon, designed by Thomas Jefferson.

⚑ Islands and Waterways

1. What name is given to the important channel formed in Virginia where the James, Elizabeth, and Nansemond Rivers flow together?
2. After Virginia joined the Confederacy, which two rivers formed the nation's northern boundaries?
3. What athletic feat did Adam Rankin Johnson perform to elude Federal capture in Ohio?
4. In what battle did Winfield Scott Featherston force Union troops off a seventy-foot Potomac River bluff onto the rocks below?
5. What six rivers were the chief battle ground in the "river war" between Confederacy and Union?
6. What was Gen. Alexander Travis Hawthorne's post-war profession after he settled on a small island in Brazil?
7. What important Carolina coastal island did Union Gen. Ambrose Burnside capture in 1862?
8. What was the main obstacle during the Union army's march up the Peninsula toward Richmond?
9. What type of people were supposed to settle on Île à Vache?
10. When Tennessee Gov. Isham Harris asked Gen. Daniel Donelson to built forts at good spots on the Tennessee River, how did Donelson respond?
11. How did Confederate troops hem in the Union gunboats on Virginia's Blackwater River?
12. What Union military goal was achieved when Port Hudson, Louisiana, surrendered in July 1863?
13. Union armies were named for rivers. What were the Confederate armies named for?
14. What type of bridges did the Union army use to cross the James River in the summer of 1864?
15. What much-hated Union general had a plan for digging a canal to bypass Rebel forts along the James River?
16. What was the original purpose of the USS *Hunchback*, part of the Union attack on New Bern, North Carolina?
17. In what battle did Confederates have a field day shooting Union men trying to swim across the Potomac River?
18. What notorious Confederate raiding ship was launched at the Azores Islands in August 1862?
19. What bizarre method was planned to block the inlets of the Albemarle Sound in North Carolina?
20. What overcrowded Richmond prison had many prisoners transferred to the new Georgia prison at Andersonville?

🖎 Islands and Waterways (answers)

1. Hampton Roads, site of the famous *Monitor* and *Merrimack* battle.
2. The Ohio and the Potomac.
3. He swam across the Ohio River.
4. Ball's Bluff, a Union defeat that caused a major stir in Washington.
5. The Cumberland, Tennessee, Yazoo, Arkansas, Red, and (of course) Mississippi.
6. Missionary.
7. Roanoke, the historic site of the "Lost Colony."
8. The high, formidable fortress at Drewry's Bluff on the James River.
9. Freed slaves. Lincoln had a scheme to have freed slaves colonize areas outside the U.S. Île à Vache was a jungle island near Haiti. The scheme failed.
10. He said there were no good spots, but went on to build Fort Donelson and Fort Henry.
11. They felled trees on the riverbanks, making the river impassable.
12. The Union had opened up the entire Mississippi River to its own forces.
13. Regions. The Union had the Army of the Potomac, Army of the Tennessee, etc., while the South had the Army of Northern Virginia, Army of Tennessee, etc.
14. Pontoons.
15. Benjamin "Beast" Butler, noted for hatching many hare-brained schemes.
16. It had been a Staten Island ferry in New York.
17. Ball's Bluff, October 1861.
18. The *Alabama*, scourge of Union shipping for two years.
19. "Stone fleets," nineteen boats loaded with stones and sunk in the channels to prevent ships from going through.
20. Belle Isle, the large island in the James River.

21. Where was the Union fortification known as Rip Rap?
22. What Gulf island of Florida was a strategic spot for blockade runners?
23. What famous fort is on Sullivan's Island near Charleston?
24. What Mississippi River island, captured by the Union in April 1862, had no name?

21. Hampton Roads, Virginia. It was a small artificial stone island.
22. Cedar Key, in the "elbow" of Florida.
23. Fort Moultrie, part of the Fort Sumter National Monument.
24. The infamous Island No. 10.

Part 4

Reminders and Mementos

♫ All Over the American Map

Old soldiers never die . . . they just get places named in their honor—cities, parks, bodies of water, etc. The American map is testimony to the affection Americans (and particularly Southerners) feel for the great names of the Confederacy.

1. What three Confederate heroes' images are carved on Georgia's Stone Mountain?
2. In what city would you (appropriately) find the Museum of the Confederacy?
3. Where can you visit the first White House of the Confederacy?
4. Where would you find the only underwater memorial to a Confederate battle?
5. What Southern capital has the Cyclorama, with a 42-foot-high, 360-degree painting of the Union-ravaged city?
6. What Mississippi town has a Confederate cemetery with 6,000 soldiers, most gravestones being marked "Unknown Soldier"?
7. What Tennessee city has the Confederama, depicting the fierce battles in and around the city?
8. Where would you find the Stonewall Jackson Shrine, the building in which the general died from the wounds of friendly fire?
9. What seaport town has a monument to South Carolina's noted Confederate general, Wade Hampton?
10. What state has a state park, a TVA dam, a wildlife refuge, *and* a lake named after Gen. Joseph ("Fightin' Joe") Wheeler?
11. Where can you tour "Stonewall" Jackson's house?
12. Where would you find the Blue and Gray Museum, formerly a retirement home for Union soldiers?
13. Where would you find the house where the Civil War finally ended?
14. In what large riverside city would you find Confederate Park, which preserves the city's defenses against Union gunboats?
15. What state capitol building has bronze stars marking the scars made by Union cannons?
16. What capital city has a state archives building with stained glass windows telling the story of the Confederacy?
17. What Mississippi city has *The Vanishing Glory*, a dramatic multimedia presentation of the city's siege by the Union?
18. What city has a controversial park named for Gen. Nathan Bedford Forrest?
19. Where would you find a state park dedicated to Confederate Vice-president Alexander Stephens?
20. What seaport city has a monument to Gen. P. G. T. Beauregard, in charge of the city's defense during the war?

✎ All Over the American Map (answers)

1. President Jefferson Davis, Generals Robert E. Lee and Thomas "Stonewall" Jackson.
2. Richmond, Virginia, naturally.
3. Montgomery, Alabama, near the state capitol building. It was Jefferson Davis's presidential home before the Confederate capital was moved to Richmond, Virginia.
4. At Hampton Roads, Virginia, the site of the battle. The Monitor-Merrimack Bridge-Tunnel is probably one of the few underwater memorials in the world.
5. Atlanta, Georgia.
6. Corinth, site of one of the bloodier battles of the Civil War.
7. Chattanooga. The Confederama sits at the foot of Lookout Mountain, near the battle sites of Chattanooga and Chickamauga.
8. Virginia. The house, kept as it was when Jackson died, is near Guinea.
9. Charleston, naturally.
10. Alabama. All of them lie along the Tennessee River.
11. Lexington, Virginia. The house is near the Virginia Military Institute, where Jackson was an instructor.
12. Fitzgerald, Georgia. The museum contains both Confederate and Union artifacts.
13. Near Durham, North Carolina. The Bennett Place State Historic Site includes the house where Gen. Joseph E. Johnston surrendered to Gen. William T. Sherman. (Note: This occurred *after* Lee's surrender to Grant at Appomattox.)
14. Memphis, Tennessee.
15. Columbia, South Carolina. The capitol—or State House, as the locals call it—suffered from Union general Sherman's cannon.
16. Atlanta. It is the Ben W. Fortson, Jr., State Archives, near the capitol building.
17. Vicksburg, whose 47-day siege pitted Union Gen. Ulysses S. Grant against Confederate Gen. John Pemberton.
18. Memphis, Tennessee. The park (or its name, anyway) has aroused racial controversy because of Forrest's post-war connections with the Klan.
19. Crawfordville, Georgia. The site contains the house Stephens lived in before the war.
20. Charleston. The city loved the general, and the general loved the city.

21. Gadsden, Alabama, has a monument to a 15-year-old girl who guided Confederate cavalry general Nathan Bedford Forrest toward Union troops. Who was she?
22. On what university campus would you find the burial place of Robert E. Lee (and also of his horse, Traveler)?
23. What city has St. Paul's Church, the church where Jefferson Davis was worshipping when he received word to evacuate immediately?
24. Where would you find the Official State Bible, on which Jefferson Davis took the oath of office as Confederate president?
25. On what bay would you find the Fort Gaines Historic Site, commemorating a 14-day siege by the Union navy?
26. Where would you find a magnificent Gothic carillon dedicated to the Confederate general who was also an Episcopal bishop?
27. In what state would you find Nathan Bedford Forrest State Park?
28. In what Virginia town would you find not one but two museums dedicated to the same battle?
29. What state has a park commemorating a naval bombardment in which the only fatality was the fort's cat?
30. Where would you find the home of Raphael Semmes, head of the Confederate navy?
31. Arlington House in Arlington, Virginia, was home to what Confederate general?
32. A New Orleans' city park has an equestrian statue of Louisiana's most famous Confederate general. Who?
33. Where is the first capitol of the Confederacy?
34. What city's enormous Hollywood Cemetery contains the graves of Jefferson Davis, Jeb Stuart, Fitzhugh Lee, George Pickett, and many other Confederate notables?
35. What state has a city named for the Confederacy's ambassador to France?
36. Where would you find the (second) White House of the Confederacy?
37. What state's university has the home of Gen. Josiah Gorgas, the Confederacy's chief of ordnance?
38. What city was a Robert E. Lee statue mounted smack in the middle of a trolley track?
39. What Southern capital has Monument Avenue, called the "most beautiful street in America" and dedicated to the Confederacy?
40. Whose monuments are found on Monument Avenue? (There are 5 altogether.)
41. Where would you find a massive chain that Rebel soldiers stretched across the Mississippi River to halt Union gunboats?

21. Emma Sansom. Forrest asked for a lock of her hair as a keepsake.
22. Washington and Lee University in Lexington, Virginia. Lee died in Lexington, serving as president of what was then known as Washington College.
23. Richmond, Virginia. The church has plaques commemorating Jefferson Davis and Robert E. Lee, who both worshipped there. The pews they normally sat in (No. 63 for Davis, No. 111 for Lee) are marked.
24. In the State Archives of Montgomery, Alabama.
25. Mobile Bay, in Alabama. The Battle of Mobile Bay was where Union admiral Farragut uttered his famous "Damn the torpedoes" line.
26. The University of the South, Sewanee, Tennessee. Bishop Leonidas Polk, later Gen. Polk, was one of the founders of the university.
27. Tennessee, Forrest's home state and the state where he carried on much of his cavalry activity.
28. New Market, site of a May 1864 battle involving cadets from the nearby Virginia Military Institute. Two different (but adjacent) museums are operated there.
29. Georgia. The Fort McAllister State Historic Park commemorates an 1863 bombardment by the Union navy. The one fatality was Tom Cat, the Confederates' mascot.
30. Mobile, Alabama—near the sea, appropriately.
31. Robert E. Lee. The house is open to tours and faces D.C. across the Potomac River.
32. P. G. T. Beauregard, the "Grand Creole."
33. Montgomery, Alabama. It served as Confederate capitol only a few months, the new capitol being in Richmond. Interestingly, the Alabama capitol is on Goat Hill.
34. Richmond, Virginia, appropriately enough. The hilly cemetery also contains an enormous pyramid-shaped monument to all the Confederate dead.
35. Louisiana. The city is Slidell, near New Orleans, and named for John Slidell.
36. Richmond, Virginia, adjacent to (appropriately) the Museum of the Confederacy.
37. The University of Alabama, which Gorgas served as president after the war.
38. New Orleans. The statue sits atop a tall column and the trolley rails actually go around the column.
39. Richmond, Virginia.
40. President Jefferson Davis, Gen. Robert E. Lee, Gen. "Stonewall" Jackson, Gen. J. E. B. Stuart, and oceanographer Matthew Fontaine Maury.
41. At Kentucky's Belmont Battlefield State Park, commemorating the 1861 Battle of Belmont.

42. What general is the subject of an outdoor drama at the Lime Kiln Theatre in Lexington, Virginia?
43. What state has Secession Lake?
44. What large Texas city is named for Robert E. Lee's home?

⚐ The Confederacy on Screen

Hollywood has a long fascination with the Confederate South, so much so that one of the great movies of all time—perhaps the greatest—is a Confederate epic. (That's Gone with the Wind, *in case you're straining.) Test your knowledge here of some well-known—and lesser-known—films about the Confederacy.*

1. In what Confederate state is *Gone with the Wind* set?
2. What film featured the Our Gang ("Little Rascals") kids in a sentimental Civil War story?
3. What Clint Eastwood film has him playing a lustful (and wounded) Yankee soldier recovering in a girls' academy in the Confederacy?
4. What stone-faced film comic played a Confederate train conductor in the 1927 film *The General?*
5. What is the only Walt Disney film set in the Confederacy?
6. What slapstick comic played a bellboy acting as a Confederate spy behind enemy lines?
7. What acclaimed 1989 film showed the attack on the Confederacy's Fort Wagner by a black regiment?
8. What four-hour 1993 film centered on a famous battle between the Confederacy and the Union?
9. In that film, actor Martin Sheen played which noted Confederate leader?
10. What lavish MGM film of the 1950s featured Elizabeth Taylor as an unhappy Confederate belle married to a schoolmaster?
11. What film starred James Caan and Harrison Ford in a tale of young Texans going off to fight in Tennessee?
12. What epic-length silent film (directed by pioneer director D. W. Griffith) still arouses controversy because of its sympathetic portrayal of the KKK?
13. What child star portrays a Confederate daughter who cajoles Abraham Lincoln into releasing her condemned father?
14. Who is the only character in *Gone with the Wind* who actually says the words "I'm a Confederate"?

42. Thomas "Stonewall" Jackson, whose home was in Lexington before the war.
43. Appropriately, South Carolina, the first state to secede. The lake is in Abbeville County.
44. Arlington, named for Arlington House in (you guessed it) Arlington, Virginia.

✎ The Confederacy on Screen (answers)

1. Georgia, of course. (Please don't admit it if you missed this.)
2. *General Spanky* (1936), with "Spanky" McFarland in the title role, and also featuring "Alfalfa" and "Buckwheat" (as a slave in search of a master).
3. *The Beguiled* (1971). It is one of Eastwood's least sympathetic roles, though at the end he does get his come-uppance in the form of poisoned mushrooms.
4. Buster Keaton.
5. *The Great Locomotive Chase* (1956), starring the former Davy Crockett (and later Daniel Boone), Mr. Fess Parker. It concerns Union spies stealing a Confederate train (the same story, in fact, as *The General* with Buster Keaton).
6. Red Skelton. The film was *A Southern Yankee* (1948).
7. *Glory*, probably the first Civil War film to show the racism of the Union side.
8. *Gettysburg*.
9. Robert E. Lee.
10. *Raintree County* (1958).
11. *Journey to Shiloh* (1966).
12. *Birth of a Nation* (1915), which traces the fortunes of one Confederate and one Union family who were formerly friends.
13. Shirley Temple in the 1935 film *The Littlest Rebel*.
14. Naughty lady Belle Watling, who makes the remark when contributing some cash to help the Southern cause.

15. What film featured Michael Landon in the story of young Confederates who take the law into their own hands at the war's end?
16. What Jimmy Stewart classic looks at the divisive effects of the Civil War on a Virginia family?
17. What off-beat film was set in a Mississippi county that threatens to secede from the state if the state secedes from the Union?
18. What John Wayne extravaganza had Wayne playing a Union cavalry office sent into Confederate territory to destroy a railroad junction?
19. What 1935 film starred western regular Randolph Scott in the story of an aristocratic Confederate family during the Civil War?
20. Besides playing Rhett Butler in *Gone with the Wind*, Clark Gable also played in a later film about the Confederacy. What was it?
21. What noted short film concerns a Confederate soldier and Union soldier who strike up a friendship on opposite sides of a river?
22. What brutal 1967 film featured Glenn Ford and George Hamilton in a tale about Confederate prisoners escaping from a Union fort?
23. What Confederate leaders appear in *Gone with the Wind?*
24. What film tells the story of the doctor who treated the Confederate-friendly assassin of President Lincoln?
25. What Gary Cooper film depicted a Quaker family whose oldest son (Anthony Perkins, pre-*Psycho*) breaks family tradition and runs off to fight the Confederacy?
26. In what film did Gary Cooper play a Union officer who goes undercover as a Confederate spy?
27. What film, based on a classic American novel, featured World War II hero Audie Murphy as a green Union soldier in his first battle against Confederates?
28. What is the only film to mention a Confederate battle site in its title?
29. What is the only French-made movie about the Confederacy?
30. What Van Heflin film has him playing poor Andrew Johnson, faced with a divided country and a devastated Confederacy after the Civil War?
31. What *very* bad movie of the 1960s featured rock star Roy Orbison in a tale of Confederate spies?
32. What TV movie of a famous Civil War novel featured Richard Thomas, John-Boy from "The Waltons"?
33. What 1961 film about Confederate prison escapees is based on a novel by science fiction author Jules Verne?
34. Why were so few Civil War films made during the World War II years?

15. *The Legend of Tom Dooley* (1959), based on the popular folk ballad.
16. *Shenandoah* (1965).
17. *Tap Roots* (1948), starring Van Heflin and Susan Hayward. It featured horror star Boris Karloff as an Indian medicine man.
18. *The Horse Soldiers* (1959), which also starred a young William Holden. The film is based on the exploits of Union Col. Benjamin Grierson, who destroyed the Confederacy's supply route in Tennessee.
19. *So Red the Rose* (whose title, incidentally, is taken from Omar Khayyam's *Rubaiyat*).
20. *Band of Angels* (1957), based on a novel by Robert Penn Warren.
21. *Time Out of War* (1954). The film was based on several occurrences during the Civil War.
22. *A Time for Killing*, based on a novel titled *Southern Blade*.
23. None. In spite of the historical accuracy of the film (and the novel on which it was based), there are no actual historical characters in it.
24. *The Prisoner of Shark Island* (1936), the story of the ill-fated Dr. Mudd who treated John Wilkes Booth.
25. *Friendly Persuasion* (1956).
26. *Springfield Rifle* (1952).
27. *The Red Badge of Courage* (1951), based on the novel by Stephen Crane. The movie's cast included war cartoonist Bill Mauldin.
28. *Journey to Shiloh* (1966).
29. *Incident at Owl Creek Bridge* (1961). Based on a story by American author Ambrose Bierce, it concerns the hanging of a Confederate spy by Union troops.
30. *Tennessee Johnson.*
31. *The Fastest Guitar Alive* (1968). It's probably one of the worst Civil War movies ever made, but it's at least mildly interesting to see Orbison on screen (with a guitar, of course).
32. *The Red Badge of Courage*, which most viewers believe was much better than the 1951 movie that starred Audie Murphy.
33. *The Mysterious Island*. The escapees' getaway balloon, blown off course, lands them on an island of gigantic animals.
34. Hollywood was under pressure to show the Allied war aim of freeing oppressed peoples. Anything remotely approving of slavery was out of the question.

35. What famous Confederate raid is the subject of the 1954 film *The Raid?*
36. What comic made the Civil War film *Mooching Through Georgia* the same year as *Gone with the Wind?*
37. What Academy Award winning film opens with actor Kevin Costner making a suicide charge into a line of Confederate soldiers?

⚑ The Cream of Memorials

Is there an "official" list of great Americans? Not really, though there are two locations where statues of an elite group of heroes and heroines are on public display. One is the Hall of Fame for Great Americans on the campus of Bronx Community College in New York. Inaugurated in 1900, the Hall of Fame has busts of great Americans, a few of whom were Confederates. Even more famous than the Hall of Fame is the Capitol in Washington, where every state has the privilege of placing statues of two of its most illustrious people. Yes, some of these were Confederates—not necessarily ones you might expect.

1. What two Confederate generals are honored with busts in the Hall of Fame?
2. What is the only state represented in the Capitol by statues of *two* Confederate leaders?
3. Who is the only Confederate governor who has a statue in the Capitol?
4. What general's statue represents Virginia in the Capitol?
5. What Confederate soldier and poet's bust is in the Hall of Fame?
6. What grand statesman's statue represents Mississippi in the Capitol?
7. What cavalry general's statue represents South Carolina in the Capitol?
8. What Confederate scientist's bust is in the Hall of Fame?
9. What state is represented in the Capitol by a statue of Gen. Edmund Kirby Smith?
10. What statesman represents Georgia in the Capitol?
11. What Southern nationalist leader has a statue in the Capitol, representing South Carolina?
12. What man's Capitol statue represents the "breakaway" state of West Virginia?

35. The raid from Canada on St. Albans, Vermont. Interestingly, the movie was directed by an Argentinian.
36. Buster Keaton. The title is a spoof of the popular Union song "Marching Through Georgia," referring to Sherman's March to the Sea.
37. *Dances with Wolves* (1990).

✎ The Cream of Memorials (answers)

1. Robert E. Lee (part of the original group in 1900) and Thomas "Stonewall" Jackson (added in 1955).
2. Alabama. One is Gen. Joseph Wheeler, the other is statesman (and later educational reformer) Jabez Curry.
3. Zebulon Vance of North Carolina.
4. Robert E. Lee, of course.
5. Sidney Lanier's, one of the lesser-known Confederate notables.
6. Jefferson Davis.
7. Wade Hampton.
8. Matthew F. Maury, naval man, oceanographer, the "Pathfinder of the Seas."
9. Florida, his birthplace.
10. Vice-president Alexander Stephens.
11. John C. Calhoun, also well-known as a senator and as vice-president of the U.S.
12. Francis Pierpont, first governor of the new state, and also governor of Union-occupied counties in northern Virginia.

⚑ Parking the Confederacy

Thanks to the U.S. National Park Service, visitors can visit battlefields and other significant sites connected with the Confederacy. In fact, a history-minded tourist with adequate time might plan an endless vacation exploring America's Confederate park sites.

1. Which national military park features the "Bloody Pond," often stained red to commemorate the men and mounts who bled and died in its waters?
2. Which park, situated on a South Carolina island, is the site of the first shots of the Civil War?
3. What is the only Civil War national park with its own navy?
4. What national park in Virginia commemorates the fateful meeting of Lee and Grant on April 9, 1865?
5. Which national battlefield park features an equestrian statue of Stonewall Jackson where he and his brigade gained their early fame?
6. What park commemorates the 1862 battle in which Stand Watie, a Cherokee leader, aided the Confederate forces?
7. What Maryland battle site commemorates one of the bloodiest Civil War battles, a rare case of Confederate forces invading the Union?
8. Which park commemorates the Mississippi River-side city that long withstood the siege of Union Gen. Ulysses S. Grant?
9. Which general's death site is on the former Fairfield Plantation, now part of the Chancellorsville battlefield park?
10. What famous Pennsylvania military battlefield lies near the farm and retirement home of President Dwight Eisenhower?
11. Which Tennessee military park is often called "Chick-Chatt"?
12. What infamous Confederate prison in Georgia is now a national historic site?
13. At what park site did Confederate and Union boat gunner exchange "iron valentines" on February 14, 1862?
14. What fort on the Gulf of Mexico never fell to the Confederates, in spite of repeated attempts?
15. What historical site in West Virginia commemorates the first major confrontation between pro-slavery and anti-slavery forces?
16. What Missouri park commemorates the first major Civil War battle west of the Mississippi River?
17. What Georgia park commemorates the Confederates' loss of one of their most important ports?
18. Which battlefield park in northern Virginia was the site of not one, but two major battles, both of which were Confederate victories?

🐚 Parking the Confederacy (answers)

1. Shiloh, in Tennessee, commemorating the battle on April 6-7, 1862.
2. Fort Sumter National Monument, near Charleston, fired on by Confederates on April 12-14, 1861.
3. Vicksburg National Military Park in Mississippi, which contains the Union iron-clad *Cairo*, sunk in 1862 and completely reconstructed in 1984.
4. Appomattox Court House. Grant and Lee met in the home of Wilmer McLean, which no longer exists. A reconstruction sits on the site.
5. Manassas National Battlefield Park in northern Virginia. It was here, on July 21, 1861, that Jackson was observed "standing like a stone wall."
6. Pea Ridge National Military Park in Arkansas.
7. Antietam National Battlefield.
8. Vicksburg National Military Park in Mississippi.
9. Stonewall Jackson, who died in a small office building on the plantation. The building is now the Stonewall Jackson Shrine. Technically, it is part of the Fredericksburg and Spotsylvania County Battlefields Memorial National Military Park. (One wonders if the National Park Service could devise shorter names for these areas.)
10. Gettysburg National Military Park.
11. The Chickamauga and Chattanooga National Military Park.
12. Andersonville, through whose gates some 45,000 Union prisoners passed in only fourteen months. The prison became, after the war, a focus of Northern resentment.
13. Fort Donelson National Battlefield, on the Cumberland River in northern Tennessee.
14. Fort Pickens, near Pensacola, Florida. It is now part of the Gulf Islands National Seashore.
15. Harpers Ferry National Historical Park, which commemorates the October 1859 raid of abolitionist John Brown. He and his followers seized the town's armory, aiming to arm (and free) the slaves. The townspeople fought back, and a Marine force led by Robert E. Lee stormed the building. Some regard Brown's raid as the beginning of the Civil War, and of the Confederacy.
16. Wilson's Creek National Battlefield, in Missouri. At the time of the battle, it was uncertain whether Missouri was to be part of the Union or the Confederacy.
17. Fort Pulaski National Monument, near Savannah. The loss of the fort (and port) was a major Confederate setback in 1862.
18. Manassas National Battlefield Park, with the victories in July 1861 and August 1862.

19. Which park contains "Bloody Lane," a road on which victorious Union soldiers could walk from one end to the other, stepping only on the bodies of the downed Confederate soldiers?
20. Which Tennessee park commemorates Union penetration of much of middle Tennessee?
21. Which park in Pennsylvania contains an enormous Cyclorama depicting the fateful battle that took place there?
22. Which Tennessee park was the site of a "Battle Above the Clouds"?
23. Which Georgia park contains Providence Spring, a clear-water spring that appeared miraculously during the hot summer of 1864?
24. Which Virginia city contains the site of Chimborazo, the Confederacy's largest military hospital?
25. Which Georgia park commemorates the Confederate's successful efforts to slow Sherman's infamous march through Georgia?
26. What Mississippi park commemorates the Confederate wild man, Gen. Nathan Bedford Forrest?
27. Which park contains the Surrender Triangle?
28. What massive Virginia park contains a 100-mile driving tour within its various segments?
29. What is the largest of the National Park Service's Civil War parks?
30. Which national battlefield in Virginia features a hollowed-out area known as "the Crater," caused by a monumental underground explosion?
31. Which park commemorates Ulysses S. Grant's famous "Unconditional surrender" ultimatum?
32. Which park contains the Hornet's Nest, the site of the battle's most vicious fighting?
33. Which battlefield contains the Dunker Church, a small building that was witness to some of the worst gore of the war?
34. What park contains the nation's oldest Civil War monument?
35. Where would you find the Old Salem Church, a Baptist church used by both Confederates and Union after the battle?
36. What park contains the High Water Mark Monument, marking where the Confederates briefly broke through the Union lines?
37. Which Georgia park contains more than 12,000 Union prisoners' graves?
38. Which battlefield site commemorates one of the few occasions that a Union general had beaten elusive cavalry leader Nathan Bedford Forrest?

19. Antietam National Battlefield in Maryland.
20. Stones River National Battlefield, near Murfreesboro. The contest occurred from December 31, 1862 to January 2, 1863.
21. Gettysburg.
22. Chickamauga-Chattanooga—or "Chick-Chatt."
23. Andersonville National Historic Site, site of the infamous Confederate prison.
24. Richmond. The Chimborazo site is part of Richmond National Battlefield Park.
25. Kennessaw Mountain National Battlefield Park. Confederate Gen. Joseph E. Johnston's actions slowed Gen. Sherman's advance toward Atlanta.
26. Brice's Cross Roads National Battlefield Site. Here, in June 1864, Forrest's troops struck at Union Gen. Sherman's. Though outnumbered two to one, Forrest inflicted massive losses.
27. Appomattox Court House, of course—the site of Lee's surrender to Grant in 1865.
28. The Richmond National Battlefield Park, which occupies several sites in and around the city.
29. Chickamauga and Chattanooga, containing more than 8,000 acres.
30. Petersburg National Battlefield. The Crater explosion was the brainchild of coal miners in the 48th Pennsylvania Infantry.
31. Fort Donelson National Battlefield in Tennessee. Here Grant faced his old friend—and now Confederate enemy—Simon Bolivar Buckner. Confronted with the demand for "unconditional surrender," Buckner did.
32. Shiloh National Military Park in Tennessee.
33. Antietam National Battlefield in Maryland. The present church is a reconstruction.
34. Stones River National Battlefield in Tennessee. The park's Hazen Monument and Cemetery were built within a year of the battle itself.
35. Fredericksburg and Spotsylvania County Battlefields Memorial National Military Park. (Has anyone suggested a shorter name for this park?)
36. Gettysburg National Military Park. The monument stands on the spot where Gen. Lewis Armistead fell, after cheering on his brigade by waving his hat atop his raised sword.
37. Andersonville National Historic Site, where the Confederacy's largest prison stood.
38. Tupelo National Battlefield in Mississippi. Forrest was wounded in the battle, and, oddly, he had not inflicted his usual resounding defeat on his Union opponent.

⚑ All Over the American Map (Part 2)

1. On the grounds of Virginia's capitol are statues of the Confederacy's most famous doctor and one of its most famous generals. Who are they?
2. In what coastal city could you visit Beauvoir, Jefferson Davis's last home?
3. Where could you find a nine-story-high Robert E. Lee?
4. What South Carolina town bills itself as the "Birthplace of the Confederacy"?
5. In what non-Confederate state would you find a plaque marking the birthplace of Confederate general "Stonewall" Jackson?
6. In what city would you find the Confederate Memorial Chapel?
7. What noted Confederate site would you find in Birmingham, Alabama?
8. Which non-Confederate state has a monument to the birthplace of Jefferson Davis?
9. What Confederate statesman's house can be toured in Washington?
10. What states have counties named for Jefferson Davis?
11. Which state capitol building has a life-size bronze statue of Robert E. Lee?
12. What famous fort lies on Sullivan's Island near Charleston?
13. What nationally famous cemetery has a large Confederate Memorial erected by the United Daughters of the Confederacy?
14. Where would you find the prison cell which confined Jefferson Davis after the fall of the Confederacy?
15. What South Carolina college's museum displays two of the largest Confederate flags in existence?
16. Where would you find the Big Shanty Museum, which houses a Confederate locomotive stolen by Union soldiers?
17. Where could you see the bullet-pierced raincoat worn by "Stonewall" Jackson when he was fatally wounded *and* Jackson's horse, Little Sorrel?
18. In what city could you tour the Beauregard-Keys House, post-war home to Gen. P. G. T. Beauregard?
19. What four noted Confederates are portrayed on the Confederate Monument in Augusta?
20. In what state would you find Lake Jeff Davis?
21. At what college does a statue of "Stonewall" Jackson overlook the parade grounds?
22. In what state would you find the Barbara Fritchie house, home of an elderly woman who defied "Stonewall" Jackson?

✎ All Over the American Map (Part 2) (answers)

1. Dr. Hunter Holmes McGuire, Stonewall Jackson's physician, and Stonewall Jackson himself.
2. Biloxi, Mississippi. The grounds contain a Confederate museum and a cemetery with more than 700 graves.
3. At Stone Mountain, Georgia, along with Thomas "Stonewall" Jackson and Jefferson Davis. All three are carved on the face of the 825-foot mound of granite.
4. Abbeville, where the first organized secession meeting took place in 1860. Ironically, the town was also the Confederacy's deathplace: Jefferson Davis held his last cabinet meeting here in 1865.
5. West Virginia. Jackson was born in Clarksburg in 1824, and at that time West Virginia was not a separate state. It seceded from Virginia in 1863.
6. Richmond, Virginia, naturally. The small building is located behind the Virginia Museum of Fine Arts.
7. None whatever. The city of Birmingham didn't exist during the Confederate era. (Is a trick question all right?)
8. Kentucky. The Jefferson Davis Monument is near Fairview and is one of the largest monuments in the U.S. Though Davis was (obviously) pro-secession, Kentucky never officially seceded from the Union. (Interestingly, Davis's birthplace is not far from Abraham Lincoln's.)
9. Robert Toombs, both a general and a congressman for the Confederacy.
10. Georgia, Louisiana, Mississippi, Texas. In Georgia and Texas the counties are actually Jeff Davis, not Jefferson Davis.
11. Richmond, Virginia. The statue stands on the spot where Lee assumed his command.
12. Fort Moultrie, part of the Fort Sumter National Monument.
13. Arlington, near D.C.
14. Fort Monroe in Hampton, Virginia.
15. The Citadel's, in Charleston.
16. Kennesaw, Georgia. The locomotive, "The General," was stolen and recaptured. Buster Keaton's movie *The General* was based on this incident, as was the Walt Disney movie *The Great Locomotive Chase*.
17. At the Virginia Military Institute Museum in Lexington, Virginia. Little Sorrel is faithfully stuffed and preserved behind glass.
18. New Orleans.
19. Robert E. Lee, Thomas "Stonewall" Jackson, William Walker, and Howell Cobb. Walker and Cobb were Georgians, and Walker was born and buried in Augusta.
20. Mississippi.
21. The Virginia Military Institute in Lexington, where Jackson was an instructor before the war.
22. Maryland, in the city of Frederick. Supposedly Barbara Fritchie dauntlessly waved her Union flag as "Stonewall" and his soldiers marched through town. ("Stonewall" being a gentleman, he did not shoot her.)

23. What state has a military installation named for Gen. Henry Benning?
24. What capital city is traversed north-south by the Jefferson Davis Highway?
25. Where would you find Robert E. Lee Boulevard running parallel to Lake Pontchartrain?
26. What army base near Fredericksburg, Virginia, is named for a Confederate general?
27. Where would you find the Tomb of the Unknown Soldier of the Confederate States of America?
28. In what inland city would you find the Confederate Naval Museum?
29. What North Carolina site commemorates a ridiculous attempt to blow up a fort using a "powder ship"?
30. What Kentucky battlefield site commemorates the state's bloodiest battle?
31. What Tennessee mountain city has the Confederate Memorial Hall?
32. What state capitol building has a Confederate spy buried on the grounds?
33. What recreational lake in Georgia is named for the Confederacy's most notable poet (and also a Confederate veteran)?
34. In what state is the Olustee Battlefield Historic Site, commemorating the largest Civil War battle in the state?
35. What state has Fort Polk, an army base name for Gen. Leonidas Polk?
36. What state has a memorial to its governor during the Civil War, a governor who kept Confederate soldiers from having adequate uniforms?
37. Lexington Presbyterian Church in Lexington, Virginia, has a pew marked with a small plaque that mentions the church's most famous deacon. Who was he?
38. In what historic city would you find Signal Mountain, used as a signaling point for the Confederate army?
39. In what state is Natural Bridge Historic Site, commemorating a battle to keep Union troops from the state capital?
40. The historic House of Delegates hall in the Virginia state capitol has statues of eight noted Confederates. Which ones? (Hint: Most, but not all, were Virginians.)
41. Thibodaux, Louisiana, contains St. John's Episcopal Church. Which Confederate general was closely connected with the church?
42. The Medical College of Virginia has a medical library named for the South's most renowned nurse. Who was she?
43. A black church in Roanoke, Virginia, has a stained glass window dedicated to a Confederate general who taught a Sunday school for slaves. Who was he?

23. Georgia—the famous Fort Benning, of course.
24. Richmond, Virginia, of course.
25. New Orleans.
26. Fort A. P. Hill, named for Gen. Ambrose Powell Hill, who was mortally wounded in the last weeks of the war.
27. At Beauvoir, Jefferson Davis's last home in Biloxi, Mississippi.
28. Columbus, Georgia. Though the town is not a seaport, it is on the Chattahoochee River, which empties into the Gulf of Mexico.
29. Fort Fisher Historic Site in North Carolina. Union Gen. Benjamin Butler had the brilliant idea that a ship loaded with 215 tons of powder would explode and destroy the fort. It failed, much to the Confederacy's relief.
30. Perryville State Historic Site, marking the 1862 battle of 17,000 Confederates versus 22,000 Federals.
31. Knoxville. The Hall was the headquarters of Gen. James Longstreet during the 1863 siege of Knoxville.
32. Tennessee's. The capitol, in Nashville, has the grave of 21-year-old Sam Davis, executed by the Yanks. (Davis's home is in nearby Smyrna, Tennessee.)
33. Lake Sidney Lanier.
34. Florida. The battle is re-enacted every February.
35. Louisiana. Gen. Polk was also Episcopal bishop of Louisiana.
36. North Carolina. The Zebulon Vance Birthplace memorializes the governor who took care to see that the produce of North Carolina's many textile mills went to clothe North Carolina soldiers.
37. Thomas "Stonewall" Jackson.
38. Chattanooga, Tennessee.
39. Florida. The Battle of Natural Bridge was fought in March 1865 to defend Tallahassee.
40. Robert E. Lee, Stonewall Jackson, J. E. B. Stuart, Joseph E. Johnston, Fitzhugh Lee, Matthew Fontaine Maury (the Virginians), and Jefferson Davis and Alexander Stephens (the only two non-Virginians honored in the room).
41. Bishop (later General) Leonidas Polk, the Confederacy's "Fighting Bishop." Polk founded the parish which contains St. John's Church.
42. Sally Tompkins.
43. Thomas "Stonewall" Jackson.

44. In what state would you find a state memorial to Confederate Cabinet member Judah P. Benjamin?
45. What city houses the locomotive *Texas*, used in the Great Locomotive Chase in which Confederates chased down Union spies who had stolen a train?
46. Where would you find Stratford Hall, the birthplace of Gen. Robert E. Lee?
47. What state has a county named for Thomas "Stonewall" Jackson?
48. What Florida city's historical museum was a church that served as a Union prison and barracks during the war?
49. What Kentucky park commemorates a Mississippi River fort that was known as the "Gibraltar of the West"?
50. In what historic Tennessee city would you find Silverdale Confederate Cemetery?
51. Richmond's St. James Episcopal Church has memorial windows dedicated to two noted worshipers: a nurse and a famous cavalry general. Who were they?
52. What large national military park is divided between Tennessee and Georgia?
53. What Confederate spy's home is now a museum in Smyrna, Tennessee?
54. What metropolis has a history center with a permanent display on the city in its Civil War years?
55. In what Florida resort town would you find Fort Zachary Taylor with its large collection of Civil War armaments?
56. What Georgia city's museum is in a building used as a Civil War hospital?
57. What Virginia city has a siege museum, showing how painful life was in the 10 months before Lee surrendered to Grant?
58. What Georgia town has a marker on the spot where the Confederate government was officially dissolved on May 4, 1865?
59. Which historic Richmond church has memorials to Jefferson Davis, Robert E. Lee, and Matthew Fontaine Maury?
60. In what state could you see the CSS *Neuse*, one of only two Confederate ironclads in existence?
61. What North Carolina port town runs the J. N. Maffitt River Cruises, named for one of the Confederacy's most renowned blockade runners?
62. In what town would you find a monument to the Confederate defenders of Fort Sumter and Fort Moultrie?
63. Front Royal, Virginia, has the memorial home of which noted Confederate spy?

44. Florida. At Ellenton is the Judah P. Benjamin Confederate Memorial Historic Site. At the end of the Civil War, Benjamin stayed in this area before fleeing to England.
45. Atlanta, in the Cyclorama museum building.
46. Stratford, Virginia, very near the birthplace of George Washington.
47. Texas. The county is named Stonewall, since Texas already had a Jackson County (named for Andrew, naturally).
48. Pensacola. The museum was originally Old Christ Church.
49. The Columbus Belmont Battlefield State Park, site of the 1861 Battle of Belmont.
50. Chattanooga.
51. Captain Sally Tompkins and Gen. J. E. B. Stuart.
52. Chickamauga and Chattanooga National Military Park. The larger part is in Georgia.
53. Sam Davis'. The twenty-one-year-old Davis was executed by the Union for failing to divulge secrets.
54. Atlanta. "Atlanta and the War, 1861–65" is housed in McElreath Hall.
55. Key West.
56. Augusta's.
57. Petersburg, south of Richmond.
58. Washington.
59. St. Paul's Episcopal, near the capitol. The church also has pew markers indicating where Davis and Lee usually sat during services.
60. North Carolina, at the Caswell-Neuse State Historic Site, near Kinston.
61. Wilmington—appropriately, since Wilmington was the center for blockade running.
62. Charleston, naturally.
63. Belle Boyd, who used the town as one of her most effective bases.

64. What South Carolina city has a mansion that belonged to Gen. Wade Hampton?
65. What two U.S. colleges are named for Confederate notables?
66. What city has the Boyhood Home of Robert E. Lee, a 1795 house open for touring?
67. What well-known cemetery has the Tomb of the Unknown Dead of the Civil War?
68. What is the significance of the Fort Hill plantation in South Carolina?
69. What Confederate general has a high peak in the Great Smoky Mountains named for him?

64. Columbia. It is known as the Hampton-Preston Mansion and is open to the public.
65. Washington and Lee University in Virginia (named, in part, for Robert E. Lee) and Jefferson Davis Community College in Alabama.
66. Alexandria.
67. Arlington National Cemetery.
68. It is a sort of shrine to secession and Southern nationalism, since it was the estate of John C. Calhoun. It became the site of Clemson University.
69. Thomas Lanier Clingman. Clingman's Dome is the highest point in Tennessee.

Part 5

The Confederacy Afloat

☗ That Blasted Blockade

The Confederacy's greatest battle was not on land. It was against a string of U.S. ships that (in theory) shut down all the South's coastal commerce. This was Lincoln's idea, and it was easier said than done. The blockade did hurt the South, but never as effectively as the North wanted. And thanks to the blockade, American history now has that brave and romantic character, the blockade runner, who ensured that Southerners with money could still buy lace, guns, and coffee.

1. Where was the first successful invasion of Confederate territory?
2. What request of Confederate diplomat John Slidell did French emperor Napoleon III refuse?
3. What general proclaimed (incorrectly) that the Union's naval blockade had been lifted in January 1863?
4. What Atlantic port became the principal goal of blockade runners after New Orleans and Charleston were bottled up?
5. What sort of Confederate ships always operated in pairs?
6. What Confederate blockade runner was named for one of the South's greatest leaders?
7. When Lincoln extended the Union blockade on April 27, 1861, which two coastal states were then included?
8. Who were the best-paid men in the service of the Confederacy?
9. What flattering inscription was found on the jewel-studded sword on the captured Confederate blockade runner *Fanny and Jenny*?
10. What restriction did the Confederate government impose on its blockade runners in March 1864?
11. What cargo was the British blockade runner *Rouen* carrying when pursued by the Union ship *Keystone State* off Wilmington, North Carolina?
12. What Rebel blockade runner was such a success because he had spent years surveying the Atlantic coast?
13. Who was the most infamous passenger aboard the blockade runner *Condor* when the Union navy caught up with it?
14. After the Union captured the port of Wilmington, how did they fool blockade runners into thinking the Confederacy still controlled the port?
15. What, according to Southern optimists, was the bright side of the Union's blockade of Southern ports?
16. What was the most important item brought in by the Confederate blockade runners?
17. What elderly Union general conceived of the Anaconda Plan against the Confederacy?

✎ That Blasted Blockade (answers)

1. At Hatteras in North Carolina, where Confederates tried to keep the inlet clear for their blockade runners. They failed.
2. French aid in breaking the Union's naval blockade of the Confederacy. The emperor did not want to offend the U.S.
3. P. G. T. Beauregard. He was quite mistaken.
4. Wilmington, North Carolina.
5. The blockade runners. The idea was that, if pursued, they would split up so that only one would be captured.
6. The *Robert E. Lee.*
7. North Carolina and Virginia. Before this, only the lower South states were included in the blockade.
8. The blockade runners who, while providing essential supplies to the country, also swelled their own personal bank accounts.
9. "To Gen. Robert E. Lee, from his British sympathizers."
10. A rule that half the runners' cargo space had to be used for government supplies.
11. Cotton, the favorite export item of blockade runners headed to Europe.
12. The brilliant John N. Maffitt, famous as the captain of the *Owl.*
13. Confederate spy queen Rose O'Neal Greenhow, who drowned when her getaway boat capsized.
14. They lit the "all clear" signal on the Mound, the port's signal hill. Being out at sea, the blockade runners had no idea of the port's capture.
15. It would stir the South to creating more of its own industries. To some extent, this did occur.
16. Probably the British-made Enfield rifles, desperately needed by the common soldiers.
17. Mexican War hero Winfield Scott, who proposed blockading the South's ports and cutting off its access to the Mississippi.

18. What historic deed was done by the USS *Sabine* in Pensacola, Florida, in April 1861?
19. When the Union's blockade of Southern ports began in 1861, what was the rate of capture?
20. How many ships did the Union use to blockade the Southern ports?
21. What did the Union offer Englishmen who provided information on Southern blockade runners?
22. About how many Confederate vessels were captured by the Union blockade?
23. What type of coal was used by blockade runners because it burned with little smoke, making concealment easier?
24. What were the two favorite foreign ports for blockade runners?
25. How many Confederate navy blockade runners were ever captured?
26. What English newspaper artist traveled with the Army of Northern Virginia and smuggled his sketches to England via blockade runners?
27. What Mexican port city was a favorite point of entry for Southern blockade runners?
28. Who lifted the blockade on May 22, 1865?
29. What nation's flag was flown by most of the Confederate blockade runners leaving the port of Nassau in the Bahamas?
30. Beginning in 1864, what Confederate port was the chief focus of the Union's blockade?
31. When Rebel blockade runner John Wilkinson sailed for the port of Wilmington, North Carolina, in 1865, where did he end up?
32. What foreign port had 588 Confederate blockade runners sail out of its harbor during the war?
33. What state was the leader in Confederate blockade running?
34. What effect did the Union blockade of Southern ports have on the Charleston *Mercury*?
35. What neighbor nation's waters were open to Southern blockade runners but closed to Union warships?
36. What was the nearest foreign port for the many Confederate blockade runners operating out of Wilmington, North Carolina?
37. How many naval vessels was Union Navy Capt. Louis Goldsborough given to blockade the coasts of Virginia and North Carolina?
38. What was the name of the U.S. naval unit responsible for blockading the coasts of Virginia and North Carolina?
39. What nations benefited most from the Union blockade of Confederate ports?
40. What famous Georgia poet had served for a while on a blockade runner?

18. It was the first Union ship to blockade a Southern port—a key component in the South's defeat.
19. About 1 in 9 Confederate ships were captured.
20. About 600.
21. A reward of 30.
22. About 1,500.
23. Anthracite. The Union attempted to cut off anthracite shipments to foreign ports where the Confederacy could buy it.
24. Nassau, in the Bahamas, and Bermuda. At these ports the runners would transfer cargo to smaller ships that could easily evade the Union blockade.
25. None.
26. Frank Vizetelly, one of the most famous Civil War artists.
27. Matamoros, near Brownsville, Texas.
28. President Andrew Johnson.
29. Great Britain's.
30. Wilmington, North Carolina.
31. Liverpool, England. Wilmington had been captured by the Federals, and the nearest port, Charleston, was closed, so Wilkinson crossed the Atlantic to find safety.
32. Nassau, the Bahamas—very close to the coast of Florida, but technically foreign soil.
33. North Carolina.
34. The blockade caused a paper shortage, thus finally reducing the newspaper to 2 pages.
35. Mexico's. The Confederates took full advantage of this.
36. Nassau, in the Bahamas, 570 miles away.
37. Thirteen, at the beginning. Needless to say, this was not adequate.
38. The North Atlantic Blockading Squadron.
39. Bermuda, the Bahamas, and the Caribbean islands that saw a neat profit from having the blockade runners trade there.
40. Sidney Lanier, who became the unofficial poet of the defeated South.

41. What Southern author was captured while running the blockade to Britain to promote his own books?
42. What mainly financed the building up of the Confederate navy?
43. What Confederate Cabinet member had a fleet of 60 ships for running the Federal blockade?
44. What position did Gen. William Beall hold that allowed him to sneak cotton through the Union blockade?
45. Vain Gen. P. G. T. Beauregard claimed that military stress had turned his black hair to gray. According to rumor, the blockade turned it gray. How?
46. What was the purpose of the CSS *David*, a 50-foot cigar-shaped torpedo boat built in Charleston?
47. What noted blockade runner commanded, at various times, the *Cecile*, the *Theodora*, the *Florie*, the *Lillian*, and the *Owl*?
48. What Gulf island was a strategic spot for blockade runners?
49. What Georgia port was closed to the Rebel blockade runners when the Union captured Fort Pulaski?
50. What North Carolina town has the J. N. Maffitt River Cruises, named for one of the Confederacy's most famous blockade runners?

⚑ Ironclads, Submarines, and Other Naval Novelties

War has brought forth many technological wonders, including ironclad ships, submarines, and many others. In the 1860s, the South, admittedly more agricultural than technical, rose to the occasion of war and made more than a few contributions to the modern navies of the world. And, incidentally, two of the most famous ships in world history happen to fall into this category of questions.

1. What new type of naval warfare began in Charleston harbor?
2. What ship, burned in the Norfolk Naval Yard in April 1861, became one of the most famous ships in the world?
3. What was the purpose of the Ladies' Gunboat Societies in the South?
4. What North Carolina town has one of only two Confederate ironclads still in existence?

41. Edward Pollard, famous for coining the phrase "The Lost Cause" for the Confederacy.
42. Cotton, shipped to Europe past the coastal blockade.
43. George Trenholm, possibly the wealthiest man in the Confederacy. He was Secretary of the Treasury.
44. He was purchasing agent for Confederate prisoners of war. With his profits from blockade running he brought supplies for Confederate prisoners.
45. The blockade cut off Beauregard's access to hair dye.
46. Breaking the Federal blockade of Charleston.
47. John Maffitt, who made his reputation by his exploits on the *Owl*.
48. Cedar Key, in Florida's "elbow."
49. Savannah.
50. Wilmington, the center of blockade running.

✎ Ironclads, Submarines, and Other Naval Novelties

(answers)

1. Submarine. The Confederate submarine *Hunley* sank the Union's *Housatonic*.
2. The ironclad USS *Merrimack*, which the Confederacy renovated. As the *Virginia*, it went on to fight the *Monitor*.
3. Raising money to build ironclads for the Confederate navy.
4. Kinston. The CSS *Neuse* is at the Caswell State Historic Site.

5. Why was Commodore T. T. Craven of the Union navy court-martialed?
6. At 209 feet long, what was the largest ironclad ship built by the Confederacy?
7. What was the fate of the Confederate ironclad *North Carolina*, docked on the Carolina coast?
8. What wooden object was commonly used by Confederates to make naval mines?
9. What new naval era was begun on March 9, 1862?
10. What was "Old Bogey"?
11. What notorious Union ironclad was called a "Yankee cheese box on a raft"?
12. What name was given to the Union gunboats that wore only a light armor of iron?
13. What important naval bureau was organized in 1862?
14. What name was given to the wave of joy that swept the North after the famous *Monitor-Merrimack* naval duel?
15. How many Union ships were sunk by Confederate naval mines?
16. What did Horace L. Hunley create?
17. What Confederate naval man invented a deep-sea sounding apparatus for mapping the ocean bottom?
18. What did President Jefferson Davis propose as a source for the iron needed for ironclad ships?
19. What did ironclad ships lack, posing a communications problem?
20. How did Union naval men convince Confederate mine expert Jeffries Johnson to tell them where mines were placed?
21. What was the original name of the Confederate ironclad *Virginia*?
22. What was the only casualty in the famous *Monitor-Merrimack* battle?
23. Where was the first aircraft carrier used?
24. What bizarre method was planned to block the inlets of the Albemarle Sound in North Carolina?
25. What sneaky explosive device was perfected by the Confederacy in early 1864?
26. How many were in the crew of the *Hunley*, the Confederacy's first submarine?
27. What purpose did the ironclad ship *North Carolina* serve after its bottom had been eaten out by worms?
28. What famous Confederate ship did Franklin Buchanan command?
29. Why were the ironclads *Georgia*, *Fredericksburg*, and *Charleston* called "ladies' gunboats"?
30. In what port was the Confederate navy the victim of its own ingenuity in planting naval mines?

5. Commanding two Union ships, he declined to fight with the fearsome Confederate ironclad *Stonewall*.
6. The CSS *Tennessee*, launched in 1864.
7. It had its bottom eaten out by worms, making it unusable.
8. Beer kegs.
9. The age of the ironclads, commencing with the battle of *Monitor* versus *Merrimack*. Ironclads had superseded wooden warships.
10. A fake ironclad ship, used by Federals to spook Confederates. It was basically timber, canvas, and skillfully applied black paint.
11. The *Monitor*.
12. "Tin-clads," though tin was not actually used.
13. The Torpedo Bureau, designed to refine the use of mines (called "torpedoes" at the time).
14. "Monitor fever." The North was relieved to learn that the Confederate ironclads were not as fearsome as they had thought.
15. There were 37, including 9 ironclads.
16. The Confederate submarine that bore his name, the *H. L. Hunley*.
17. John M. Brooke, who also advocated the use of ironclads by the Confederacy.
18. Railroad rails. His proposal was never acted on.
19. Masts. On normal ships, signal flags were run up the masts.
20. They fastened him to the bow of a ship headed up the James River where the mines were planted. He told all.
21. The USS *Merrimack*, the name it usually goes by in histories.
22. A Confederate shell hit one of the *Monitor*'s viewing slits, temporarily blinding the commander, John Worden.
23. Hampton Roads, Virginia, where the Union ship *Fanny* had a reconnaissance balloon launched from its deck in August 1861.
24. "Stone fleets," nineteen boats loaded with stones and sunk in the channels to prevent ships from going through.
25. The "coal torpedo," painted to resemble lumps of coal and thus explode in the firebox of Union ships' boilers.
26. Nine—one to steer, eight to work the hand-cranked propeller.
27. The Rebels used it as a stationary gun platform.
28. The CSS *Virginia*, better known by its earlier name, the *Merrimack*.
29. They had been built with funds raised by the Ladies' Gunboat Societies throughout the South.
30. Savannah, Georgia. When Sherman's Union troops occupied the city, the Rebel navy couldn't successfully remove all the mines, so they destroyed their ships rather than leaving them for the Union.

31. What was the distinction of the USS *Commodore Jones*, destroyed by Confederate naval mines in the James River?
32. What was the Confederate ship *Teaser* equipped to launch?
33. When scanning the rivers for Confederate naval mines, what would the Federals look for?
34. What did U. S. Grant send out on the Mississippi River to draw the fire of the Vicksburg artillery batteries?
35. When the submarine *Hunley* was sent to Charleston in August 1863, what general believed (wrongly) that he had the best weapon for destroying the Union fleet?
36. Once the Union had captured Mobile Bay, what dangerous job had to be done?
37. When Confederate naval officer Tattnall was court-martialed in Richmond, what was his offense?
38. What Rebel ram ship, named for a famous general, was the object of an intense Federal search in early 1865?
39. What momentous event in the world's naval history occurred on February 17, 1864?
40. What was the source of power in the Confederacy's first submarine?
41. What was significant about the sinking of the Union ship *Cairo* in December 1862?
42. What type of metal was used in the armor of the gunboats called "tin-clads"?
43. What contribution did Samuel M. Pook make to the war against the Confederacy?
44. What powerful iron ram ship was introduced to defend Vicksburg?
45. What world-famous Confederate ship went down in flames, blown up by its own crew?
46. Why were Union ship captains told not to anchor their ships in the deepest parts of channels?
47. What 34-foot submarine, which never saw battle, eventually ended up at the Louisiana State Museum?
48. What were the South's most uncomfortable ships in summertime?
49. What future Confederate naval officer proposed the idea of ironclad ships to the U.S. Navy in 1846 but had the proposal rejected?
50. In what Southern bay did Union naval man David Farragut utter his famous words "Damn the torpedoes! Full speed ahead!"?
51. What was the South's chief problem in constructing ironclads?
52. What ironclad, with a very appropriate name, played a key role in the defense of Charleston?
53. What would the Federals do when they located the Confederates' naval mines?

31. The explosion lifted the entire ship completely out of the water.
32. Observation balloons made of silk.
33. Wires anchoring the mines to the riverbanks.
34. A fake "gunboat" made of logs and barrels. It worked.
35. P. G. T. Beauregard.
36. Clearing all the naval mines the Rebels had planted there.
37. He had ordered the destruction of the *Virginia* (better known as the *Merrimack*). He was acquitted, since there was really no other choice but to destroy the ship after Norfolk was occupied.
38. The CSS *Stonewall*.
39. The first combat sinking of a ship by a submarine. The CSS *H. L. Hunley* sank the USS *Housatonic*.
40. Hand-cranking a propeller.
41. It was the first ship sunk by the Confederates' mines.
42. Iron, not tin. The boats were not called ironclads because their iron armor was thinner than the regular ironclad ships.
43. He designed ironclad gunboats, known as the "Pook turtles" from their shape.
44. The *Arkansas*.
45. The *Virginia*, better known as the *Merrimack*. When the Norfolk Navy Yard was evacuated, the ship was found to be too deep to make it up the James River.
46. Confederate submarines would move under the boats and leave an explosive mine behind.
47. The CSS *Pioneer*.
48. The ironclads, which became like floating ovens.
49. John L. Porter, who helped design the world's first ironclad, the CSS *Virginia*.
50. Mobile Bay, Alabama. The "torpedoes" were what we now call mines.
51. Getting enough iron, a chronic problem for the Confederacy.
52. The CSS *Palmetto State*.
53. Using the wires that anchored the mines to the shore, they would drag the mines to shore, or blow them up.

54. What did Confederates release into the Cape Fear River in early 1865?

55. What noted Confederate ironclad was sunk in the Roanoke River in October 1864?

56. What famous ship was found in 1973 off North Carolina, lying in 220 feet of water?

57. What general name described land mines, naval mines, and time-bombs?

58. What was the fate of the triumphant Confederate submarine *Hunley* after it sank the Union ship *Housatonic*?

59. What energetic Confederate naval officer had started his career at the age of 15?

60. What key naval man in the Confederacy was born and died in the important naval city of Portsmouth, Virginia?

61. What extremely modern agency was headed by Gen. Gabriel Rains?

62. What name was given to ships specifically designed to ram other ships?

63. How many Union ships did the awesome ram CSS *Stonewall* sink?

64. Why did the Confederate navy destroy most of its ships in Savannah harbor?

65. What happened to the Union steamer *Greyhound* as it carried Union Gen. Benjamin Butler up the James River?

66. What reward did the Union offer for the capture of the Confederacy's "David" torpedo boats?

67. What Confederate ironclad had to be towed away before its completion because of threatening Federals?

68. What major Southern city became the name of the ship *Fingal*, originally used as a blockade runner?

69. What feared Confederate ship sank in water so shallow that part of the ship was still visible?

70. What was unusual about three members of the crew of the ironclad *Chicora*?

71. What ram ship, named for a Confederate general, had been a Union ship built in Cincinnati?

72. What Confederate ship had the distinction of being built near the place it was named for?

73. What ironclad went into service against the Union fleet even before its completion?

74. What Confederate ship set the Congress on fire?

75. What optimistic announcement did Gen. P. G. T. Beauregard make after the ironclad *Chicora* attacked Federal blockade ships off Charleston?

54. Floating mines, causing severe damage to Union boats.
55. The CSS *Albemarle*.
56. The USS *Monitor*, famous for its duel with the Confederate ironclad *Virginia* (*Merrimack*).
57. "Infernal machines." In the 1860s most men still considered such weapons to be ungentlemanly.
58. It sank.
59. Catesby ap Roger Jones, who helped developed the plating for the Confederacy's first ironclad.
60. John L. Porter, who helped design ironclads for the Confederacy.
61. The Torpedo Bureau, concerned with land and naval mines, a new concept in the 1860s.
62. Rams, appropriately enough. They were equipped with massive iron "beaks" for ramming.
63. None. By the time it reached America, the war had ended.
64. They themselves had mined the harbor, and when Union troops occupied the city in December 1864, the ships would have fallen into Union hands.
65. There was a major explosion, caused by a Confederate "coal torpedo," a bomb made to look like coal and placed on an enemy boat's fuel box.
66. $30,000. The Union really feared these 50-foot wonders.
67. The CSS *Arkansas*, which was towed from Memphis to Yazoo City, Mississippi.
68. The CSS *Atlanta*, an ironclad.
69. The CSS *Albemarle*.
70. They were freed blacks.
71. The CSS *Gen. Sterling Price*, which patrolled the Mississippi River.
72. The CSS *Albemarle*, built near the Albemarle Sound in North Carolina.
73. The CSS *Louisiana*, which, appropriately, was supposed to protect New Orleans.
74. To be precise, the CSS *Virginia* set the USS *Congress* on fire.
75. He declared the Union blockade was at an end. It definitely wasn't.

76. What ill-fated ship was blown up by its own commander, in an explosion that rocked the nearby Union ships?
77. What two ram ships, both named for Confederate generals, accidentally collided while fighting Union ships?
78. What Confederate weapons were sent to the U.S. Naval Academy for display in its museums?

⚑ Raiders of the Lost Cause

What were the raiders? They weren't warships, blockade runners, merchant ships, or passengers ships. They were, to put it mildly, designed to prey on the cargo of Union ships. And why not, since the Union had seen fit to blockade the Confederacy's coastline. If the raiders helped the cause only a little in terms of obtaining supplies, they were great morale-builders, striking terror into every Union seaman.

1. What did the owners of U.S. commercial ships do to avoid the danger of capture by Confederate raiders?
2. What Confederate raiding ship had such a reputation that the U.S. Navy offered a $500,000 reward for its capture?
3. What infamous Confederate raiding ship had to be abandoned at Gibraltar?
4. What Confederate prize did the Union navy capture in Bahia, Brazil?
5. What notorious Confederate raiding ship, named for a state, was launched in England in May 1862?
6. What Union naval officer was court-martialed for capturing a Confederate ship?
7. What was the chief claim to fame of the Union ship *Kearsarge*?
8. What Confederate raiding ship sent New York shipping agents into a panic?
9. What Confederate raiding ship was out preying on Union whaling ships after the surrender of Lee?
10. What famous Confederate ship never docked in a Confederate port?
11. What was the official name of the Confederacy's raiding ships?
12. What was awarded to Union Capt. John Winslow for sinking the infamous Confederate raider CSS *Alabama*?
13. What role did U.S. ambassador William Dayton play in the war against the Confederacy?

76. The CSS *Louisiana*, which had not even been completed.
77. The CSS *Gen. Sterling Price* and CSS *Beauregard*.
78. A Confederate torpedo (mine) boat and several types of torpedo.

✎ Raiders of the Lost Cause (answers)

1. Changed their ships' registration to other nations—meaning the ships would no longer fly the U.S. flag.
2. The CSS *Alabama*, commanded by the energetic Raphael Semmes.
3. The CSS *Sumter*, which had caused significant damage to Union shipping.
4. The great raider *Florida*.
5. The *Alabama*.
6. Napoleon Collins, who captured the feared Rebel raider, the *Florida*. Since he captured it in Brazilian waters, he violated international law, so he was court-martialed.
7. It sank the seemingly indomitable Confederate raider *Alabama*.
8. The CSS *Tallahassee*, which captured and burned several Union ships in the New York area.
9. The CSS *Shenandoah*. The crew had no idea that the surrender had occurred.
10. The CSS *Alabama*, which sailed every ocean on its raiding voyages.
11. Cruisers.
12. The official U.S. Thanks of Congress.
13. As minister to France, Dayton managed to stop French manufacture of Confederate ships and the French providing sanctuary for Confederate sea raiders.

14. What noted naval officer was a grandson of President Zachary Taylor?
15. What commodity did Union Navy Secretary Welles tell Lincoln had to be cut off from the Confederacy?
16. What notorious Confederate raiding ship was the prime focus of the Union navy's warships?
17. What sort of armor did the USS *Kearsarge* wear in its famous battle against the CSS *Alabama*?
18. What valuable item did the CSS *Florida* capture from the Union ship *Harriet Stevens* in 1864?
19. What famous Confederate raiding ship finally surrendered in November 1865, six months after the Civil War had ended?
20. How many Union ships did the Confederate cruisers destroy?
21. Before the notorious raider *Alabama* sank in June 1864, how many Union ships had it captured and sunk?
22. What type of U.S. commercial ships were the preferred prey of the Confederate ship *Alabama*?
23. What was the *Florida* missing when it left England in 1862?
24. What famous Confederate ship was originally known as "290"?
25. What state lent its name to the first Confederate cruiser built abroad?
26. What was distinctive about the Union ship *Jacob Bell*, captured by the CSS *Florida*?
27. What notable Rebel ship, named for a state capital, destroyed 30 Union ships in a two-week period?
28. What remarkable piece of Confederate technology was eventually owned by the sultan of Zanzibar?
29. What infamous Confederate raiding ship had to be abandoned at Gibraltar?
30. What ship, named for a state, was built in Scotland and originally named the *Japan*?
31. What name was given to the government-approved pirate ships that ranged the coast from Maine to Mexico?
32. What Confederate naval hero was given instructions to "do the enemy's commerce the greatest injury in the shortest time"?
33. What incredible Confederate defeat did the people of Cherbourg, France, witness in June 1864?
34. In what Latin American country's waters was the infamous raider *Florida* sailing when captured by the Union?
35. What notorious Confederate privateer was named for one of the key men of the Confederacy?
36. What type of sailors could, if captured by the Union, be hanged as pirates?

14. John Taylor Wood, one of the Confederacy's most feared coastal raiders.
15. Anthracite coal. Exported from the Union to foreign ports, it was bought by Confederates and used in their ships. Since it produced little smoke, it allowed them a "stealth factor" in raiding.
16. The infamous CSS *Alabama*, commanded by the intrepid Raphael Semmes.
17. Heavy chains, which fended off most of the *Alabama*'s shots. The Union ship won the battle.
18. Opium, desperately needed in the Southern hospitals.
19. The CSS *Shenandoah*, which had continued to capture Union whaling ships well after the war ended.
20. About 200.
21. To the Confederacy's delight, 55.
22. Whaling vessels.
23. Guns. They were sent by a separate ship. The Confederates were trying to hide the purpose of their new ship.
24. The CSS *Alabama*, since it was the 290th vessel made at England's Laird Shipyards.
25. Florida. The CSS *Florida* was built in England.
26. It was valued at $1.5 million, the most valuable ship taken by a Confederate cruiser.
27. The CSS *Tallahassee*.
28. The formidable commerce destroyer, the CSS *Shenandoah*.
29. The CSS *Sumter*, which had caused significant damage to Union shipping.
30. The CSS *Georgia*.
31. Privateers. Unlike real pirates, they (in theory) turned over their spoils to the Confederate government.
32. Raphael Semmes. He did as he was told.
33. The sinking of the supposedly unsinkable Confederate raider *Alabama*.
34. Brazil's.
35. The *Jefferson Davis*, which raided many Northern ships before meeting its end in Florida in August 1861.
36. Crew of privateers, private vessels that preyed on the Union's commercial ships.

37. What cumbersome cruiser, which captured no Union ships at all, was named for a river in Virginia?
38. When the Confederate cruiser *Magnolia* was captured by a Union ship, what cargo was it carrying?
39. What naval hero arrived in a Cuban port with seven Union ships as trophies?
40. Legally speaking, what allowed the Confederacy to engage in privateering?

♎ . . . And Other Nautical Matters

The blockade, ironclads, and raiders are covered in separate chapters. Here we cover the issue of Confederate naval matters in general. Keep in mind that when the Confederacy became a nation in 1861, it was not known for its seafaring tradition—but neither was the Union. Both South and North had to learn mostly from experience, not tradition. They had to "make it up as they went," and the nautical side of Confederate life is one of the most interesting, and least studied, aspects of the Civil War.

1. What color uniform was worn by the Confederate navy in summer?
2. What was the unusual (and appropriate) location of the Confederate naval academy?
3. When Lincoln ordered a Thanksgiving Sunday in September 1864, what two Confederate defeats were being celebrated?
4. What Confederate naval hero had been born at sea?
5. What city was captured by Union gunboats in 1862 and occupied for the rest of the war?
6. What small individual was the only fatality in the Union navy's bombardment of Fort McAllister?
7. Where was the U.S. Naval Academy relocated during the war?
8. What noted Union naval man was a Tennessean by birth?
9. How did the people of New Orleans greet Union naval man David Farragut in 1862?
10. What did the Confederates do to the Norfolk Navy Yard before evacuating it?
11. What did Confederate naval captain Edward Fuller do when his warship ran low on gunpowder bags?
12. What Canadian province gave a warm welcome to naval commander Matthew Maury?

37. The *Rappahannock*.
38. Cotton, what else?
39. Raphael Semmes.
40. The U.S. had not signed the Treaty of Paris of 1856, which outlawed privateering. As a (former) part of the U.S., the Confederacy had never formally agreed not to privateer. So it did.

✎ . . . And Other Nautical Matters (answers)

1. White, naturally. (Some things never change.)
2. On a ship.
3. The capture of Atlanta and the naval victory at Mobile.
4. The brassy John N. Maffitt, son of a sailor.
5. Memphis.
6. Tom Cat, the garrison's mascot.
7. Newport, Rhode Island. Annapolis, in Maryland, was regarded as an unsafe location, being so near the Confederacy.
8. David Farragut, probably one of the most famous American admirals.
9. They set the waterfront on fire, forcing him to anchor his fleet far from the flames.
10. Set it on fire, naturally.
11. He had his men cut off their pants legs to use for bags.
12. Nova Scotia. Maury noted that the Nova Scotians were "strongly secesh."

13. What American Revolution hero was the Confederate Naval Academy's training ship named for?

14. What Southern port was the destination of the 77-ship fleet that set sail in October 1861?

15. What naval incident brought the U.S. and Britain to the brink of war?

16. What type of coal allowed Confederate ships to approach with stealth?

17. How did Confederate troops hem in the Union gunboats on Virginia's Blackwater River?

18. What self-appointed Confederate navy man hijacked a Union cargo ship, sold its cargo, and had the ship returned to its rightful owners?

19. When the U.S. steamship *St. Nicholas* was captured by Confederates, what method was used?

20. What famous Confederate artifact is found at the Belmont Battlefield Park?

21. What happened to the Union ship *Queen of the West*, which had made an armor for itself out of cotton bales?

22. What essential cargo was the Union ship *Hercules* hauling when captured by Confederates near Memphis?

23. What was the fate of the crew of the Confederate ship *J. P. Chapman* when discovered in San Francisco?

24. Having no money to buy ships in Europe, what did the Confederates attempt to use as credit?

25. In what river was the Confederate ship *Chattahoochee* when it exploded and sank?

26. What noted Rebel horsemen claimed he had set up his own "Confederate navy"?

27. What Latin American country made Confederate and Union officials promise not to have a naval battle in its waters?

28. When Confederate Navy Secretary Stephen Mallory was arrested in May 1865, what was he charged with?

29. What six rivers were the chief battleground in the "river war" between Confederacy and Union?

30. What noted woman died after leaving a captured ship and capsizing in her getaway boat?

31. What Rebel general fled an occupied city by using a bridge made of rice boats?

32. What Georgia city, a major shipbuilding site for the Confederacy, was wrecked by Federals in April 1865?

33. What imposing fort prevented the Union's James River flotilla from advancing on to Richmond?

13. Patrick Henry (a Virginian, famed for his "Give me liberty or give me death" speech).
14. The heavily defended Port Royal, South Carolina. The 77-ship fleet was the largest American fleet assembled up to that time.
15. The *Trent* affair, in which Confederate diplomats on the British ship *Trent* were seized by a Union ship. The act was seen as an act of aggression against Britain.
16. Anthracite, which burns with little smoke. Other types of coal used as ship fuel burned with more smoke, making ships easier to see from a long distance.
17. They felled trees on the riverbanks, making the river impassable.
18. Thomas E. Hogg, who had pulled off the operation with only four comrades. He later became, officially, a Confederate naval officer.
19. The Confederate navy men boarded disguised as passengers. The leader was disguised as a woman.
20. The chain stretched by the Confederates across the Mississippi to try to stop Union gunboats.
21. Confederates fired into the bales, setting them on fire.
22. Coal—seven barges full, in fact.
23. They wound up jailed on Alcatraz Island.
24. Cotton certificates—that is, pledges of future shipments of cotton.
25. The Chattahoochee.
26. Cavalry general Nathan Bedford Forrest, who captured three Union boats, which he used in an 1864 raid on a Union depot in Tennessee.
27. Brazil. The Union naval commander broke the promise.
28. Organizing "piratical expeditions," and also treason.
29. The Cumberland, Tennessee, Yazoo, Arkansas, Red, and (of course) Mississippi.
30. Noted Rebel spy Rose O'Neal Greenhow, who was carrying secret documents at the time.
31. William Hardee, who chose to evacuate Savannah, seeing that he was faced by William Sherman's army of 62,000 Federals.
32. Columbus, which produced arms as well as ships.
33. The fort at Drewry's Bluff on the James.

34. Why was Confederate naval officer John Braine called on the carpet for capturing the Union ship *Roanoke*?

35. What was Union General William T. Sherman's aim in reaching the ocean at Savannah?

36. What was the name of the captured Confederate high-speed boat that the Federals used as a courier ship between D.C. and City Point, Virginia?

37. What famous navy man was crippled and never able to serve at sea after 1839?

38. What select group of men were given the task of escorting the Confederate treasury's gold when Richmond was evacuated?

39. In what sea was the Confederate Naval Academy ship anchored?

40. What valuable items were under the protection of naval Lt. William H. Parker?

41. What name was given to iron shot that was heated in a furnace and fired at wooden ships?

42. What European country was most receptive to Confederate ships docking there?

43. What former Confederate warship was used in the Union's assault on Alabama's Fort Morgan?

44. What was the first combined army-navy operation in the war?

45. What contribution did John Mercer Brooke make to the Confederate navy?

46. What was the usual shore duty of the Confederate Marines?

47. What was Stephen Mallory's best qualification for serving as Secretary of the Navy?

48. What is the claim to fame of the Union ship *San Jacinto*?

49. What modification in ships reduced the effectiveness of "hot shot"?

50. About how many Confederate Marines were there?

51. What general was responsible for torching the Norfolk Navy Yard and evacuating the city?

52. What old naval friend of Richard L. Page demanded that Page surrender Fort Morgan to the Union?

53. What South Carolina soldier had to defend Port Royal against an attack from his brother?

54. In what Caribbean locale did Confederate naval officer John Braine capture the Union ship *Roanoke*?

55. Who was paid more, marines or regular soldiers?

56. What was the true mission of the *Star of the West*, a cargo steamer sailing from New York to New Orleans?

57. What Confederate Cabinet member was (appropriately) born on an island?

34. He captured it near Havana, Cuba—a neutral port. Worldwide, the act was seen as a violation of neutrality.
35. Linking up with the Union navy, making it easier to get supplies for his troops.
36. The *Bat*.
37. Matthew F. Maury, known for his work in oceanography.
38. The cadets of the Confederate Naval Academy.
39. It wasn't. It was at Drewry's Bluff on the James River.
40. The Confederate archives and treasury, after the evacuation of Richmond.
41. Hot shot, appropriately enough. It was widely used at coastal forts.
42. France. The port of Brest was a favorite harbor for Confederate ships.
43. The (formerly CSS) *Tennessee*.
44. The Union's capture of the Confederate forts guarding the important Hatteras Inlet in North Carolina.
45. The Brooke rifle, a heavy artillery piece. Brooke was made chief of the Confederate navy's Ordnance Bureau.
46. Guarding naval stations and manning naval shore batteries.
47. He had served in the U.S. Senate as chairman of the Committee on Naval Affairs.
48. It captured Confederate diplomats Slidell and Mason on board the British ship *Trent*, kicking off the infamous *Trent* affair.
49. Iron plating. The furnace-heated iron "hot shot" was only effective at penetrating wooden vessels.
50. Just over 500.
51. Benjamin Huger, who believed the city could not resist a Union invasion.
52. David Farragut, who asked for unconditional surrender. Page refused.
53. Thomas Drayton, whose brother, Union Cmdr. Percival Drayton, commanded the lead Union warship.
54. Near Havana, Cuba.
55. Regular soldiers.
56. It was in fact carrying reinforcements and supplies to Fort Sumter near Charleston. The soldiers were hidden below deck to keep the mission a secret. Northern newspapers let the story leak.
57. Stephen Mallory, secretary of the navy, who was born on Trinidad in the West Indies.

58. What large Virginia port had its naval yard burned when the city was evacuated by Gen. Benjamin Huger?
59. What naval officer had been the first head of the U.S. Naval Academy at Annapolis?
60. What non-Confederate state contributed many men to the Confederate navy?
61. What inland city was the site of a Confederate naval works?
62. What land-based job was given after the war to, ironically, one of the Confederacy's best naval men?
63. What world-renowned Confederate naval leader ended his days as a professor of meteorology?
64. What ship, sunk in the James River to block navigation, was dredged up by the U.S. Navy in 1939?
65. What type of Union ships were burned by naval Lt. James Waddell in the Arctic Ocean?
66. What naval officer, forced to abandon his river post, took his men to fight at the land battle of Sayler's Creek?
67. What two ships were engaged in the 1862 Battle of Hampton Roads?
68. What was the fate of the CSS *Bat*, a high-speed steamer?
69. What Confederate naval man made his reputation not by commanding ships but by writing books on navigation?
70. What noted naval man fled the South after the war, escaping to Cuba in a lifeboat?
71. What riverside city was the site of an 1862 sinking of a Confederate fleet?
72. What group of women held raffles, auctions, and benefit concerts to raise money to build fighting ships for the Confederacy?
73. What blockade running ship covered its activities by taking part in yacht regattas?
74. What type of ships were "cottonclads"?
75. Besides cotton, what farm product would warships sometimes wear as "armor"?
76. What non-nautical position was Rear Admiral Raphael Semmes given in the war's last days?
77. What new tactic did the Confederates use to keep the Union from capturing Confederate steamers on the Santee River, South Carolina?

58. Norfolk.
59. Franklin Buchanan.
60. Maryland, naturally enough, with its long coastline, its pro-Southern sympathies, and (of course) the site of the U.S. Naval Academy.
61. Charlotte, North Carolina.
62. President of Maryland Agricultural College, Franklin Buchanan.
63. Matthew F. Maury, who taught at the Virginia Military Institute.
64. The CSS *Patrick Henry*, the ship that served as the Confederacy's Naval Academy.
65. Whaling ships. Most were burned after the war had ended, before Waddell had heard the news.
66. John Randolph Tucker, who went on to become an admiral for the navy of Peru.
67. The CSS *Virginia* (formerly the *Merrimack*) and the USS *Monitor*.
68. It was taken by the Federals and used as a courier ship between D.C. and City Point, Virginia.
69. Matthew F. Maury. Crippled in 1836, he could not lead the seafaring life.
70. John Taylor Wood. Between Florida and Cuba he encountered pirates and a violent storm.
71. Memphis.
72. The Ladies' Gunboat Societies.
73. The *Camilla*, which had won the Queen's Cup in its pre-Confederate days. The lovely schooner was later captured by the Union.
74. Any ship that used cotton bales as protection against enemy fire. Although it caught fire easily, it made great padding and was much cheaper than iron.
75. Bales of hay—specifically, *wet* hay, which wouldn't necessarily burn if hit.
76. He was made a brigadier general in the Confederate army and told to defend Danville, Virginia.
77. They secured the steamers to the docks with concealed chains. As the Union men worked to undo the chains, the Confederates opened fire on them.

Part 6

Things of the Spirit

ᛋ Chaplains, and Other Men of the Cloth

"There are no atheists in foxholes," says the old proverb. Indeed, war makes some people more religious, confronting them with the brevity of life and the need for spiritual support. The Confederacy's men of the cloth played an important role . . . not always spiritual.

1. What Episcopal bishop was also a Confederate general?
2. What renowned Presbyterian theologian had once been Stonewall Jackson's chief of staff?
3. What famous Northern preacher was noted for shipping rifles to Kansas to use against pro-slavery settlers?
4. What clergyman became an artillery chief and named four of his guns "Matthew, Mark, Luke, and John"?
5. At the beginning of the war, how many chaplains did the Confederate army officially have?
6. What religious group was not represented among Confederate chaplains?
7. What was the monthly pay of the Confederate chaplain?
8. What insignia was worn by Confederate chaplains?
9. Roughly, how many men joined the Confederate armies as chaplains?
10. What author of such noted books as *Power Through Prayer* was a Confederate chaplain?
11. What chaplain of Lee's army was headed to China as a missionary when the war broke out?
12. Besides preaching and fighting, what other purpose did chaplains serve?
13. What distinguished chaplain from Tennessee was also famous as a physician?
14. What Presbyterian clergymen wrote one of the first biographies of Stonewall Jackson, whom he had served under?
15. What Tennessee general was also a Baptist minister?
16. What pro-slavery Southern minister gained the name "Apostle to the Slaves"?
17. What office did Presbyterian pastor Thomas V. Moore hold?
18. What Confederate general almost resigned his command in mid-war to enter the ministry?
19. What did the Federals occupying northern Alabama do to keep Confederate guerrillas from shooting at passing trains?
20. What Confederate spy disguised himself as a minister, allowing him to move fairly freely among Northern troops?
21. What Mississippi Catholic bishop withstood demands from Union officers to pray for the president of the U.S.?

✎ Chaplains, and Other Men of the Cloth (answers)

1. Leonidas Polk, bishop of Louisiana, who died from a cannon shot in Georgia.
2. Robert Dabney, whose *Systematic Theology* was (and still is) a standard theological text. He was head of Richmond's Union Theological Seminary.
3. Henry Ward Beecher, brother of author Harriett Beecher Stowe. Beecher's shipments of rifles were known as "Beecher's Bibles."
4. William Pendleton, an Episcopal clergyman who often preached to his troops.
5. Officially, none. Like the Union army, the Confederate army had no policy regarding chaplains.
6. Jews. However, there was no actual restriction against Jewish chaplains.
7. $50. Since this was less than soldier's pay, many chaplains chose to serve as soldiers on the front.
8. A gold or brass Maltese cross on the side of the collar (although there was, officially, no insignia for chaplains).
9. About 600.
10. E. M. Bounds, who was captured at the Battle of Franklin.
11. John William Jones, who wrote *Christ in the Camp*, an account of the Confederate revivals.
12. Taking dictation for illiterate soldiers who wanted to write home. Some chaplains also taught reading and writing to soldiers.
13. Dr. Charles Todd Quintard of the First Tennessee Regiment.
14. Robert Dabney, who also gained fame as a theological author.
15. Mark Perrin Lowrey, who was active in the Great Revival.
16. Charles Colcock Jones of Georgia, who defended slavery but also evangelized slaves.
17. Chaplain to the Confederate Congress.
18. Edmund Kirby Smith, one of the key figures in the western Confederacy.
19. Arrested local pastors and placed one on each train passing through—assuming that the guerrillas wouldn't want to accidentally kill a minister. They were wrong.
20. The notorious Thomas Nelson Conrad, who was, in fact, an ordained Methodist.
21. William Elder, bishop of Natchez, Mississippi, who was exiled by the occupying Federal general but later returned to his post.

22. What Methodist pastor, also a newspaper editor, was one of the most pro-Union men in the Confederacy?
23. What object was Chaplain Tucker Lacy given to bury in May 1863?
24. Which denomination contributed the most chaplains to the Confederacy army?
25. What renowned general married twice, both times to daughters of Presbyterian ministers?

⚑ The Mix: Politics, Propaganda, and Religion

During the Civil War, the Confederacy and the Union had one thing in common: They believed God was on their side. Pastors both South and North preached sermons about the rightness of their side. Wartime, indeed, became a time when politics and religion mixed together quite often.

1. What general said he would fight only "more ordinary battles" on Sunday?
2. What large denomination split in 1861 because of the South's secession?
3. What denomination did Robert E. Lee belong to?
4. What general organized and taught a Sabbath school for slaves?
5. Religiously speaking, how did the Confederate Constitution differ from the U.S. Constitution?
6. What apostle commanded slaves to obey their masters (which the Confederates constantly quoted)?
7. What very large denomination is still divided today as a result of the North-South split?
8. When the Methodists experienced a North-South split, what name did the Southern branch take?
9. What two very large denominations never experienced a North-South split?
10. Where was Jefferson Davis sitting when he received word that he must evacuate Richmond?
11. What item was donated free to almost every Confederate soldier?
12. What noted Christian group in the North continued to supply materials to both North and South?
13. What were the *Soldier's Visitor* and *Soldier's Friend?*

22. William Brownlow, known as "Parson," editor of the Knoxville *Whig*.
23. The amputated left arm of his commander, Gen. Thomas "Stonewall" Jackson.
24. The Methodists, about 200 in all.
25. The devout Presbyterian deacon, Thomas "Stonewall" Jackson.

✎ The Mix: Politics, Propaganda, and Religion (answers)

1. Thomas "Stonewall" Jackson.
2. The Presbyterians, who did not reunite until 1983.
3. The Episcopal church—as did most wealthy Virginians of his day.
4. Thomas "Stonewall" Jackson.
5. It specifically mentions "Almighty God." God is not mentioned in the U.S. Constitution.
6. Paul (Letter to the Ephesians 6:5-8).
7. The Baptists. The American Baptists and Southern Baptists have been split since 1845. (Ironically, there are now Southern Baptists in all 50 states, not just in the South.)
8. The Methodist Episcopal Church, South. The Northern church was simply the Methodist Episcopal Church.
9. The Episcopalians and the Roman Catholics.
10. Richmond's St. Paul's Episcopal church, next to the Virginia capitol.
11. A Bible, of course.
12. The American Bible Society. (There was, by the way, a separate Bible Society of the Confederate States.)
13. Christian newspapers encouraging the soldiers in clean living.

14. What three moral evils were most condemned in tracts given to soldiers?
15. What name was given to the men who gave away (or sold very cheaply) religious books and tracts?
16. What patriotic song was found (without a title) in Confederate hymnals?
17. What foreign group aided the Confederacy by contributing Bibles?
18. What was "Bible gleaning"?
19. What American general was often referred to in tracts as an example of the Christian soldier?
20. President Jefferson Davis ordered a nationwide day of "fasting, humiliation, and prayer" in 1863. In what month?
21. What great Southern statesmen had predicted that the North-South splitting of denominations was an omen of the South's secession?
22. What leader, referring to North and South, said, "Both read the same Bible"?
23. What was sometimes called the South's "invisible institution"?
24. What kind of aid did the Confederacy hope to get from Pope Pius IX?
25. Why was there a noticeable Bible shortage in the Confederacy when the war began?
26. What denomination's publishing house had its Bible-printing plates confiscated by the Federals?
27. What arrangement was made to get Bibles from the North into the Confederacy?
28. What denomination had to issue a revised prayer book after the war began?
29. What Virginia region was home to the most Mennonites, who were pacifists?
30. In what denomination did U.S. Secretary of War Edwin Stanton intervene?
31. What U.S. president's father had been an openly pro-slavery Presbyterian pastor during the war years?
32. What devout general usually slept through sermons?
33. What item did Richmond's Second Baptist Church donate to the Confederacy to make cannons?
34. What church wanted to have an artillery battery named for it?
35. What capital city's churches decorated with evergreens to celebrate secession?
36. What major Tennessee battle took its name from a small Methodist church on the battle site?

14. Drinking, cursing, and gambling—which were all too common among soldiers of both South and North.
15. Colporteurs.
16. "My Country, 'Tis of Thee." The song had the words changed from "Land of the Pilgrim's pride" to "Land of the Southron's pride."
17. The British and Foreign Bible Society, which gave the Confederacy credit without interest for the purchase of Bibles.
18. Going over battlefields to collect Bibles from the dead soldiers of both sides. Due to a shortage of Bibles, Confederate chaplains and soldiers had to do this quite often.
19. George Washington, of course. He was put forward as a role model in both Southern and Northern tracts.
20. August.
21. John C. Calhoun, who had referred to the denominations as "a strong cord" that "held the Union together."
22. Abraham Lincoln, in his second inaugural address, 1865.
23. The religion of the slaves, who generally did not worship in the same churches as their masters.
24. They wanted him to interfere with Federal recruiting of German and Irish Catholics for the Union army.
25. There were no Bibles printed in the South at that time. Southern publishers had to purchase printing plates and have them sent south.
26. The Southern Methodists', whose publishing house in Nashville was a key supplier of Bibles for the Confederacy.
27. They passed under a flag of truce at Fort Monroe, Virginia. Remember that Lincoln had banned all trade with the Confederacy.
28. The Episcopalians, which had formed the Confederate States Protestant Episcopal Church. The former Book of Common Prayer specifically mentioned prayer for the U.S. president—which obviously had to be changed.
29. The Shenandoah Valley.
30. The Methodists. He told Northern Methodist bishops to assume control over Southern Methodist churches in occupied areas. Southern Methodists deeply resented this, naturally.
31. Woodrow Wilson's.
32. Thomas "Stonewall" Jackson, who rarely missed a service.
33. The church's bronze bell. The church also promised to donate money to buy artillery.
34. Richmond's Second Baptist, which promised to donate money to buy the artillery. (Wasn't Jesus the "Prince of Peace"?)
35. Jackson, Mississippi.
36. Shiloh.

⚑ Revivals and Baptisms

Religious revivals in an army? That hardly fits well with our image of the modern military. But revivals were common in the South in the 1800s, and as the war wore on, the need for spiritual support became more deeply felt. More so than the North, the South felt its own weakness and the need for divine aid. It was true for everyone, and perhaps especially the war-weary boys in gray.

1. What year did the "Great Revival" in the Confederate army begin?
2. What general, having lost the use of one arm and having one leg amputated, was baptized?
3. What fellow general performed his baptism?
4. Roughly, how many Confederate soldiers claimed to be converted during the army's revival?
5. What title did Baptist minister John William Jones give to his book concerning the Confederate revivals?
6. What noted general, a devout Presbyterian, had been baptized in an Episcopal church?
7. What army organization was noted for holding prayer meetings as often as three times per week?
8. What material was used for building the soldier's chapels?
9. What name was given to buildings constructed for preaching and prayer meetings?
10. What general is noted for baptizing three other generals?
11. What tone-deaf general enjoyed singing hymns at the top of his lungs?
12. When Union troops opened fire on a Confederate group holding a prayer meeting during the Seven Days' campaign, what did the Confederate soldiers do?
13. What name was given to religious meetings where soldiers told of how they were converted?
14. What foul-mouthed general became a Christian during the war and cleaned up his vocabulary?
15. What general was head of the soldiers' Temperance Society?
16. Who wrote *A Narrative of the Great Revival Which Prevailed in the Southern Armies*?
17. What noted leader finally became a church member at the ripe age of 53?

🖎 Revivals and Baptisms (answers)

1. In 1863 (not surprisingly, a year when many soldiers began to feel a strong need for spiritual consolation).
2. John Hood, baptized in the fall of 1864.
3. Gen. (and Bishop) Leonidas Polk.
4. About 100,000.
5. *Christ in the Camp.*
6. Thomas "Stonewall" Jackson, who was baptized before he made his decision to join the Presbyterian fold.
7. The Army Christian Association.
8. Logs, usually.
9. Tabernacles.
10. Again, Bishop-Gen. Leonidas Polk, who not only baptized Gen. Hood (mentioned above) but also Joseph E. Johnston and William Joseph Hardee.
11. "Stonewall" Jackson.
12. Sought for cover while keeping their eyes still closed, since the prayer had not yet been concluded.
13. "Experience meetings."
14. Richard Stoddert Ewell.
15. Braxton Bragg, who became a Christian during the war.
16. William W. Bennett, who had led the Methodist Soldiers' Tract Association. His book is one of the best accounts of the Confederate revival.
17. President Jefferson Davis, who was confirmed at Richmond's St. Paul's Episcopal Church.

Part 7

The Political Scene

⚑ Grand Old Flags

A flag, as everyone knows, it much more than a piece of cloth. It is a symbol, one that evokes love and respect (from patriots) or rage and disgust (from the enemy). From the beginning of the Confederacy, the new nation knew it had to design a new flag to rally under. In the course of the war, the flag changed, as did the nation it flew over.

1. What was Nicola Marschall famous for?
2. Why was the Stars and Bars replaced by another flag?
3. What happened when the U.S. flag at Fort Sumter was shot down on April 12, 1861?
4. What rash act did Confederate Colonel William Mumford commit at New Orleans' U.S. Mint building?
5. What became of the first Confederate flag ever made?
6. What did the owners of U.S. commercial ships do to avoid the danger of capture by Confederate raiders?
7. What Federal fort in Virginia became the normal point of entry between Federals and Confederates under a flag of truce?
8. What honor was given to Major Atherton Stevens of Massachusetts?
9. Where was the first Confederate flag, the original Stars and Bars, raised on March 4, 1861?
10. What important date pressured the Confederates to create a national flag?
11. What general was credited with designing the Confederate battle flag, with its familiar blue X?
12. What size was the Confederate flag used by the infantry?
13. What was the nickname of the new Confederate flag introduced in May 1863?
14. Where was the last Confederate flag lowered?
15. What post-war U.S. president shocked Northerners by approving the return of captured Confederate flags to the South?
16. What would a regiment have stitched into its flag?
17. What price did Union Col. Elmer Ellsworth pay for removing the Confederate flag flying over the Marshall House Hotel in Alexandria, Virginia?
18. What secessionist flag was raised at Stockton, California, in January 1861?
19. What nation's flag was flown by most of the Confederate blockade runners leaving the port of Nassau in the Bahamas?
20. In April 1862, what two far western cities were flying the Confederate flag?

❧ Grand Old Flags (answers)

1. She designed the Stars and Bars, the first official Confederate flag.
2. It resembled the Union flag, causing some confusion on the battlefield.
3. A sergeant nailed it up again.
4. He took down the U.S. flag and destroyed it. This led to his execution by the Federals.
5. It draped the casket of Thomas "Stonewall" Jackson.
6. Changed their ships' registration to other nations—meaning the ships would no longer fly the U.S. flag.
7. Fort Monroe, in Hampton, which was held by the Federals throughout the war.
8. He raised the Union flag over the Richmond Capitol.
9. Over the Capitol in Montgomery, Alabama.
10. Lincoln's inauguration. The Confederacy wanted to have its new symbol ready when Lincoln took office.
11. P. G. T. Beauregard.
12. A 4-by-4-foot square.
13. The Stainless Banner.
14. In Liverpool, England, on board the CSS *Shenandoah*, November 6, 1865.
15. Grover Cleveland, in 1887. The public outcry was so great that the flags were not actually returned until 1905.
16. The names of battles in which it had fought.
17. The hotel owner killed him on the stairway with a shotgun.
18. The flag of the pro-secession "Pacific Republic."
19. Great Britain's.
20. Santa Fe and Albuquerque in New Mexico.

21. What animal sometimes appeared on secessionist flags?
22. What color flags were used to mark field hospitals?
23. What was the most dangerous battle duty in any regiment?
24. What became of the U.S. flag lowered at Fort Sumter on April 13, 1861?
25. What acid-tongued general fled to Mexico after the war, swearing he would never live under the U.S. flag?
26. What welcome item did Confederate authorities send under a flag of truce to Northern prisons?
27. What honor did the Confederacy give to the granddaughter of former President John Tyler?
28. What song about a flag was the South's unofficial national anthem?
29. What size was the original Confederate flag?
30. What is the claim to fame of William Porcher Miles?
31. Why were some of the original Confederate battle flags pink?
32. According to tradition, who wrapped himself in a Confederate flag before committing suicide?

⚑ Fire-eaters, Secessionists, and Such

The Civil War did not begin because Fort Sumter was fired on. It began much earlier in the North-South sectional conflicts, and throughout the 1850s many Southerners had urged the course of secession. The most prominent pro-secession agitators, the "fire-eaters," were a major influence, galvanizing public opinion on both sides. Had there been no fire-eaters, there would have been no Confederacy.

1. What South Carolina aristocrat was dubbed the "Father of Secession"?
2. What animal sometimes appeared on secessionist flags?
3. What word was inscribed on the gavel used at the South Carolina secession convention?
4. What name was given to the bipartisan U.S. Senate committee that met in December 1860 to avert secession?
5. What was the first convention at which South Carolina proposed secession of all Southern states?
6. Before South Carolina had actually seceded, what other Southern state had indicated that it would gladly follow suit?
7. What infamous Alabama secessionist formed the League of United Southerners to encourage Southern Nationalism?
8. What is the claim to fame of David F. Jamison?

21. A rattlesnake, which had also been used in the Revolution, with the slogan "Don't tread on me."
22. Yellow. The flags often had a large "H" in the center also.
23. Carrying the colors, considering the effort the enemy would make to shoot down flags, and the men carrying them.
24. Four years later the same flag was hoisted again over the fort.
25. Jubal Early, who eventually did return to his native Virginia.
26. Cotton, to be sold to buy warm clothing, which Confederate prisoners badly needed.
27. Raising the first Confederate flag over the capitol in Montgomery.
28. "The Bonnie Blue Flag," by English entertainer Harry McCarthy.
29. Nine by fourteen feet.
30. He proposed the basic Confederate flag design of a blue X (known as "St. Andrew's cross") with thirteen stars on a red field.
31. At the time there was a shortage of red silk in Richmond.
32. Elderly secession agitator Edmund Ruffin, who chose to shoot himself rather than return to Federal rule. The flag story is colorful but not true.

✎ Fire-eaters, Secessionists, and Such (answers)

1. Robert Barnwell Rhett, noted "fire-eater" who, ironically, never had a post in the Confederate government.
2. A rattlesnake, which had also been used in the Revolution, with the slogan "Don't tread on me."
3. "Secession," appropriately enough.
4. The Committee of Thirteen, which included Mississippi Senator Jefferson Davis. Split by the pro-slavery and anti-slavery senators, the committee proved useless.
5. The Nashville Convention, 1850, a meeting of delegates from the slave states to discuss Southern unity.
6. Florida, whose governor was gung-ho secessionist Madison Perry.
7. William L. Yancey, who wrote his home state's ordinance of secession.
8. He presided at the South Carolina secession convention.

9. What symbolic gift did aged secessionist Edmund Ruffin receive from the South Carolina secession convention?
10. What plant emblem was a widely used symbol of secession?
11. What important pro-secession document was issued in 1860 by Senators James Pugh of Alabama and Louis Wigfall of Texas?
12. Why was South Carolina's Secession Ordinance passed at Charleston instead of at the capital, Columbia?
13. According to the Peace Democrats in the North, what had forced the Southern states to secede?
14. What name was given to the U.S. House committee assigned to prevent secession?
15. What name is given to the statement by Christopher Memminger on behalf of South Carolina's secession?
16. What was Arkansas Governor Henry Rector doing while the state legislature debated secession?
17. What secession agitator left his native Virginia because the state hadn't yet seceded?
18. What state rejected in January 1861 a proposal to join the South in seceding?
19. What prominent secession advocate died eleven years before the Confederacy came into being?
20. What South Carolina newspaper was the South's chief voice of secession?
21. What secession governor billed the U.S. for his work done as U.S. minister to Russia?
22. In what Georgia city did the secession convention meet? (No, it wasn't Atlanta.)
23. At the February 1861 gathering of seceded states in Montgomery, who was elected president by the delegates?
24. What noted compromiser in the U.S. Senate chaired the Border Slave State Convention held in Kentucky?
25. Who claimed that secession was "the most glorious event in the history of Florida"?
26. What town bills itself as the "Birthplace of the Confederacy"?
27. What future general, stationed in Texas when it seceded, left the state for his native Virginia?
28. What government service continued for some time after secession?
29. What five states did the Confederacy try to woo into secession by promising to keep the Mississippi River open for commerce?
30. Who, speaking of President Jefferson Davis, said, "The man and the hour have met"?
31. What state's voters rejected secession by a 4-1 vote in January 1861?

9. The pen that had signed the Ordinance of Secession.
10. The palmetto frond, after South Carolina's state tree.
11. The Southern Manifesto, which claimed the Southern states had been denied rights by the North and had no choice but to secede and form a new nation.
12. There was a smallpox epidemic in Columbia at the time.
13. The Republicans, by calling for troops to put down the "rebellion."
14. The Committee of Thirty-three (one congressman from each state). Two proposals from the committee eventually passed both houses of Congress: admitting New Mexico as a slave state, and guaranteeing no interference with slavery in the existing states. Before any of this took effect, the country had already been split.
15. Declaration of Immediate Causes, in which Memminger stated that the Union was not perpetually binding on the states.
16. Seized Fort Smith and the Federal arsenal for the Confederacy.
17. Edmund Ruffin, who fired the first shot at Fort Sumter.
18. Delaware.
19. Senator and Vice-president John C. Calhoun, who had laid all the groundwork for the secession movement. He died in 1850.
20. The *Mercury*, founded in 1822.
21. Francis W. Pickens of South Carolina. The U.S. issued a check drawn on a South Carolina bank—which the state had already seized.
22. Milledgeville, the state capital at that time.
23. Howell Cobb of Georgia. He was president of the convention, *not* of the Confederacy.
24. John J. Crittenden, who had no luck in dissuading states from seceding.
25. Florida's governor, John Milton.
26. Abbeville, South Carolina. The first organized secession meeting took place there in 1860.
27. Robert E. Lee.
28. The U.S. mail service.
29. Indiana, Ohio, Michigan, Illinois, Wisconsin. There was a belief that the Midwest was as anti-East Coast as the South was.
30. Noted secessionist William L. Yancey.
31. Tennessee, which eventually did join the Confederacy.

32. What immigrant group of Texans strongly opposed the state's secession?
33. What near-legendary American hero did Texas Lt. Gov. Edward Clark replace as governor after Texas seceded?
34. What is the claim to fame of Alabama delegate Christopher Sheats?
35. What was secessionist agitator Robert Barnwell Rhett's beef against President Jefferson Davis?
36. What contribution did J. D. B. DeBow make to the Confederacy?
37. What James River plantation, home of secession agitator Edmund Ruffin, was destroyed during the war?
38. What state, before it seceded, called for a Southern convention to "discuss the problem"?
39. What is the significance of the Fort Hill plantation in South Carolina?
40. What Knoxville, Tennessee, newspaper editor declared that he would "fight the secessionist leaders till hell froze over"?
41. Which state's House of Delegates voted 53 to 13 against secession in April 1861?
42. Which Confederate state authorized a Union government in November 1861?
43. What Canadian province gave a warm welcome to naval commander Matthew Maury?
44. Who called for Georgia to hold a secession convention?
45. What slave state was the scene of the Civil War's first bloodshed?
46. What was Mississippi's status between the time it seceded and the time it joined the Confederacy?
47. What state's secession convention voted to stay in session to direct the state's war effort?
48. What state was the birthplace of Missouri's strongly pro-secession governor, Thomas C. Reynolds?
49. What honor was given to 67-year-old secessionist Edmund Ruffin on April 12, 1861?
50. What notable secessionist from Alabama had high hopes of becoming president of the Confederacy but was considered too radical?
51. Why were Union troops eager to enter South Carolina?
52. Why did the citizens of Charleston rush out to buy the newspaper of December 20, 1860?
53. Which state's secession convention called for a meeting of all seceding states?
54. What was the first aggressive act of the pro-secession government in Arkansas?
55. What governor had his life threatened by pro-secessionists mobs?

32. Germans. As recent immigrants to the U.S., they felt a loyalty to the Union.
33. Sam Houston, who lost his post for opposing secession.
34. He tried to get his home county, Winston County, to secede from Alabama.
35. In spite of being one of most flamboyant secessionists, Rhett was never given a post in the Confederate government.
36. His pro-secession magazine *DeBow's Review* was an active force in urging on the South toward secession.
37. Evelynton. As Ruffin's home, its destruction was inevitable.
38. Virginia.
39. It is a sort of shrine to secession and Southern nationalism, since it was the estate of John C. Calhoun. It became the site of Clemson University.
40. William G. Brownlow, one of the South's most famous Unionists.
41. Maryland, a slave state with a lot of pro-Southern sentiment.
42. North Carolina. The Union convention held in Hatteras repudiated the state's secession and established a rival government.
43. Nova Scotia. Maury noted that the Nova Scotians were "strongly secesh."
44. Its pro-secession governor, Joseph E. Brown.
45. Maryland. On April 19, 1861, pro-secession civilians pelted the 6th Massachusetts Militia with stones on its march to Washington.
46. It called itself the Republic of Mississippi.
47. Arkansas'.
48. Appropriately enough, South Carolina, the birthplace of secession.
49. Firing the first shot on Fort Sumter.
50. William L. Yancey, who did become a senator in the Confederate Congress. He died in 1863.
51. It had been the birthplace of secession and, somehow, had escaped most of the war's fighting.
52. It carried the announcement of the state's secession.
53. Alabama. The meeting convened in Montgomery.
54. Seizing the Federal arsenal at Little Rock.
55. Maryland's Thomas Hicks, who was slow to act in his badly divided state.

56. What western state had a pro-secession group wanting to form a separate "Pacific Republic"?
57. What state's capital celebrated secession with a torchlight parade?
58. Why did Secretary of War John Floyd send Major Robert Anderson to command Fort Sumter?
59. What Alabama county was the scene of some of the worst fighting between pro-Union and pro-Confederate forces?
60. What city, in a state that never seceded, was treated as occupied territory till the end of the war?
61. What Confederate congressman had at one time left his state of Mississippi and gone to California to get away from secessionists?
62. What valuable service did Thomas Hicks do for the Union?
63. Which state, long a hotbed of secessionists, escaped the war largely unharmed until the final year?
64. What prompted Arkansas to rethink secession after it had already voted not to secede?
65. When Florida seceded in January 1861, what percentage of the population was slave?
66. What state's secession convention was egged on by speakers from South Carolina, Alabama, and Mississippi, which had already seceded?
67. How did North Carolina Gov. John Ellis react to a telegraph from U.S. Secretary of War Simon Cameron, requesting troops for the Union?
68. Who was the "Secesh Cleopatra"?
69. What capital city's churches decorated with evergreens to celebrate secession?
70. When Gov. Claiborne Jackson of Missouri moved the state capital from Jefferson City, where was the new capital?
71. What was the signal for South Carolina to secede?
72. What state was the "Lone Star State" before Texas was?
73. What Confederate state was not invaded until 1865?
74. What happened to pro-Union Alabama delegate Christopher Sheats when he argued against secession?
75. What secession leader failed both as a Confederate statesman and as a soldier, and spent the rest of the war harassing the government?
76. What longtime advocate of Southern nationalism died before the Confederacy did?

56. California.

57. Florida's. The capital is Tallahassee.

58. Floyd, already preparing for secession, thought that Anderson would act for the South since he was a Kentuckian married to a Georgia woman. Floyd was wrong.

59. Winston County, which had tried to secede from the state.

60. Baltimore, which was strongly pro-Southern.

61. Henry Foote, harshest critic of the Davis administration.

62. As Maryland governor, he worked to keep his divided state from seceding.

63. South Carolina. In 1865, Sherman's troops made up for lost time.

64. Lincoln's call for 75,000 volunteers to put down the rebellion.

65. About 50 percent.

66. Georgia's.

67. Ellis replied, "You can get no troops from North Carolina." The state then seceded.

68. Noted Confederate spy Belle Boyd of Virginia.

69. Jackson, Mississippi.

70. Neosho, where pro-Southern legislators passed a secession ordinance.

71. The election of a Republican (Lincoln) to the presidency.

72. Mississippi, which chose the single star as its symbol after secession. The star symbolized its independent nation status.

73. South Carolina—ironically, the first state to secede.

74. He was dragged from the convention floor and jailed. He was released after the state seceded.

75. Robert Toombs of Georgia.

76. William L. Yancey, who died in July 1863.

◪ Hail to the Chief: Jefferson Davis

The Confederacy's one president, Jefferson Finis Davis, has been called the "Sphinx of the Confederacy," since so few people have understood him. He was considered a true gentleman, but never a particularly warm person, and as the war progressed, the poor man bore much of the blame for the Confederacy's fall. Even so, by most human standards, he was a great man: West Point graduate, Mexican War hero, faithful husband and father, distinguished senator from Mississippi, leader of a new and fragile nation, and, finally, public symbol of the Lost Cause.

1. What was Jefferson Davis doing when news of his election arrived?
2. How many years was President Davis's term of office, according to the Constitution?
3. What general had the nerve to threaten to run for president against his commander-in-chief, Jefferson Davis?
4. What earth-shaking proclamation was issued by Davis on May 6, 1861?
5. What important early battle had Davis as a spectator?
6. What caused Davis's sore hand on New Year's Day, 1862?
7. How many children did Jefferson and Varina Davis have?
8. On what holiday did Davis take office in 1862?
9. What Confederate loss led President Davis and his cabinet members to send their families off to North Carolina?
10. When Jefferson Davis declared Union generals Hunter and Phelps to be felons, what was their offense?
11. What relation was Jefferson Davis to Jefferson Davis?
12. What kind of reception did President Davis give to Clement Vallandigham, the Ohio politician who had been banished to the South?
13. Why did Davis visit Gen. Braxton Bragg's headquarters after the defeat at Chattanooga?
14. What city was Davis visiting while its nearby fort received Union bombardment at the rate of 33 shells per hour?
15. What sent President Davis into mourning in May 1864?
16. What general was removed from command for his ill-advised criticism of two of Davis's pet generals?
17. Why was the Confederate Supreme Court never formed?
18. What was, by proclamation of President Davis, the special purpose of April 8, 1864?
19. In July 1864, Davis wrote to Robert E. Lee that "Johnston has failed. It seems necessary to relieve him." What was Johnston's notable failure?

✎ Hail to the Chief: Jefferson Davis (answers)

1. Pruning rosebushes.
2. Six years. He did not serve six.
3. P. G. T. Beauregard. At that time, Davis had been elected by the secession convention, not popular vote. Beauregard apparently thought he could ride the wave of popularity after his victory at First Manassas.
4. The declaration of a state of war between Confederacy and U.S.
5. First Manassas. Several U.S. Congressmen were also present.
6. He had hosted a reception, shaking hands with literally thousands of people in Richmond.
7. Six.
8. Washington's Birthday.
9. The Union capture of Norfolk, only 100 miles from Richmond.
10. They were organizing slaves for the Union army.
11. None. One was the president of the Confederacy, the other was a Union general.
12. Chilly. The poor man had been banished from the Union, and in the Confederacy he was classed as an "alien enemy."
13. He hoped to stifle the grumbling among Bragg's subordinates. Bragg was a constant source of friction in the Confederate army.
14. Charleston, where nearby Fort Sumter was still being bombed heavily.
15. His five-year-old son, Joe, was killed at the Confederate White House in Richmond.
16. Daniel Harvey Hill, who rather foolishly griped about his superiors, Robert E. Lee and Braxton Bragg.
17. There was a fear that President Jefferson Davis would pack the court with his "pets."
18. A day of fasting, prayer, and humiliation to invoke God's aid.
19. He had withdrawn his army all the way to Atlanta, leaving the path open for Sherman's Union troops.

20. How many guns saluted President Davis's first arrival in Richmond?
21. What was the original name of the White House of the Confederacy?
22. What reward did the Federals offer for anyone delivering Jefferson Davis to the U.S. military authorities?
23. What snide slogan did Federal soldiers paint on the front of Davis's Mississippi plantation house?
24. What officer ran afoul of Jefferson Davis for referring to Mrs. Davis as "an old squaw"?
25. What mission did Davis give to Henry Hopkins Sibley?
26. Where was Davis sitting when he received word from Robert E. Lee that Richmond had to be evacuated?
27. What general wrote a whining nine-page letter to Davis for not being placed first on a seniority list?
28. Was Davis more popular with the soldiers or the civilians?
29. Why did Davis so seldom suspend habeas corpus (much less than Lincoln did, in fact)?
30. Who bore all the blame for the Union plot to burn Richmond and kill Davis and the Confederate Cabinet in March 1864?
31. What regulation army item came in "a few standard sizes that fit most men"?
32. Who was "Winnie"?
33. What Union general so scandalized the South that Jefferson Davis ordered that he be executed immediately if captured?
34. What relation to Jefferson Davis was Gen. Joseph Robert Davis?
35. What world figure sent a polite letter to Jefferson Davis, addressing him as "President of the Confederacy"?
36. What occurred in the U.S. Senate when Davis gave his farewell speech?
37. What officer was promoted immediately to brigadier general after President Davis witnessed him in action?
38. What general suggested to President Davis that the president himself might take an active command in the Confederate army?
39. What despised Union general had once proposed Jefferson Davis for the U.S presidency?
40. What occurred on July 4, 1864, at Davis's Mississippi plantation?
41. Where was Davis on the day of Lee's surrender to Grant?
42. What did Davis authorize General Joe Johnston to do on April 12, 1865?
43. Where was Davis when Lincoln was shot?
44. What feisty cavalry general suggested to Davis that he move west of the Mississippi and keep up the fight?

20. Eleven—one for each state in the Confederacy.
21. The Brockenbrough mansion.
22. $100,000 in gold.
23. "The House That Jeff Built."
24. Abraham C. Myers, who apparently was referring to Varina Davis's dark complexion. Myers regretted the remark.
25. Run the Federals out of the New Mexico Territory and open the door to California for the Confederates.
26. In a pew at Richmond's St. Paul's Episcopal Church.
27. Joseph E. Johnston, who, in the pre-war U.S. army, had the highest rank.
28. Generally speaking, the soldiers.
29. The strong feeling for states rights in the Confederacy ruled out any widespread national suspension of habeas corpus.
30. A dead Union man, Col. Ulric Dahlgren, on whose body were found the papers describing the plot. The Union command said they had no knowledge of the plot, thus Dahlgren bore all the blame.
31. The Davis boot, named for Jefferson Davis while he was secretary of war under Franklin Pierce.
32. This was the nickname of the "Daughter of the Confederacy," Varina Anne Jefferson Davis.
33. Benjamin "Beast" Butler, governor of occupied New Orleans.
34. Joseph was Jefferson's nephew.
35. Pope Pius IX.
36. A great deal of weeping. Davis was a good orator.
37. George Burgwyn Anderson. Davis witnessed his brave charge at Williamsburg in May 1861.
38. John B. Hood, who hobnobbed often with the Davis family.
39. Benjamin Butler, later known as the "Beast of New Orleans."
40. Federals hosted a picnic on the grounds for Davis's liberated slaves.
41. In Danville, Virginia. He departed the next day for Greensboro, North Carolina, hoping to escape the Union cavalry on his heels.
42. Meet with Union General Sherman to discuss surrender.
43. Greensboro, North Carolina, still on the lam from the Federals.
44. Wade Hampton. Davis did not act on this suggestion.

45. In what state did Davis rendezvous with his wife after they separated at the evacuation of Richmond?
46. What unpleasant bit of news did Gen. Henry Harrison Walker convey to Davis?
47. What medal was Davis carrying on him until he was imprisoned at Fort Monroe?
48. What were Davis's words at the time of his capture?
49. Where were Davis's children sent after his capture?
50. What family sued Davis after the war?
51. What items did Davis give to Gen. George Gibbs Dibrell for safe-keeping?
52. What Kentucky town holds the Jefferson Davis Birthday Celebration on the first Sunday in September?
53. In what Tennessee city would you find a statue of Jefferson Davis, Confederate president and, after the war, a local resident?
54. What army fort has the cell in which Davis was imprisoned after the war?
55. What medal was given to Jefferson Davis at the Texas State Fair in 1875?
56. What color was the White House of the Confederacy while Davis lived there?
57. What leaders' images are carved on Georgia's Stone Mountain, along with Davis's?
58. What Southern city has a large Jefferson Davis Monument at the intersection of Monument Avenue and Davis Street?
59. What state has a monument commemorating Davis's birthplace?
60. What city has Davis's *first* presidential home?
61. Where is Davis buried?

45. Georgia.
46. The surrender of Robert E. Lee.
47. One of the Davis Guard Medals awarded to the valiant Texas artillery unit.
48. "God's will be done."
49. To Canada, for safety's sake.
50. The kin of Sarah Anne Dorsey, who had willed Davis her estate, Beauvoir. The family lost the suit.
51. The Confederate archives.
52. Hopkinsville.
53. Memphis.
54. Fort Monroe, at Hampton.
55. A Davis Guard Medal, replacing the one taken from him when he was captured by the Union in 1865.
56. Confederate gray, not white.
57. Robert E. Lee and Thomas "Stonewall" Jackson.
58. Richmond, of course.
59. Kentucky. The Jefferson Davis Monument is near Fairview and is one of the largest monuments in the U.S. (Interestingly, Davis's birthplace is not far from Abraham Lincoln's.)
60. Montgomery, Alabama. The first White House of the Confederacy is near the state capitol.
61. Hollywood Cemetery in Richmond, where many Confederates are buried. He had been buried originally in New Orleans.

♙ States Men: The Governors

Can you name three or more Confederate generals? Probably. They are the "stars" of the Confederacy, no doubt. What about naming governors? We neglect these powerful men who were, for better or worse, key players in the new nation. Since states' rights was a cornerstone of secession, naturally the governors liked to exercise power. They always did this in the interest of their own states—and not always in the interest of the Confederacy as a whole.

1. What venerable American figure, the governor of Texas, refused to take the oath of allegiance to the Confederacy?
2. What governor stated "Tennessee will furnish not a single man for the purpose of coercion"?
3. Who wrote to President Jefferson Davis, stating that it was in the interest of "honor and safety" to seize Fort Sumter?
4. What former governor, fearing arrest by the Federals, signed not one but two oaths of loyalty to the Union?
5. What state's governor complained to the Confederate government that the Confederate cavalry in his state was doing immeasurable harm?
6. What governor served in three different state capitals during his term?
7. What Southern governor was most consistently supportive of President Jefferson Davis during the war?
8. What general was threatened with arrest if he suggested the surrender of his army to the Union?
9. What did Andrew Johnson appoint for the former Confederate states in June 1865?
10. Which state choose to join the Confederacy because Lincoln had chosen to "inaugurate the war"?
11. What feisty Confederate governor issued an order repudiating all debts owed to Northern interests?
12. What pro-Southern governor of a border state paid $60,000 for weapons that wouldn't fire?
13. What governor, who had ordered the execution of abolitionist John Brown, became a very incompetent Confederate general?
14. In what state did a pro-Union governor take office in March 1864?
15. What secession governor billed the U.S. for his work done as U.S. minister to Russia?
16. What act of the Virginia governor left Robert E. Lee without a job?
17. What distinctive office did Francis H. Pierpont hold?
18. What future Copperhead governor had once been a strong abolitionist and a supporter of John Brown?

✎ States Men: The Governors (answers)

1. Sam Houston.
2. Isham Harris.
3. Gov. Francis Pickens of South Carolina.
4. John Pettus of Mississippi.
5. North Carolina. Gov. Zebulon Vance claimed that the cavalry's seizure of horses and food was like "another plague on the Egyptians."
6. Thomas Moore. Fleeing the Union, the Louisiana capital moved from Baton Rouge to Opelousas to Shreveport.
7. Virginia's John Letcher, who subordinated state interests to the needs of the Confederacy.
8. Edmund Kirby Smith. The threat came from the governors of Arkansas, Louisiana, and Mississippi—Smith's territory.
9. Provisional governors.
10. Virginia. The governor claimed that the state's people "are free men, not slaves," and would supply no troops for Lincoln.
11. Joseph Brown of Georgia.
12. Beriah Magoffin, who planned to give the guns to secessionists.
13. Henry Wise of Virginia, a good politician but a bad commander.
14. Louisiana.
15. Francis W. Pickens of South Carolina. The U.S. issued a check drawn on a South Carolina bank—which the state had already seized.
16. All state troops (which Lee commanded) were transferred to the Confederate government. For a while Lee was only an advisor to the governor.
17. Provisional governor of the area that would eventually be called West Virginia.
18. Clement Vallandigham of Ohio.

19. What border state saw its strongly pro-Southern governor replaced by a strongly pro-Union one in July 1861?
20. Which governor was elected to the Confederate Congress after he found himself powerless as governor?
21. Why did few men respond to the Georgia governor's plea for help in defending the state from Sherman's troops?
22. What Tennessean threw out Nashville's mayor and councilmen for not taking an oath of loyalty to the Union?
23. What governor groused about his state's regiments being assigned commanders from other states?
24. What mule-headed Southern governor refused President Jefferson Davis's request for more troops to aid in the defense of Georgia?
25. Which governor carried his state into the Confederacy though the state had already voted to remain in the Union?
26. What state's superintendent of education prevented the state from diverting school money to the war fund?
27. What pro-Southern governor was informed by Lincoln that Lincoln would definitely *not* remove pro-Union forces from the state?
28. When Tennessee governor Isham Harris had to evacuate Nashville, where did he move the state government?
29. What honor was awarded to Ohio Democrat Clement Vallandigham, the man Lincoln banished to the Confederacy for expressing his pro-Southern sympathies?
30. What Confederate leaders did Union Gen. William T. Sherman invite to discuss terms of surrender with him in Atlanta?
31. Which state had a Confederate government-in-exile headed by Gov. Claiborne Jackson?
32. Which Confederate governor was a governor without a state?
33. In what border state did the legislature call for the governor to order all Confederate troops from the state?
34. What shocking move did Gov. Joseph Brown make that affected the Army of Tennessee?
35. What Confederate officer proclaimed himself military governor of Arizona in August 1861?
36. What near-legendary American hero did Texas Lt. Gov. Edward Clark replace as governor after Texas seceded?
37. What man elected "governor of Virginia" never served in that post?
38. How did North Carolina Gov. John Ellis react to a telegraph from U.S. Secretary of War Simon Cameron, requesting troops for the Union?
39. Who were "Joe Brown's Pets"?
40. When Gov. Claiborne Jackson of Missouri moved the state capital from Jefferson City, where was the new capital?
41. Where was Kentucky's Confederate capital?

19. Missouri. Hamilton Gamble replaced Claiborne Jackson.
20. Tennessee's Isham Harris who, after 1862, had no real authority in his state.
21. It would have seemed futile, since Sherman was marching through Georgia with 60,000 men.
22. Andrew Johnson, the Union governor of occupied Tennessee.
23. North Carolina's Zebulon Vance. His gripe was foolish, since such assignments are common in the military.
24. The infamous Joseph Brown, Georgia's governor and strong opponent of the central Confederate government.
25. Tennessee's Isham Harris. He pushed the state into the Confederacy after Lincoln called for Union troops.
26. North Carolina's. Superintendent Calvin Wiley convinced Gov. Zebulon Vance that such a policy was "suicidal."
27. Beriah Magoffin of Kentucky.
28. Memphis.
29. The Ohio Democrats nominated him for governor.
30. Georgia governor Joseph Brown and Confederate vice-president Alexander Stephens. Both were noted critics of the Davis administration. Both declined to meet with Sherman.
31. Missouri, which, like Kentucky, also had a pro-Union government.
32. Tennessee's Isham Harris was, after 1862, pretty much out of command of his state. In fact, having no power in Tennessee, he got himself elected to the Confederate Congress.
33. Kentucky. The legislature did *not* call for the removal of Union troops.
34. He recalled the 10,000-man Georgia militia that was part of the Army of Tennessee and gave each man a 30-day furlough.
35. Lt. Col. John Baylor. His act was not authorized by the Confederate government.
36. Sam Houston, who lost his post for opposing secession.
37. Francis H. Pierpont, who was in fact elected by the breakaway counties that formed the new state of West Virginia.
38. Ellis replied, "You can get no troops from North Carolina." The state then seceded.
39. Georgia militiamen. Gov. Joe Brown worked to exempt them from Confederate service.
40. Neosho, where pro-Southern legislators passed a secession ordinance.
41. At Russellville, where Gov. Beriah Magoffin's provisional government ratified the Confederate Constitution.

42. What Southern governor died just as his state was gearing up for war?
43. Finding himself without any authority, what service did Tennessee Gov. Isham Harris perform during the war?
44. How did Texas Gov. Sam Houston respond while he was called forward to take a loyalty oath to the Confederacy?
45. What state's governor joined the Confederate army after the Union army had left him with no state to govern?
46. Who appointed Robert E. Lee commander of all state troops in Virginia?
47. Where was the cloth factory that Texas Gov. Francis Lubbock operated to help the state and the Confederacy?
48. What governor proposed arming soldier with pikes, 18-inch knives carried on 6-foot poles, as in the Middle Ages?
49. What state governor was deposed by the Federal government after he moved the state capital to another city?
50. What made Kentucky Gov. Beriah Magoffin receive assassination threats in 1862?
51. What did Louisiana Gov. Thomas Moore do with any cotton accessible to Union troops?
52. What pro-secession governor was ousted from office by his state's secession convention, two years before his term expired?
53. What did Texas Gov. Francis Lubbock do to appease German Texans after several were massacred in 1862?
54. What consolation prize did the Confederacy give to Tennessee Gov. Isham Harris for his being "a governor without a state"?
55. What generous offer did William T. Sherman make to the governor of Georgia?
56. What position did Thomas Watts take after resigning as Confederate attorney general?
57. What Unionist newspaper editor in Tennessee received his reward by being elected governor of the state after the war?
58. What wealthy judge and slave-owner in Tennessee was elected governor but never served because of the Union occupation of Nashville?
59. What Confederate governor had for a time been an official in the Republic of Texas?
60. What North Carolina governor put his state's defense in jeopardy by transferring its military and naval forces to Virginia?
61. What pro-secession governor was ousted from office by his state's secession convention, two years before his term expired?
62. What border state governor aided Confederate generals Jo Shelby and Sterling Price in their invasions of his state?
63. What state had the same governor during the entire Civil War?

42. North Carolinian Gov. John W. Ellis.
43. He was an aide-de-camp to several generals, including Braxton Bragg and Joseph Johnston.
44. He whittled while his named was called repeatedly. He never took the oath, and he ceased to be governor.
45. Kentucky. The pro-Confederate Gov. George Johnson was elected but never allowed to serve. He died at the Battle of Shiloh.
46. Gov. John Letcher.
47. At the state penitentiary in Huntsville.
48. Joseph Brown of Georgia. A few were actually issued to Georgian soldiers.
49. Claiborne Jackson, the pro-Southern governor of Missouri.
50. He wanted to let the states' voters decide whether to be Confederate or Union. The Union-dominated state legislature wanted no part of this.
51. Ordered that it be burned.
52. Henry Rector of Arkansas.
53. Exempted them from the draft.
54. An honorary seat in the Confederate Congress.
55. Sherman's troops would spare Georgia any destruction *if* Gov. Brown would withdraw Georgia's troops from the Confederate army. Brown didn't.
56. Gov. of Alabama.
57. William "Parson" Brownlow, who had had his presses trashed because of his pro-Union views.
58. Robert Caruthers.
59. Edward Clark.
60. Henry Toole Clark. He was not reelected.
61. Henry Rector of Arkansas.
62. Thomas C. Reynolds of Missouri.
63. Georgia. Joseph Brown held office from November 1857 to May 1865.

◫ Constitutional Matters

One of the first accomplishments of the Confederacy was drafting a new Constitution, which they deliberately modeled on the U.S. Constitution. And why not, since it was familiar to people and worth keeping (except in one or two important areas, of course). Of course, in the four-year life span of the Confederacy, many parts of the Confederate states were occupied by the Union, meaning that that other *Constitution (the U.S.) was in force . . .*

1. What part of the U.S. Constitution was adopted verbatim into the Confederate Constitution?
2. Under the Confederate Constitution, how many terms could the president serve?
3. How many U.S. laws were allowed to remain in force in the Confederacy?
4. What part of the Confederate Constitution provides for a cabinet?
5. How long did it take the first Confederate Congress to draft a constitution?
6. What future Confederate Cabinet member chaired the committee that drafted the Confederate Constitution?
7. Under the Confederate Constitution, how many states' approval were needed for a constitutional amendment?
8. What type of veto power did the Confederate president have that the U.S. president does not have?
9. What institution is specifically mentioned in the Confederate Constitution, while not mentioned at all in the U.S. Constitution?
10. According to the Confederate Constitution, what type of tax was to fund the federal treasury?
11. How many states submitted the Confederate Constitution to the people for a vote?
12. In what two key areas did the Confederate Constitution differ from the U.S. Constitution?
13. What majority was needed in the Confederate Congress to admit a new state to the Confederacy?
14. What did the Confederate Constitution prohibit being imported?
15. What important institution was authorized in Article III of the Confederate Constitution?
16. According to the Confederate Constitution, which cabinet department had to pay its own way after March 1863?
17. What Alabama governor had a hand in writing the Confederate Constitution?
18. Where was Kentucky's Confederate capital when the state ratified the Confederate Constitution?

✎ Constitutional Matters (answers)

1. The first 12 Amendments.
2. One.
3. All, unless they specifically conflicted with the new Confederate Constitution.
4. None. It does provide for 6 executive departments, which became (obviously) the cabinet.
5. Six weeks.
6. Christopher Memminger, who became secretary of the treasury.
7. Only three.
8. The line-item veto.
9. Slavery, of course.
10. An export tax on cotton and tobacco.
11. None. It was ratified by the states' legislatures.
12. States' rights and slavery, naturally.
13. Two-thirds in both houses.
14. Slaves.
15. A Supreme Court, which never came to exist, due to the ongoing debate over states' rights.
16. The Postal Service.
17. John Shorter, who served only one 2-year term.
18. At Russellville, where Gov. Beriah Magoffin's provisional government had moved. The pro-Union government was still at Frankfort.

19. What important person, not mentioned in the U.S. Constitution, is mentioned in the Preamble of the Confederate Constitution?
20. What man's name heads the list of signers of the Confederate Constitution?
21. How many states are named in the Confederate Constitution?
22. Why would anti-slavery agitators sometimes burn the U.S. Constitution in public?
23. What radical Constitutional amendment was proposed in the U.S. Congress in January 1864?
24. What slave state was home to the U.S. senator who proposed a Constitutional amendment outlawing slavery in the U.S.?
25. What Confederate state made Lincoln giddy with delight in January 1864?
26. What slave state abolished slavery in October 1864?
27. What 1788 law of South Carolina was repealed in December 1860?
28. What Northern politician originated the idea of "Southern suicide," claiming the Southern states had given up all their constitutional rights when they seceded?
29. What Confederate statesman wrote *A Constitutional View of the Late War Between the States* after the war?

⚐ Confederates Abroad: Foreign Affairs

The Confederacy declared itself a nation in 1861. Declaring is one thing—getting formal recognition from other nations is another. The ruling powers in Europe and Latin America preferred a "watch and wait" strategy. They were uncertain about whether the Confederate States of America really could maintain itself as a nation, or would merely prove to be a short-lived rebel movement. This "watch and wait" strategy proved to be one of the Confederacy's greatest frustrations. It did not stop the new nation from transacting some "under the table" business abroad.

1. What naval incident sent the British Parliament into an uproar?
2. What renowned European queen announced that her country was strictly neutral in the Civil War?
3. What was the prime reason the nations of Europe would not give diplomatic recognition to the Confederacy?
4. What native New Yorker became the Confederacy's commissioner to France?
5. What was significant about the ship *Florida*, which left Liverpool, England, in March 1862?

19. God—to be specific, "Almighty God."
20. Howell Cobb of Georgia.
21. Seven, the ones that had joined at the time of the drafting of the Constitution—South Carolina, Georgia, Florida, Alabama, Mississippi, Louisiana, and Texas.
22. They claimed it was horrible because it protected slavery.
23. The abolition of slavery throughout the U.S. This would eventually become the Thirteenth Amendment.
24. Missouri. The senator was John B. Henderson.
25. Arkansas, whose Constitutional Convention had just passed an anti-slavery measure. Lincoln wanted the state back in the Union immediately.
26. Maryland. The new constitution, which abolished slavery, passed by only 375 votes.
27. The ratification of the United States Constitution.
28. Pompous and self-righteous Charles Sumner of Massachusetts.
29. Vice-president Alexander Stephens.

✎ Confederates Abroad: Foreign Affairs (answers)

1. The *Trent* affair, in which Confederate diplomats on the British ship *Trent* were seized by a Union ship.
2. Britain's Queen Victoria.
3. Fear of antagonizing the U.S., mainly.
4. John Slidell, who was living in New Orleans when the war began.
5. It was the first Confederate warship built in England.

6. What name was given to the Confederate policy of withholding cotton from Europe in the hope that Europe would give official recognition to the Confederacy?
7. What U.S. official informed the British government that supplying ships to the Confederacy would be considered an act of war?
8. What nation considered setting itself up as a mediator between the Confederacy and the Union?
9. What world figure sent a polite letter to Jefferson Davis, addressing him as "President of the Confederacy"?
10. Having no money to buy ships in Europe, what did the Confederates attempt to use as credit?
11. What secession governor billed the U.S. for his work done as U.S. minister to Russia?
12. What Union official was the Confederacy's chief obstacle to buying guns and ships in Europe?
13. What act of the Lincoln administration insured that the Confederacy would never be recognized by Great Britain?
14. What request of Confederate diplomat John Slidell did French emperor Napoleon III refuse?
15. What ruler of a huge empire informed Washington that his nation was neutral in the Civil War?
16. In what exotic spot was the raiding ship *Alabama* when it captured a Union ship bearing coal?
17. What were the Confederate warships built in England not allowed to have?
18. What did Confederate diplomats offer French emperor Napoleon III in exchange for French aid in breaking the Union blockade of the South?
19. What notorious international incident came to an end on New Year's Day, 1862?
20. What Union official had the most extensive spy network in Europe—a constant thorn in the Confederacy's side?
21. What did French diplomat Mercier offer U.S. Secretary of State William Seward?
22. Why did Lincoln reject Confederate Vice-president Alexander Stephens' notion of ousting the French forces from Mexico?
23. Where was the CSS *Ajax* when it was denied armaments on the ground that it was nothing more than a pirate ship for the Confederacy?
24. What Latin American country made Confederate and Union officials promise not to have a naval battle in its waters?
25. What was Britain doing that the U.S. government considered a violation of Britain's official neutrality in the war?

6. "Cotton diplomacy." It failed completely when Europe bought cotton from other nations.
7. Charles Francis Adams, U.S. minister to Britain.
8. Great Britain debated this in Parliament but decided not to.
9. Pope Pius IX.
10. Cotton certificates—that is, pledges of future shipments of cotton.
11. Francis W. Pickens of South Carolina. The U.S. issued a check drawn on a South Carolina bank—which the state had already seized.
12. Charles Francis Adams, the U.S. ambassador to Britain.
13. The Emancipation Proclamation, which was greeted with great enthusiasm in Britain. The British had clearly become pro-Union.
14. French aid in breaking the Union's naval blockade of the Confederacy. The emperor did not want to offend the U.S.
15. Alexander II, Czar of All the Russias.
16. The coast of Brazil.
17. Guns. The ships could be built in England, but the guns had to be added later, outside England.
18. Cotton, naturally. The emperor declined.
19. The captured Confederate diplomats Mason and Slidell were finally released from U.S. custody. The *Trent* affair was at an end.
20. Charles Francis Adams, U.S. ambassador to Britain. His spies worked to frustrate the Confederacy's efforts to purchase ships and armaments.
21. He offered to mediate between North and South. His offer was not accepted.
22. Stephens' plan was based on the idea of *two nations*, U.S. and Confederacy, cooperating. In Lincoln's view, the Confederacy was not a nation, but merely a part of the U.S. in rebellion.
23. Bermuda, a possession of Britain.
24. Brazil. The Union naval commander broke the promise.
25. Building ships for the Confederacy.

26. What European country was most receptive to Confederate ships docking there?
27. What famous Confederate ship sank in the English Channel after having captured 55 Union ships?
28. What flattering inscription was found on the jewel-studded sword on the captured Confederate blockade runner *Fanny and Jenny?*
29. What foreign ruler did diplomat Ambrose Mann beg for aid to the Confederacy?
30. What naval hero arrived in a Cuban port with seven Union ships as trophies?
31. What incident provoked the British government to send 8,000 soldiers to Canada and to build new forts along the U.S.-Canadian border?
32. Where did Ohio politician Clement Vallandigham go after he found himself unwelcome in both the South and the North?
33. Where did U.S. naval commander William Ronckendorff catch the great prize of the Confederate navy, the CSS *Alabama?*
34. What Canadian province gave a warm welcome to naval commander Matthew Maury?
35. What neighboring government refused to recognize the legitimacy of the Confederacy?
36. What incredible Confederate defeat did the people of Cherbourg, France, witness in June 1864?
37. When the Confederate raiding ship *Tallahassee* docked in Nova Scotia for refueling, what did the U.S. Consul attempt to do?
38. Why did the Confederacy allow the use of coins from France, Britain, Spain, and Mexico?
39. What was the most important item brought in by the Confederate blockade runners?
40. What essential substance did the Confederacy have to bring in from Mexico?
41. What did the Union offer Englishmen who provided information on Southern blockade runners?
42. What notorious Rebel raiding ship finally met its match in June 1864?
43. Where was the last Confederate flag lowered?
44. What European language was the main source of military terms for both Confederacy and Union?
45. What were the two favorite foreign ports for blockade runners?
46. What two formidable Confederate ships, built in England, never saw service because the English claimed they violated the neutrality laws?

26. France. The port of Brest was a favorite harbor for Confederate ships.
27. The notorious *Alabama*, sunk in June 1864.
28. "To Gen. Robert E. Lee, from his British sympathizers."
29. The pope, Pius IX. Mann wanted him to interfere with Federal recruiting among Irish and German Catholics.
30. Raphael Semmes.
31. The *Trent* affair, in which Confederate diplomats on the British ship *Trent* were seized by a Union ship. The act was seen as an act of aggression against Britain.
32. To Canada.
33. At Martinique in the Caribbean. However, the *Alabama* managed to escape.
34. Nova Scotia. Maury noted that the Nova Scotians were "strongly secesh."
35. The Spanish government of Cuba.
36. The sinking of the supposedly unsinkable Confederate raider *Alabama*.
37. Coerce the Canadians into refusing coal to the Confederate ship. They did not refuse.
38. One reason being that the Confederacy never minted its own coins, so silver or gold from elsewhere was quite acceptable.
39. Probably the British-made Enfield rifles, desperately needed by the common soldiers.
40. Mercury, used in percussion caps.
41. A reward of 30 pounds.
42. The CSS *Alabama*, sunk by the USS *Kearsarge* off the French coast.
43. In Liverpool, England, on board the CSS *Shenandoah*, November 6, 1865.
44. French, which in those days was the language of war, not love.
45. Nassau, in the Bahamas, and Bermuda. At these ports the runners would transfer cargo to smaller ships that could easily evade the Union blockade.
46. The infamous Laird rams, built by John Laird & Co.

47. What neighbor nation's waters were open to Southern blockade runners but closed to Union warships?
48. Why was Confederate naval officer John Braine called on the carpet for capturing the Union ship *Roanoke*?
49. What did Lord Russell, Britain's foreign secretary, demand from the U.S. government in order to rectify the *Trent* affair?
50. What did the commander of the CSS *Stonewall*, docked in Cuba, do when he learned of the surrender at Appomattox?

⚐ Mr. Secretary: The Confederate Cabinet

The new government continued the U.S. tradition of a Cabinet of advisors for the president. As with the U.S. Cabinet, President Davis had to choose men not just for their ability but for their geographical spread and, of course, for their presumed political loyalty. In four short years, fourteen men served as Cabinet members. Some burned out, some changed positions, and some hung on till the bitter end. Though none are as well known as the most famous generals, they deserve to be, for their influence on Confederate life was enormous.

1. What Confederate Cabinet member had once challenged Jefferson Davis to a duel?
2. How many of the original six Confederate Cabinet members were slave-owners?
3. What Confederate Cabinet member convinced Jefferson Davis to institute a draft?
4. What technological wonder was introduced into the Secretary of War's office in October 1862?
5. How did President Jefferson Davis and his cabinet respond to the Union capture of Norfolk?
6. Of President Jefferson Davis's original cabinet, how many were in the same position at the war's end?
7. Who was the wealthiest man in the Confederacy at the beginning of the war?
8. What did the Confederate Secretary of War have in common with the U.S. Secretary of War?
9. Of the eleven Confederate states, how many had men in the Confederate Cabinet?
10. Of the fourteen men who served in the Confederate Cabinet, how many had been slave-owners?

47. Mexico's. The Confederates took full advantage of this.
48. He captured it near Havana, Cuba—a neutral port. Worldwide, the act was seen as a violation of neutrality.
49. The release of the seized Confederate diplomats, and an apology from the U.S. government.
50. Turned the ship over to the governor of Cuba, who paid him for the ship.

✎ Mr. Secretary: The Confederate Cabinet (answers)

1. Judah Benjamin. This occurred when both were U.S. senators. The duel never took place. Supposedly Benjamin considered himself a bad shot, and Davis wasn't.
2. Six.
3. Secretary of War George W. Randolph.
4. The telegraph, which at that time extended no farther than Warrenton, Virginia.
5. Being only 100 miles away, in Richmond, they sent their families away to Raleigh, North Carolina, for safety.
6. Two. Navy Secretary Stephen Mallory and Postmaster General John Reagan.
7. Probably George Trenholm, a Charleston banker who served for a while as Confederate secretary of the treasury.
8. Neither Judah Benjamin nor Edwin Stanton had any military background.
9. Nine. Only Tennessee and Arkansas were not represented.
10. Fourteen.

11. What restriction did Confederate Senator Robert Johnston of Arkansas try to place on the Confederate Cabinet?
12. Of the fourteen men who had served in the Confederate Cabinet, how many were imprisoned at the war's end?
13. What vicious Union plan to burn Richmond and kill Jefferson Davis and the entire cabinet ended up being a morale-booster for the Confederacy?
14. What future Confederate Cabinet member drafted the Declaration of Immediate Causes, claiming that the Union was not perpetually binding on the states?
15. How did Charleston newspaper editor Robert Barnwell Rhett respond to Secretary of War Pope's request that newspapers not publish military information?
16. What Southern newspaper was so consistently pro-Davis that readers believed its articles had been written by Jefferson Davis and his cabinet members?
17. Which member of the Confederate Cabinet was a Texan?
18. What cabinet member gained his office mainly because President Jefferson Davis needed a member from Alabama?
19. What man with military experience replaced Judah Benjamin, who had no military experience, as secretary of war?
20. Which three of the Confederate Cabinet's original members held office till the end of the Confederacy?
21. What cabinet department received the most attention from President Jefferson Davis?
22. What cabinet member was called by Jefferson Davis, "the most accomplished statesman I have ever known"?
23. What Confederate Cabinet member resigned because he thought President Jefferson Davis didn't consult him enough?
24. When President Jefferson Davis was captured in 1865, who was the only cabinet member with him?
25. What cabinet member was said to look like "a man who has been in his grave a month"?
26. What Southern state was the birthplace of Secretary of the Treasury Christopher Memminger?
27. What cabinet member and former general organized the Confederacy's evacuation of Richmond?
28. What was the key reason behind the appointment of North Carolinian George Davis to the Confederate Cabinet?
29. What U.S. president was grandfather of Confederate Secretary of War George W. Randolph?
30. What failed general served as secretary of war for a few days between George W. Randolph and James Seddon?

11. A two-year term limit for each member. This was never done.
12. Six (Hunter, Mallory, Reagan, Trenholm, G. Davis, Seddon).
13. The plan found on the body of Union Col. Ulric Dahlgren. The so-called Dahlgren papers rallied the South behind its leaders.
14. Christopher Memminger, who became secretary of the treasury.
15. Rhett screamed "Censorship!" and said the public had the right to any war-related information.
16. The Richmond *Enquirer*, one of the few reliably pro-Davis papers in the South.
17. Postmaster General John H. Reagan.
18. Secretary of War Leroy P. Walker, who had the nickname "Slow Coach."
19. George W. Randolph, who had both army and navy experience.
20. Judah Benjamin, John H. Reagan, and Stephen Mallory.
21. The War Department—naturally enough, since Davis had been U.S. Secretary of War once. (And besides, the country was at war.)
22. Judah Benjamin, who held three different positions in the Cabinet.
23. Attorney General Thomas Bragg, brother of Gen. Braxton Bragg.
24. Postmaster General John Reagan.
25. Secretary of War James Seddon, who had a rather gaunt look due to poor health.
26. None. He was born in Germany, but grew up in Charleston.
27. John C. Breckinridge, who accompanied the cabinet in its flight to North Carolina.
28. Politics. Jefferson Davis was aching for support from North Carolina, so he gave George Davis the position of attorney general. (George and Jefferson were not related, by the way.)
29. Thomas Jefferson.
30. Gustavus W. Smith, who was not the best field commander in the Confederacy.

31. What Confederate Cabinet official changed from secretary of war to secretary of state in March 1862?
32. What Confederate Cabinet department controlled the issuing of the passports required for moving about in the Confederacy?
33. When President Jefferson Davis met with his cabinet in Charlotte, North Carolina, what did they agree to do?
34. What former Confederate Cabinet member went on to serve as mediator between the Confederate government and the North Carolina government?
35. What Confederate Cabinet member was born (appropriately) on an island?
36. What cabinet member dropped out of the Confederate-Cabinet-on-the-run on April 27, 1865?
37. What Confederate general became secretary of war—the Confederacy's last—in February 1865?
38. What Confederate official was arrested by the Federals and charged with instigating "piratical expeditions"?
39. What Confederate Cabinet member resigned his post on May 3, 1865, and headed for safety in England?
40. What cabinet member resigned under pressure from Virginia representatives who wanted General Joseph Johnston restored to a high command?
41. How had Judah Benjamin, the only Jewish member of the Confederate Cabinet, supposedly affect President Jefferson Davis's public prayers?
42. Who was President Jefferson Davis's first choice for secretary of state?
43. What was Stephen Mallory's best qualification for serving as secretary of the navy?
44. What position did Judah Benjamin hold before joining the Confederate Cabinet?
45. What cabinet member played referee between President Jefferson Davis and temperamental generals like Johnston and Beauregard?
46. What Confederate Cabinet member had a fleet of 60 ships for running the Federal blockade?
47. When the Confederate Cabinet agreed to re-form west of the Mississippi, which member chose to head home?
48. What Confederate Cabinet member had been born in the Virgin Islands?
49. What likable Virginian was a congressman, secretary of state, and senator for the Confederacy?
50. Which states were represented in the first cabinet?

31. Judah P. Benjamin, noted for holding several positions in the Cabinet.
32. The War Department.
33. Escape to the west of the Mississippi River.
34. Former Attorney General Thomas Bragg, brother of Gen. Braxton Bragg.
35. Stephen Mallory, secretary of the navy. He was born on Trinidad in the Caribbean.
36. Treasury Secretary George Trenholm.
37. John C. Breckinridge, once vice-president of the U.S.
38. Navy Secretary Stephen Mallory. The charge was based on the damage done by the Confederacy's notorious commerce raiders.
39. Judah Benjamin, who had served three different positions in the Cabinet.
40. Secretary of War Seddon, even after President Jefferson Davis begged him to stay.
41. He had, allegedly, convinced Davis to omit any mention of Christ.
42. Robert Barnwell of South Carolina, who declined, saying he was not qualified for the post. Barnwell was a loyal Davis supporter.
43. He had served in the U.S. Senate as chairman of the Committee on Naval Affairs.
44. U.S. senator from Louisiana.
45. Secretary of War James Seddon.
46. George Trenholm, possibly the wealthiest man in the Confederacy. He was secretary of the treasury.
47. Attorney General George Davis (no relation to Jefferson Davis, by the way).
48. Judah Benjamin, who grew up in Louisiana.
49. Robert M. T. Hunter. In his days in the U.S. Senate, he, Jefferson Davis, and Robert Toombs were known as the "Southern Triumvirate."
50. Florida (Stephen Mallory, secretary of the navy), Texas (John Reagan, postmaster general), Georgia (Robert Toombs, secretary of state), Alabama (Leroy Walker, secretary of war), South Carolina (Christopher Memminger, secretary of state), and Louisiana (Judah Benjamin, attorney general). Mississippi was represented by President Davis.

⚑ The Quarrelsome Congress

Who is more famous, Robert E. Lee or Robert Toombs? Thomas "Stonewall" Jackson or Thomas Bocock? It is unfortunate that Toombs and Bocock and their Congressional kin aren't better known, for they played a major role in the Confederacy. Many—but not all—of the South's best leaders took a military command. A few labored in Richmond to keep the new nation afloat. A few, alas, seemed to do everything in their power to sink the ship of state.

1. What former U.S. president was elected to the Confederate Congress?
2. What building was the first meeting place for the Confederate Congress?
3. What four non-Confederate states were recognized as part of the Confederacy by the Confederate Congress?
4. Which governor was elected to the Confederate Congress after he found himself powerless as governor?
5. How many hotels did Montgomery, Alabama, have when the Confederate Congress met there in February 1861?
6. Sensing that the Confederate government felt cramped in Montgomery, what did the state of Alabama offer to build?
7. What act of the Confederate Congress finally pushed Virginia to join the Confederacy?
8. According to a February 1863 resolution of the Confederate Congress, what was to be done with captured black Union soldiers?
9. What did the Confederate Congress ask the wealthy men of the South to contribute in August 1861?
10. What right did the Confederate Congress confer upon President Jefferson Davis in February 1862?
11. What infamous law passed the Confederate Congress in April 1862?
12. What was the monthly pay of a soldier, according to the October 1862 act of the Confederate Congress?
13. How many senators and representatives were in the first Confederate Congress?
14. What was the worst handicap of the Confederate Congress?
15. What were the "imaginary districts" of the Confederate Congress?
16. Who was the most noted absentee in the Confederate Senate?
17. According to an act of the Confederate Congress, what was to be done with a captured Union officer who had commanded black troops?
18. What was the purpose of the citizens' "mass meetings" in Richmond in October 1863?

✎ The Quarrelsome Congress (answers)

1. John Tyler of Virginia, who died in 1862.
2. The Alabama state capitol in Montgomery.
3. The four border (and slave) states: Kentucky, Missouri, Maryland, and Delaware. The Congress also authorized raising troops in those states.
4. Tennessee's Isham Harris who, after 1862, had no real authority in his state.
5. Two, which was hardly adequate.
6. A capital district in the state, corresponding to the Union's District of Columbia.
7. The Congress voted to move the capital to Richmond.
8. They were to be sold as slaves, the proceeds going to reimburse Confederate slave-owners who had lost their property.
9. A loan of 100 million dollars to finance the war.
10. The right to suspend habeas corpus—a right that Lincoln already exercised.
11. The conscription (draft) bill.
12. $4.
13. There were 28 senators and 122 representatives, mostly from the planter class.
14. Poor leadership, mostly because the best leaders in the South were serving in the army.
15. Districts that were in Union-occupied areas. As the war progressed, there were more and more of these districts.
16. Vice-president Alexander Stephens who was (as in the U.S.) president of the Senate. After 1862, Stephens was rarely present.
17. Execution. This was never actually done.
18. They wanted the Confederate Congress to enact price controls.

19. What generous offer of the Confederate Congress did U. S. Grant accept in January 1865?

20. What law did the Congress pass in March 1865 that would radically change the Confederate army?

21. What key bill was introduced in the Congress by Walter Brooke on May 1, 1861?

22. What Indian tribe sent a delegation to the Confederate Congress in Montgomery?

23. How many sessions of the Confederate Congress were there?

24. How were the representatives to the first Confederate Congress elected?

25. How long did it take the first Confederate Congress to draft a constitution?

26. What was the "Great Debate" of the first Confederate Congress?

27. How many houses did the first Confederate Congress have?

28. According to a law passed in 1862, what was to be published after each battle to recognize particularly brave soldiers?

29. What much-hated law passed the Confederate Congress on April 24, 1863?

30. How were Confederate senators elected?

31. What two unofficial political parties developed within the Confederacy?

32. What Richmond prison had such a bad reputation that the Confederate Congress ordered an investigation of its commandant?

33. What city invited the Confederate Congress to relocate there on April 27, 1861?

34. What body met for the first time on February 18, 1862?

35. What cantankerous Confederate official was almost (but not quite) removed from office by the Senate in 1864?

36. What notable secessionist from Alabama had high hopes of becoming president of the Confederacy but was considered too radical?

37. What Confederate congressman, Davis's most vocal opponent, set off for Washington to negotiate a surrender?

38. What power was removed from President Jefferson Davis by the Congress in January 1865?

39. What majority was needed in the Confederate Congress to admit a new state to the Confederacy?

40. What post did Virginian Thomas Bocock hold in the Confederate government?

41. What former congressman returned from Canada to learn that he was charged with involvement in Lincoln's assassination?

19. An exchange of prisoners between South and North. Grant had previously forbidden exchanges, hoping to keep the South's soldier power tied up as long as possible.
20. The Congress authorized using blacks in the army. By the end of March, some were already in uniform.
21. A proposal to move the Confederate capital from Montgomery to Richmond.
22. The Choctaws.
23. Three.
24. They weren't. The first delegates were appointed by their states' secession conventions.
25. Six weeks.
26. The matter of admitting non-slave states to the Confederacy.
27. Only one. Later the Congress had two.
28. A Roll of Honor. This was important, since the Confederacy gave no medals.
29. The tax-in-kind law, requiring that 10 percent of agricultural products and livestock be given to the Confederate government.
30. By state legislatures, the same as in the U.S. at that time.
31. A pro-Davis and anti-Davis.
32. Castle Thunder, whose commandant, Capt. George Alexander, had been charged with "harshness, inhumanity, and tyranny."
33. Richmond. The offer was accepted.
34. A bicameral Confederate Congress.
35. Lucius Northrop, the Confederacy's commissary general, widely accused of incompetence.
36. William L. Yancey, who did become a senator in the Confederate Congress. He died in 1863.
37. Henry Foote of Tennessee. He was apprehended and brought back to face a reprimand from the Confederate Congress.
38. His title of commander in chief of the armed forces. The title was given to Robert E. Lee.
39. Two-thirds in both houses.
40. Speaker of the House.
41. Clement Clay of Alabama, who was imprisoned along with Jefferson Davis. His case was never tried.

42. What office did Presbyterian pastor Thomas V. Moore hold?
43. What act of Congress provided for organizing companies of partisan fighters?
44. How did Georgia governor Joseph Brown react when the Confederate Congress passed a law allowing the governor to exempt *essential* state officers from the draft?
45. Who was elected by the Cherokees to represent them in the Confederate Congress?
46. What Confederate congressman was sent to Europe on a mission of winning European recognition by promising to abolish slavery?
47. What Tennessee congressman was censured by Congress for making "treasonous overtures" to the Federal government?
48. What general and former Confederate congressman led some Georgia reserves in a spunky attempt to halt William T. Sherman's march up the Georgia coast?
49. What Louisiana general had lost a U.S. Senate election to Judah Benjamin by one vote?
50. What Richmond newspaper's offices became a favorite meeting place for Confederate congressmen opposed to President Jefferson Davis?
51. Who received the first Thanks of the Confederate States Congress in February 1861?
52. What member of the Confederate Congress went on after the war to be president of a college for blacks?
53. What close friend and Confederate House member was President Jefferson Davis's fellow prisoner after the war ended?
54. What noted Indian fighter spent most of the war as a Confederate congressman, begging for permission to invade New Mexico?
55. What hot-tempered South Carolina general left military life to become a Confederate congressman and, later, governor of his state?
56. What award did Gen. Francis Cockrell and his Missouri troops receive for their devotion to the Southern cause?
57. What redheaded Irishman achieved fame for beating back an attempted Union invasion of the Texas interior?
58. What Southern governor failed in his bid to be elected to the Confederate Congress?
59. Who was President Jefferson Davis's staunchest defender in the Confederate Congress?
60. How did the Confederate Congress respond to repeated stories of theft by partisan fighters?
61. What Confederate congressman took it on himself to meet with Lincoln to negotiate a peace settlement?

42. Chaplain to the Confederate Congress.
43. The Partisan Ranger Act of 1862.
44. He promptly decided that almost all of them were essential, thus exempting most of Georgia's civil officials and militiamen.
45. Elias Boudinot, who had a committee voice but no House vote.
46. Duncan Kenner of Louisiana, who believed emancipation was necessary for the Confederacy to survive. His mission failed.
47. Henry Foote, President Jefferson Davis's longtime critic and adversary.
48. Lucius J. Gartrell, a better politician than a soldier.
49. Henry Gray, who went on to serve in the Confederate army and the Congress.
50. The Richmond *Whig*, noted for its harsh criticism of Davis's war policies.
51. The state of Alabama, for loaning $500,000 to the Confederacy.
52. Jabez Curry of Alabama, who was president of Howard College in D.C.
53. The loyal Clement Clay of Alabama. The two remained lifelong friends.
54. John Robert Baylor of Texas.
55. Milledge Bonham, who was a thorn in the side of the Confederate government.
56. The official Thanks of the Confederate Congress.
57. Richard Dowling, who won the official Thanks of the Confederate Congress.
58. John Letcher of Virginia.
59. Probably Thomas Bocock, Speaker of the House.
60. They repealed the Partisan Ranger Act in 1864, thus removing the official status of the partisans.
61. Henry Foote, Jefferson Davis's harshest critic. Lincoln refused to meet with Foote.

62. What anti-Davis congressman from North Carolina had five sons serving as Confederate army officers?
63. What likable Virginian was a congressman, secretary of state, and senator for the Confederacy?
64. What name was given to the hospitals established by Congress at railroad junctions?
65. What two Confederate officials actually came to blows in Richmond over their disagreements?
66. What deed of Englishman John Lancaster garnered an official Thanks from the Confederate States Congress?
67. What general was offered the dictatorship of the Confederacy by a congressional delegation?
68. What two generals received the official Thanks of Congress for the victory at Bull Run?
69. What was the main source of Congressman Henry Foote's hatred for Jefferson Davis?
70. Who was the first general to receive a Thanks of Congress from the Confederacy?
71. What 300-pound Kentuckian served in the Confederate Congress after making a poor showing as a soldier?
72. Who was the last man to receive the official Thanks of Congress from the Confederacy?
73. What radical idea was proposed for drafting more soldiers for the Confederate army?
74. What congressman had at one time left his state of Mississippi and gone to California to get away from secessionists?
75. What Texas senator in the Confederate Congress led the movement to have Jefferson Davis stripped of his powers as commander-in-chief?

⚑ States Men: The Governors (Part 2)

1. What Southern governor had been born in New Jersey?
2. What governor was invited to Richmond by President Jefferson Davis to be an advisor on Trans-Mississippi affairs?
3. What border state governor had his hands full trying to keep pro-Confederate and pro-Union forces from destroying the state?
4. What German-born politician became governor of Union-occupied Louisiana?

62. William Graham, who, ironically, was constantly working for Confederate surrender.
63. Robert M. T. Hunter.
64. "Way hospitals." These were especially used by soldiers on medical furlough.
65. Senator Henry Foote, a constant critic of the Davis administration, and Lucius Northrop, the Confederacy's commissary general.
66. Rescuing the renowned Capt. Raphael Semmes after the sinking of the CSS *Alabama*.
67. Robert E. Lee, who was horrified by the offer.
68. Joseph E. Johnston and P. G. T. Beauregard.
69. Davis had been appointed secretary of war by Franklin Pierce, a post Foote had wanted. He held his grudge for years.
70. P. G. T. Beauregard for his action in the taking of Fort Sumter.
71. Humphrey Marshall, who had been U.S. ambassador to China.
72. Gen. Wade Hampton, for his defense of Richmond. The thanks was granted March 17, 1865.
73. Drafting slaves. First proposed by General Patrick Cleburne, the plan was adopted by Congress in 1864. It was assumed that slaves who fought would eventually be given their freedom.
74. Henry Foote, harshest critic of the Davis administration.
75. Louis Wigfall, not one of Davis's staunchest supporters.

✎ States Men: The Governors (Part 2) (answers)

1. Harris Flanagin of Arkansas.
2. Texas Gov. Francis Lubbock.
3. Hamilton Gamble of Missouri.
4. Michael Hahn.

5. What governor fled to England after the war because he was charged with treason?
6. What border state was declared neutral by the state's pro-Southern governor?
7. What governor had to flee Union armies just a few hours after being inaugurated?
8. What governor accused Lincoln of leading an "unholy crusade" against the South?
9. Who served as governor of a Southern state for three years without ever having been elected?
10. What political honor did Tennessean William Bate decline, preferring to hold to his field command?
11. Who called for Georgia to hold a secession convention?
12. What state governor had run on a compromise platform but was strongly pro-secession?
13. What Virginia general was elected governor in the middle of the war?
14. What was the most prominent occurrence in Henry Wise's term as governor of Virginia?
15. What Georgia statesman was urging his state toward secession while his brother, the governor, urged compromise?
16. Which Southern governor had the most extreme views of states' rights?
17. What record did Thomas Fletcher hold as governor of Arkansas?
18. What Virginia governor volunteered for the Confederate army though he had no military experience at all?
19. What Alabama governor had a hand in writing the Confederate Constitution?
20. What former Southern governor shocked his state by becoming a Republican after the war?
21. What governor had been U.S. ambassador to Brazil?
22. In what position did Alabama Gov. Andrew Moore serve after leaving office in 1861?
23. What Virginia governor had, in pre-war days, supported a movement to make western Virginia a separate state?
24. What governor enlisted thousands of slaves to help build coastal defenses for his state?
25. What Southern governor was accused of breaking his neutrality pledge by letting Confederate recruiters operate in the state?
26. Who was secretary of state in the short-lived Republic of South Carolina?
27. Who claimed that secession was "the most glorious event in the history of Florida"?

5. Isham Harris of Tennessee.
6. Kentucky. Army recruiters from both sides operated in the state, ignoring Beriah Magoffin's declaration of neutrality.
7. Richard Hawes, elected pro-Confederate governor of Kentucky.
8. Claiborne Jackson of Missouri.
9. Andrew Johnson, appointed by Lincoln as governor of Union-occupied Tennessee.
10. Candidate for governor. After the war, he was elected governor twice.
11. Its pro-secession governor, Joseph E. Brown.
12. Claiborne Jackson of Missouri.
13. William "Extra Billy" Smith.
14. John Brown's raid on Harpers Ferry and, afterward, Brown's execution.
15. Thomas Cobb, brother of Howell Cobb. Both became Confederate generals.
16. Georgia's Joseph Brown, a great admirer of John C. Calhoun. Brown often locked horns with the Confederate government.
17. He served for only 11 days.
18. Henry Wise, who was immediately made a brigadier general.
19. John Shorter.
20. Joseph Brown of Georgia.
21. Henry Wise of Virginia, who was also a Confederate general.
22. Aide to his successor, Gov. John Shorter.
23. John Letcher, who, in 1863, watched the movement actually come to pass, to his deep regret.
24. Francis Lubbock of Texas.
25. Beriah Magoffin of Kentucky.
26. Andrew Magrath, who became governor of the state in 1864.
27. Florida's governor, John Milton.

28. What state governor had been a wealthy sugar plantation owner?
29. What governor fled his capital because of Sherman's troops in February 1865?
30. What former governor was imprisoned by the Federals but released because of his poor health?
31. What governor had helped organize the Washington Peace Conference to try to prevent war between South and North?
32. What Southern governor committed suicide rather than surrender to the Union?
33. What western governor fled to Mexico by escape arrest by Federals?
34. What proclamation did Georgia Gov. Joseph Brown make in November 1864?
35. What governor was kind enough to share the guns he captured from Federal arsenals with another state?
36. What Southern governor had his home burned by the troops of Union Gen. David Hunter?
37. Before South Carolina had actually seceded, what other Southern state had indicated that it would gladly follow suit?
38. What two-term Mississippi governor left office to become a private in the 1st Mississippi Infantry?
39. What governor had wanted to serve in the Confederate army but couldn't because of poor health?
40. What position did Francis Pierpont hold after a brief spell as first governor of West Virginia?
41. What Southern governor managed to keep his seat for a few months after the Union occupied his capital?
42. What border state governor was inaugurated but never performed any official duties?
43. After the evacuation of Nashville in 1862, what Tennessean was named Military Governor of his home state?
44. What Southern governor failed in his bid to be elected to the Confederate Congress?
45. What fretful governor often received no replies to his requests to the Confederate government to send guns for his state's coastline?
46. In what state was a pro-Northern provisional governor inaugurated on January 22, 1864?
47. What Southern governor continually protested having his state's soldiers serving in other Confederate states?
48. What former governor fled to Mexico and became an attorney for the Emperor Maximilian?

28. Thomas Moore of Louisiana.
29. Andrew Magrath of South Carolina.
30. Alabama's Andrew Moore.
31. John Letcher.
32. John Milton of Florida, who died April 1, 1865.
33. Pendleton Murrah of Texas.
34. He called on every able-bodied man to defend the state against Sherman's troops.
35. Louisiana's Thomas Moore, who shared the loot with Mississippi's John Pettus.
36. John Letcher, whose home was in Lexington, Virginia.
37. Florida, whose governor was gung-ho secessionist Madison Perry.
38. John Pettus, who eventually reached the rank of colonel.
39. Pendleton Murrah of Texas.
40. He was "governor of Virginia"—at least in the northern Virginia counties occupied by Federals.
41. Harris Flanagin of Arkansas.
42. Richard Hawes, who had to flee Union armies just hours after his inauguration.
43. Andrew Johnson, later to be Lincoln's vice-president.
44. John Letcher of Virginia.
45. John Milton of Florida.
46. Arkansas, which had just passed an antislavery law.
47. Joseph Brown of Georgia, a staunch states rights advocate.
48. Thomas C. Reynolds, who was fortunate in being fluent in Spanish and French.

⚐ Confederates Abroad: Foreign Affairs (Part 2)

1. What subversive pro-Southern fraternity had originally been founded to extend slavery into Mexico?
2. What nations benefited most from the Union blockade of Confederate ports?
3. What anti-Confederate action by the Union almost brought it to war with Great Britain?
4. What deed of Englishman John Lancaster garnered an official Thanks from the Confederate States Congress?
5. What English statesman, speaking of the Confederacy, stated, "They have made a nation"?
6. How did Britain react when the U.S. government protested the building of Confederate ships in England?
7. What role did U.S. ambassador William Dayton play in the war against the Confederacy?
8. What was the most pro-Confederate newspaper in England?
9. In what country did Gen. Alexander Hawthorne try to establish a post-war Confederate community?
10. What diplomatic position was held by Lucius Quintus Cincinnatus Lamar?
11. What diplomatic post was given to Kentucky general William Preston?
12. What governor had been U.S. ambassador to Brazil?
13. What did Southerners hope would be the result of the *Trent* affair?
14. What was Edwin de Leon's mission in France?
15. What Confederate soldier went on to become a member of Britain's Parliament?
16. What position did naval officer Samuel Barron hold?
17. What Caribbean island was the U.S.—particularly the South— interested in acquiring in the 1850s?
18. What countries' cotton replaced Confederate cotton in the world's markets?
19. What was French-born general Camille Armand Jules Marie de Polignac doing in Europe when he learned of Lee's surrender?
20. What Confederate official's favorite expression was *Tout va bien*?
21. What Confederate diplomat failed in his attempt at a Franco-Confederate military alliance?
22. What did Union Secretary of State Seward offer to do to unite the U.S. against the Confederacy?

✎ Confederates Abroad: Foreign Affairs (Part 2) (answers)

1. The Knights of the Golden Circle.
2. Bermuda, the Bahamas, and the Caribbean islands that saw a neat profit from having the blockade runners trade there.
3. The USS *San Jacinto* had boarded the British ship *Trent* to seize two Confederate diplomats. This was a violation of Britain's neutrality, and the British government was outraged.
4. Rescuing the renowned Capt. Raphael Semmes after the sinking of the CSS *Alabama*.
5. William Gladstone.
6. They ordered that the ships then being constructed would be kept in port.
7. As minister to France, Dayton managed to stop French manufacture of Confederate ships and the French providing sanctuary for Confederate sea raiders.
8. The *Index*, financed by the Confederate government and edited by the capable Henry Hotze.
9. Brazil.
10. Commissioner to Russia.
11. Ambassador to the court of Maximilian, France's puppet emperor in Mexico.
12. Henry Wise of Virginia, who was also a Confederate general.
13. War between the U.S. and Britain. Technically, the U.S. had committed an act of aggression by seizing Confederate diplomats from the British ship *Trent*.
14. Spreading Confederate propaganda, which he failed at rather badly.
15. Henry Morton Stanley, born in Wales, who had fought in the 6th Arkansas Infantry. He is most famous for tracking down missionary David Livingstone in Africa.
16. He was called "flag officer commanding naval forces in Europe." His actual duties involved getting Confederate ships built in England and France.
17. Cuba, a possession of Spain. Southerners saw it as a potential slave state for the U.S.
18. India, Egypt, and Brazil.
19. Seeking aid for the Confederacy from Emperor Napoleon III.
20. Diplomat Pierre Rost, working in France. *Tout va bien* is "all goes well," the unrealistic response Rost gave to Europeans' inquiries about the Confederate war effort.
21. John Slidell, the Confederate diplomat in France.
22. Start a war with France or Spain. Lincoln did not think this was wise.

23. What French ruler received the Confederate diplomat but refused to formally recognize the Confederacy?
24. Aside from diplomatic recognition, what did the Confederacy hope to gain by its policy of withholding cotton from the nations of Europe?
25. What French-born Confederate diplomat was assigned to Spain after embarrassing the Confederacy in his native France?
26. What was John Slidell's chief asset as Confederate diplomat in France?
27. Why did the U.S. seize Confederate diplomats Mason and Slidell, provoking the notorious *Trent* incident?
28. The South had had a bumper cotton crop in 1860. What problem did this cause in the Confederacy's relations with other countries?
29. Besides the aching need for more soldiers, why did the Confederacy decide to recruit blacks for the army?
30. What was the Confederacy's chief reason for wanting to be recognized as an independent nation by the nations of Europe?
31. Who wrote *Three Months in the Confederate Army* as a propaganda piece for Europeans?
32. What Confederate congressman was sent to Europe on a mission of winning European recognition by promising to abolish slavery?
33. Who was the Confederacy's chief purchasing agent in Europe?
34. What nation enabled the Europeans to be less dependent on cotton from the Confederacy?
35. What Civil War incident brought the U.S. and Britain to the brink of war?
36. What was accomplished by the Union occupation of Brownsville, Texas, in November 1863?
37. In what exotic location was the CSS *Alabama* when it captured and burned the Union ship *Emma Jane*?
38. When Charleston was being bombarded, what foreign officials sent messages to the Union commanders, asking them to stop the bombing?
39. Where was the notorious Rebel raiding ship *Alabama* docked when the fatal battle with the USS *Kearsarge* began?
40. When diplomat Ambrose Mann left Richmond in 1861, when did he promise to return?
41. What Confederate diplomat had ten years' experience on the U.S. Senate Foreign Relations Committee?
42. What energetic Confederate diplomat never succeeded in getting Britain to recognize the Confederacy as an independent nation?
43. What Confederate official had come to America because of his disappointment at the fall of Napoleon?

23. Napoleon III. Slidell, the diplomat, also wanted French aid in breaking the Union's naval blockade.
24. Military aid against the Union.
25. Pierre Rost, who was intensely disliked by his fellow French.
26. His marriage to a French Creole woman.
27. Both diplomats were headed to Europe to drum up support for the Confederacy.
28. Since other nations had plenty of cotton in warehouses, the Confederacy's threat of a cotton embargo carried little weight.
29. The hope that this seemingly liberal policy would bring recognition and approval from Europe.
30. As an independent nation, it could forge military alliances, which would have meant trouble for the U.S.
31. Propaganda-master and publisher Henry Hotze, who presented an idealized picture of Southern morale and patriotism.
32. Duncan Kenner of Louisiana, who believed emancipation was necessary for the Confederacy to survive. His mission failed.
33. Caleb Huse, who bought guns and equipment from any nation that would accept Confederate business.
34. India. Although Indian cotton was inferior, it was more readily available during the Civil War.
35. The *Trent* affair, in which Confederate diplomats on the British ship *Trent* were seized by a Union ship. The act was seen as an act of aggression against Britain.
36. The Mexican border area was securely under Union control.
37. The coast of Malabar, India.
38. The British and Spanish consuls. The Union refused.
39. Cherbourg, in France.
40. When the South achieved true independence. Sure enough, he never returned. He died in Paris.
41. James Mason, a close friend of President Jefferson Davis.
42. James Mason.
43. Diplomat Pierre Rost, born in France, later resident of Louisiana.

44. What was John Slidell's chief asset as Confederate diplomat in France?
45. What kind of aid did the Confederacy hope to get from Pope Pius IX?
46. What name was given to the $8 million loan given for the Confederacy's use in Europe?

Ⓑ Blessed Are the Peacemakers

Was every resident of the Confederacy gung-ho for independence? Hardly. From the beginning, some believed that the South would inevitably be defeated by the North, so why not try to negotiate an honorable peace and return to the Union? As the war progressed and Confederate defeats accumulated, more people were won to the cause of waving the white flag. To many ardent Confederates, these peaceniks were weakminded at best, downright traitors at worst. They played an important, and too often forgotten, role in the Confederate nation.

1. What former U.S. president presided over a D.C. peace conference in February 1861, hoping to prevent a war?
2. In what state did a Peace Convention meet in February 1861, hoping to forestall a complete separation from the U.S.?
3. What peace-making Kentucky senator remained in the U.S. Senate as long as possible, hoping for a peaceful solution to the North-South problem?
4. What governor had helped organize the Washington Peace Conference to try to prevent war between South and North?
5. What was the Order of the Heroes of America?
6. What Confederate official said to Lincoln's face, "Is there no way of putting an end to the present trouble?"?
7. What phrase, used in a January 1865 letter from President Jefferson Davis to Lincoln, made Lincoln shut down peace negotiations?
8. What Confederate congressman took it on himself to meet with Lincoln to negotiate a peace settlement?
9. When, according to Confederate money, could the bill actually be cashed in?
10. What was the purpose of the Peace and Constitutional Society?
11. What city hosted a peace conference in February 1861, hoping to avert war?

44. His marriage to a French Creole woman.
45. They wanted him to interfere with Federal recruiting of German and Irish Catholics for the Union army.
46. The Erlanger Loan, negotiated by the Confederacy and Emile Erlanger and Co. of Paris. The loan was secured by government-owned cotton in the Confederacy.

✎ Blessed Are the Peacemakers (answers)

1. John Tyler, who later became a Confederate congressman.
2. Virginia. The convention was (obviously) unsuccessful.
3. John C. Breckinridge, former vice-president of the U.S., and later a Confederate general.
4. John Letcher of Virginia.
5. One of the alleged "peace societies" aimed at convincing the Confederacy to surrender peacefully.
6. Vice-president Alexander Stephens, part of the informal "peace conference" that met with Lincoln at Fort Monroe, Virginia.
7. Davis used the phrase "two nations." From Lincoln's point of view, no peace could be had unless the Confederacy admitted that there was only one nation, the U.S.
8. Henry Foote, Jefferson Davis's harshest critic. Lincoln refused to meet with Foote.
9. "Six months or two years after the ratification of a treaty of peace between the Confederate States and the United States"—which never occurred.
10. Encouraging Confederate soldiers to desert and encouraging civilians to support the Federal army.
11. Washington. The conference led to nothing.

12. What fateful conference met at Fort Monroe, Virginia, on February 2, 1865?
13. What Confederate official, hoping to negotiate a peace after the Battle of Gettysburg, was refused by the Federal government?
14. Who were the "Red Strings"?
15. What Confederate official left Richmond for good after the failure of his peace talk with Lincoln?
16. What Southern peace society was started at Union instigation and included U. S. Grant and Lincoln in its membership?
17. What plan did sixty members of the Peace Society have for Christmas Day 1863?
18. What American political party supplied many of the Confederacy's peace agitators?
19. What type of flag did peace demonstrators in North Carolina march under in March 1862?
20. What was Bryan Tyson's claim to fame?
21. What did the peace agitators insist on retaining if the Confederacy returned to the Union?
22. Who was the Confederate Congress's most outspoken peace advocate?
23. What flag was usually flown at meetings of peace activists?
24. What fate befell William Holden, pro-peace editor of the *North Carolina Standard*?
25. According to most Southern peace agitators, when was the proper time to approach Washington concerning peace negotiations?
26. What state governor was a noted leader in the peace movements?
27. What unofficial offer did Lincoln's friend Francis Blair make to the peace faction in the Confederate Congress?

12. The North-South peace meeting, discussing terms to reconcile the two nations. Lincoln was insistent that the South *must* recognize Federal authority. The South wouldn't. The conference floundered.
13. Vice-president Alexander Stephens.
14. Men belonging to the peace society the Heroes of America. They wore a red string on their lapels.
15. Vice-president Alexander Stephens, who remained on his Georgia estate until arrested by the Federals.
16. The Order of the Heroes of America, a thorn in the Confederacy's side.
17. They planned to mutiny against their commander, Gen. James Clanton and head home. The plan failed.
18. The Whigs, which, as a party had ceased to exist by 1860. Many former Whigs were strongly anti-secession and became diehard Unionists.
19. A white one, of course.
20. He published *A Ray of Light*, one of many books claiming that Confederate defeat was inevitable, and thus surrender was the sensible thing to do.
21. Slavery, naturally.
22. James T. Leach of North Carolina, a state noted for its many peace activists.
23. The U.S. flag, what else?
24. He had his presses destroyed by Confederate troops.
25. After any Confederate military victory.
26. Joseph Brown of Georgia, a constant thorn in Jefferson Davis's side.
27. The possibility of gradual (instead of immediate) emancipation of slaves if the seceded states returned to the Union.

🏴 Grumbling, Griping, Dissenting

Being a Southerner and being a proud Confederate weren't necessarily the same thing. Not everyone south of the Potomac waved the Bonnie Blue Flag with enthusiasm. The dissenters ran the gamut from downright traitors to lukewarm Unionists who kept their feelings to themselves. Even more common were the average Joes who resented the discomforts that the war brought into their lives. Perhaps the motto "United we stand, divided we fall" would have been a great help to the poor Confederacy, had the people taken it seriously.

1. What Confederate state saw its entire northwestern portion break off to form a new state?
2. What radical move was taken by Winston County, Alabama?
3. What independent-minded state governor refused to observe Jefferson Davis's national day of fasting?
4. What Confederate policy was most resented as an infringement on independence?
5. Before the breakaway territory from Virginia took the name West Virginia, what was the name?
6. What was the cause of the protest that frightened the Virginia legislature into adjourning?
7. What name was given to the practice of seizing citizens' food and supplies to give to soldiers?
8. What high-level Confederate official made clear his opposition to such national policies as secession, the draft, and martial law?
9. Why was the list of exemptions for the draft so resented?
10. What city was the scene of the notorious 1863 Bread Riot, in which a mob of angry women rampaged into stores and took food and clothing?
11. Who confronted the Bread Riot mob and emptied out his pockets to them?
12. What was the primary cause of soldiers deserting the Confederate ranks?
13. What was the widely resented Twenty-Negro Law?
14. What percentage of grains, produce, and meats did the Confederate government lay claim to?
15. What constantly griping Confederate congressman compiled a "shocking catalog" of questionable arrests when habeas corpus was suspended?
16. When did the Confederate Congress authorize the income tax?
17. What document was required of any Confederate citizen traveling through a war zone?

🖎 Grumbling, Griping, Dissenting (answers)

1. Virginia, naturally. The new state was West Virginia.
2. It voted to secede from the state—a futile move, since it was surrounded by Confederate territory.
3. Joseph E. Brown of Georgia. Oddly, a week later Brown proclaimed his own fast day.
4. Conscription, that is, the draft, which had never existed on a national basis in the U.S.
5. Kanawha.
6. It was a protest against suspension of habeas corpus—that is, the guarantee that a person will not be detained illegally. (This occurred in the North also, where Lincoln did not mind suspending habeas corpus.)
7. Impressing. The practice was much hated, needless to say.
8. Vice-president Alexander Stephens.
9. It appeared that the draft exemptions favored the wealthy and influential—which they did. The poor and middle class had no way of buying their way out of the draft.
10. Richmond.
11. President Jefferson Davis. However, he also ordered them to disperse or be fired upon. They dispersed.
12. Pleading letters from their poor afflicted families.
13. It provided a draft exemption for any planter with more than twenty slaves. In theory, the law was designed to keep slavemasters around so the slaves would not revolt. The law was widely hated, since it obviously favored the wealthy.
14. Ten percent. This "tax in kind" hurt small farmers much more than plantation owners.
15. Jefferson Davis's longtime adversary, Henry Foote.
16. Spring 1863. This was long before the U.S. had a national income tax.
17. A passport. This requirement was widely resented, since anyone without a passport had to be held for questioning.

18. Can you complete this famous phrase: "A rich man's — and a poor man's —"?
19. What offense caused Virginia politician John Minor Botts to be jailed for eight weeks?
20. What was probably the most dangerous group of Confederates?
21. How did Georgia governor Joseph Brown react when the Confederate Congress passed a law allowing governor to exempt *essential* state officers from the draft?
22. What areas were most liked by Confederate deserters?
23. What high-ranking official told Gen. Braxton Bragg that he had no constitutional right to declare martial law in Atlanta?
24. What was the "Republic of Jones"?
25. What was the most common form of protesting (and evading) the draft?
26. What fateful meeting took place in Wheeling, Virginia, in June 1861?
27. How did the pro-Union people of east Tennessee respond to lack of Federal help?
28. What river was the dividing line between Arkansas' pro-Union and pro-Confederate governments?
29. What section of Tennessee was mostly pro-Union?
30. What happened to pro-Union Alabama delegate Christopher Sheats when he argued against secession?
31. In what state were some pro-Union German citizens massacred?
32. What Tennessee editor ran a newspaper called the *Rebel Ventilator*, taking the Union side?
33. What east Tennessee city was placed under martial law by Gen. William Henry Carroll?
34. What group met in Bill Looney's tavern in Winston County, Alabama, in April 1861?
35. What did twenty-three Arkansas counties establish in 1864?
36. What were "Tories"?
37. What did Lincoln plan to offer Louisiana planters who were willing to pledge loyalty to the Union?

18. "A rich man's war and a poor man's fight"—the common gripe about how easy it was for the rich to be exempt from the draft.
19. Openly challenging the legality of the Confederate government.
20. Probably the army deserters, who often became bands of brutal fugitives. Since they were often being hunted down by Confederate officials, they became increasingly desperate and bloodthirsty.
21. He promptly announced that almost all of them were essential, thus exempting most of Georgia's civil officials and militiamen.
22. Isolated hills and hollows, where they could easily evade the Confederate authorities. There were several "fugitive kingdoms" in the Appalachians.
23. Vice-president Alexander Stephens.
24. A gang of pro-Union guerrillas in Jones County, Mississippi. They burned bridges, sank boats, and harassed Confederates along the roads.
25. Passive resistance—that is, simply not showing up. Confederate officials had a devil of a time rounding up the draftees.
26. The pro-Union meeting that led to the formation of the state of West Virginia.
27. They went on their own anti-Confederate rampage, burning bridges and harassing the local Confederate commander, Gen. Felix Zollicoffer.
28. Roughly, the Arkansas River.
29. The eastern section.
30. He was dragged from the convention floor and jailed. He was released after the state seceded.
31. Texas, in October 1862.
32. The infamous William "Parson" Brownlow, one of the most famous Unionists in Tennessee.
33. Knoxville, which had a sizable pro-Union population.
34. Unionists from northern Alabama, Georgia, Mississippi, and Tennessee, discussing secession from their home states.
35. A new pro-Union state government, with the capital at Little Rock.
36. White Southerners serving in the Union army. The name recalled the Tories of the Revolutionary War, colonists who took the British side.
37. The chance to sell cotton to the Union.

⚑ Copperheads and Such: Friends in the North

Was every Northerner a staunch supporter of Lincoln and the war effort? Hardly. Many people openly or secretly made their Southern sympathies plain. They were branded as disloyal or downright traitorous by Lincoln's Republican administration. A propaganda machine cranked up to smear the treasonous "Copperheads," and the machine functioned rather effectively. The Confederacy, needless to say, encouraged any Northern expression of sympathy for the new nation.

1. What U.S. political party was frequently accused of disloyalty during the war years?
2. What Atlantic coast state was strongly pro-Southern, with pro-Union sympathies only in (ironically) its southern counties?
3. What Midwestern city's newspaper was shut down for publishing pro-Southern statements?
4. According to the Peace Democrats in the North, what had forced the Southern states to secede?
5. What Northern city had five of its pro-Southern newspapers charged with disloyalty?
6. What subversive pro-Southern fraternity had originally been founded to extend slavery into Mexico?
7. What Northern state had the most Copperheads in its legislature?
8. Why did the Peace Democrats in the North fear the abolition of slavery?
9. In what Northern city did the mayor declare that his city would become a "free city," trading with both North and South?
10. What border state governor had his hands full trying to keep pro-Confederate and pro-Union forces from destroying the state?
11. What were the two wings of the Democratic Party during the war?
12. What is the claim to fame of George Bickley?
13. What did Peace Democrats in the North sometimes wear as an identification badge?
14. What pro-Southern governor was informed by Lincoln that Lincoln would definitely *not* remove pro-Union forces from the state?
15. How did the Union government deal with pro-Southern men in the Maryland legislature?
16. What future Copperhead governor had once been a strong abolitionist and a supporter of John Brown?
17. What Union head of the Secret Service gained a nasty reputation in the North for harassing and arresting suspected Southern sympathizers?

✎ Copperheads and Such: Friends in the North (answers)

1. The Democrats, or, more specifically, the Peace Democrats who advocated letting the Confederacy alone.
2. New Jersey. The Quakers in the southern counties were anti-slavery and, thus, pro-Union.
3. Chicago. This caused a howl of protests about freedom of speech.
4. The Republicans, by calling for troops to put down the "rebellion."
5. New York, which was notoriously pro-Southern.
6. The Knights of the Golden Circle.
7. Illinois, whose state legislature was a constant irritation to the state's pro-Lincoln governor, Richard Yates.
8. They feared that ex-slaves would migrate to the Midwest, playing havoc with the economy.
9. New York City.
10. Hamilton Gamble of Missouri.
11. The War Democrats, who backed the fight against the Confederacy, and the Peace Democrats, who would accept an independent Confederacy.
12. He founded the Knights of the Golden Circle, a subversive pro-Southern fraternity that had chapters in both South and North.
13. Copper pennies, since they were often called Copperheads.
14. Beriah Magoffin of Kentucky.
15. They had them arrested for disloyalty, thus insuring that Maryland remained in the Union.
16. Clement Vallandigham of Ohio.
17. Lafayette Baker, who was more widely hated in the North than in the South.

18. What pro-Union fraternity in the North was dedicated to ferreting out Southern sympathizers and whipping up support for the North?
19. According to the platform adopted by the Peace Democrats at the Democratic Convention in 1864, how was the war against the Confederacy to be continued?
20. What happened in May 1861 to push many Missouri residents into the pro-Confederate camp?
21. What Maryland city saw its mayor arrested for his pro-Southern sympathies?
22. What state governor was deposed by the Federal government after he moved the state capital to another city?
23. What city, angry at Lincoln's call for troops, cut off its telegraph lines to D.C. and tore up rail tracks?
24. What caused a rash of protests about freedom of speech in the North in 1863?
25. What Northern politician, banished to the Confederacy for his pro-Southern sympathies, had stated that he did not care to live in a country where Lincoln was president?
26. In the 1864 U.S. presidential election, which party had a "peace plank" in its platform, showing openness to the possibility of leaving the Confederacy alone?
27. Which part of Maryland remained decidedly pro-South throughout the war?
28. What border state saw its strongly pro-Southern governor replaced by a strongly pro-Union one in July 1861?
29. What honor was awarded to Ohio Democrat Clement Vallandigham, the man Lincoln had banished to the Confederacy for expressing his pro-Southern sympathies?
30. The Union League of America was dedicated to squelching sympathy Northern support for the South. It went by the initials ULA. What did Southerners say ULA stood for?
31. What subversive pro-Southern fraternity in the North were the Peace Democrats supposed to be collaborating with?
32. Where was pro-Southern politician Clement Vallandigham living while he campaigned for governor of Ohio?
33. Besides "Copperheads," what other slang term referred to pro-Southern people in the North?
34. What border state was declared neutral by the state's pro-Southern governor?
35. What future president spent most of the war fighting pro-Southern guerrillas in West Virginia?

18. The Union League of America, which wielded considerable power.
19. It wouldn't. The Peace Democrats called the war "a failure" and said it should be ended, with the South left in peace.
20. An invasion by Union troops.
21. Baltimore.
22. Claiborne Jackson, the pro-Southern governor of Missouri.
23. Baltimore, strongly pro-Southern.
24. Federal troops shut down the Chicago *Times* for criticizing Lincoln and expressing sympathy for the South.
25. The infamous Clement Vallandigham of Ohio.
26. The Democrats. However, Lincoln, the Republican, won easily.
27. The Eastern Shore, which had much in common with the Southern states.
28. Missouri. Hamilton Gamble replaced Claiborne Jackson.
29. The Ohio Democrats nominated him for governor.
30. Uncle Lincoln's Asses.
31. The infamous Knights of the Golden Circle.
32. In Windsor, Canada. Lincoln had banished him from the U.S. for his criticism of the Union war effort.
33. "Butternuts," so called from the home-dyed uniforms of many Confederate soldiers.
34. Kentucky. Army recruiters from both sides operated in the state, ignoring Beriah Magoffin's declaration of neutrality.
35. William McKinley.

36. What Maryland city gave a chilly greeting to the first companies of Pennsylvania troops headed south to defend Washington?
37. Who was arrested for being a Southern sympathizer while he was still a U.S. senator?
38. What Federal military victory was a major blow to the Copperheads?
39. What pro-Southern organization met in groups called "castles" and was responsible for subversive activity in the North?
40. What organization was founded by Harrison Dodd of Indianapolis?
41. What Northern state's governor was Lincoln's most outspoken foe in the war years?
42. In what Illinois town did a band of about one hundred Copperheads attack Union soldiers on leave?

36. Baltimore, which was strongly pro-Southern throughout the war.
37. Future general John C. Breckinridge of Kentucky.
38. Gettysburg. Copperheads were at their peak when the Union army was losing.
39. The Knights of the Golden Circle.
40. The Sons of Liberty, sympathetic to the South and widely accused by Republicans of plotting a revolution against the Federal government.
41. New York. Horatio Seymour, a Democrat, constantly criticized Lincoln for violating the rights of state and local governments.
42. Charleston.

Part 8

Daily Life
in
Wartime

⚐ Popular Parlance

A people's vocabulary is enriched (for better or worse) by war and other times of stress. From 1860 to 1865 Confederate civilians, like Confederate soldiers, added immensely to their language. Some expressions and phrases passed into history, while a few found a permanent place in the English dictionary.

1. What was "white gold"?
2. What were "Sherman's neckties"?
3. What were the "imaginary districts" of the Confederate Congress?
4. What was the "land of the lash"?
5. What city was, in the 1860s, considered "an American Rome"?
6. What phrase did author David Christy contribute to the Southern vocabulary?
7. What was "Confederate coffee"?
8. What were the "shell roads" so common in coastal areas?
9. Who were the "Red Strings"?
10. What were the "ornamentals" taught to girls on Southern plantations?
11. What people became "contraband of war"?
12. What were the "two-bale laws" passed in some Confederate states?
13. What were the "hells" in Richmond?
14. Who were "Uncle Lincoln's Asses"?
15. What were "corduroy roads"?
16. What was the "flock of black sheep"?
17. What was the "Breadbasket of the Confederacy"?
18. What was "Little Dixie"?
19. What type of Northerners were called "butternuts"?
20. What was "ram fever"?
21. What was the "government on wheels"?
22. What was the collective nickname for Southern Republicans?
23. Who was "Little Aleck"?
24. What name was given to state laws governing the lives of freed blacks in the South after the war?
25. What name was given to U.S. Gen. Winfield Scott's plan for bringing the South to its knees?
26. Who was the "Arkansas Comedian"?
27. What was the "Great Debate" of the first Confederate Congress?
28. What pro-slavery organization met in groups called "castles" and was responsible for subversive activity in the North?
29. What Virginia town was called the "Granary of the Confederacy"?

✎ Popular Parlance (answers)

1. Cotton, of course.
2. Confederate railroad rails, which Sherman's Union troops heated and wrapped around trees, making them unusable.
3. Districts that were in Union-occupied areas. As the war progressed, there were more and more of these districts.
4. The entire South, according to Northern abolitionists, who believed that slave-owners were all sadists.
5. Richmond. Like Rome, Richmond sat on seven hills.
6. "King Cotton," from his 1855 book *Cotton Is King.*
7. Some substitute for the real thing, which was hard to obtain—chicory, or any weed that tasted remotely like coffee.
8. Roads paved with crushed oyster shells.
9. Men belonging to the peace society the Heroes of America. They wore a red string on their lapels.
10. The "feminine arts"—piano, singing, drawing, painting, and French.
11. Slaves freed by Union occupation.
12. Laws forbidding any farmer to plant more than two bales of cotton per field hand. This was to encourage farmers to plant more food crops instead of cotton.
13. Gambling houses.
14. Members of the ULA—Union League of America, dedicated to squelching Northern sympathies for the South.
15. Laying parallel logs or boards on dirt (and mud) roads to provide a steady surface.
16. The horde of blacks—mostly women and children—that had followed Sherman's armies through the Carolinas. Observers called them "black sheep."
17. The Shenandoah Valley of Virginia, with its many farms and grain mills.
18. The southern portion of Missouri, loyal to the Confederacy.
19. The Peace Democrats, who wanted to end the war and let the South remain independent.
20. A widespread fear among Northern civilians that Southern ironclads would move against Northern cities. It was a great morale-booster for the South.
21. The name Jefferson Davis gave to his administration as they evacuated Richmond and headed south.
22. "Scalawags," of course.
23. Vice-president Alexander Stephens, who was rather short.
24. "Black codes." Interestingly, some Northern states passed laws to keep out blacks during this period.
25. The "Anaconda Plan," involving a blockade of Southern ports and the capture of the Mississippi River valley.
26. English-born Harry McCarthy, a variety entertainer who penned the famous "Bonnie Blue Flag," unofficial anthem of the Confederacy.
27. The matter of admitting non-slave states to the Confederacy.
28. The Knights of the Golden Circle.
29. Edinburg.

30. What was Virginia's "Seesaw Town" during the war?
31. What South Carolina aristocrat was dubbed the "Father of Secession"?
32. Why were the ironclads *Georgia*, *Fredericksburg*, and *Charleston* called "ladies' gunboats"?
33. What journalist coined the term "Lost Cause" to describe the South's failed attempt to create a separate nation?
34. What state was the "bleeding" state, so called because of the fighting over slavery in the 1850s?
35. What were "niter beds"?
36. What sort of people received "Sherman's land grants"?
37. What was "Oil of Gladness"?
38. Who was "the photographer of the Confederacy"?
39. What town bills itself as the "Birthplace of the Confederacy"?
40. Who was "Captain Sally"?
41. What sort of soldiers were "Tories"?
42. What were bank notes of low denominations called?

ꙮ Camp-sick: Confederate Medicine

Medicine in the 1860s was, needless to say, not very advanced. The whole notion of bacterial infection was unknown, and some of the "cures" were downright laughable, and often did more harm than good. Ordinary civilians suffered the usual illnesses and infections, but the military men, living with inadequate food, clothing, and shelter, suffered even more.

1. For every Confederate soldier who died of battle, how many died of disease?
2. At the beginning of the war, what sort of physical exam was administered to Confederate recruits?
3. Who suffered more from disease, the city-bred soldiers or the rustics?
4. What name was given to latrines?
5. What pestilent insect had the nickname of "gallinippers"?
6. Soldiers attributed malaria not to mosquitoes but to what?
7. What pest went by such colorful names as "graybacks," "tigers," and "Bragg's bodyguard"?
8. What childhood disease was especially common among soldiers from rural areas?
9. What common and (now) easily remedied affliction caused a tenth of its victims to die in the Confederate army?

30. Winchester, which was occupied by Confederates, then Federals, then Confederates . . . and so on, many times.
31. Robert Barnwell Rhett, noted "fire-eater" who, ironically, never had a post in the Confederate government.
32. They had been built with funds raised by the Ladies' Gunboat Societies throughout the South.
33. Edward Pollard, whose 1866 book was titled *The Lost Cause.*
34. Kansas. "Bleeding Kansas" was the scene of the notorious massacre by fanatic abolitionist John Brown.
35. Trenches and holes outside communities where people could dump urine, used in the making of niter needed for gunpowder.
36. Freed slaves, who could receive 40 acres of Union-occupied land between Charleston and Jacksonville.
37. One of many names for bootleg whiskey.
38. George S. Cook, noted for his dramatic pictures of Fort Sumter.
39. Abbeville, South Carolina. The first organized secession meeting took place there in 1860.
40. Hospital administrator Sally Tompkins, given the honorary rank of captain by Jefferson Davis.
41. White Southerners who served in the Union army. The name recalls the Tories of the Revolutionary War, colonists who supported the British.
42. "Shinplasters." The Confederacy had no metal coins, but lots of "paper coins."

Camp-sick: Confederate Medicine (answers)

1. Three, according to most estimates.
2. None. Not until fall 1862 was a program for exams begun.
3. Oddly enough, the rustics. Though they were of tough constitution, they knew little about hygiene, and the toughest outfits of the war were units composed of city-bred youths.
4. "Sinks."
5. Mosquitoes, a major problem for the Confederacy.
6. The miasma, or swamp mist. (They were at least correct in that there was a connection between swamps and malaria—since swamps breed mosquitoes.)
7. The all-too-common body lice.
8. Measles, which attacked in epidemic proportions and led to thousands of deaths.
9. Dysentery and diarrhea. Men afflicted composed from one-sixth to one-fourth of all hospital admissions.

10. What type of disease inevitably increased for soldiers stationed near cities?
11. What distasteful ingredient was often added to drinking water as a disease preventive?
12. What would soldiers wear to ward off the bad effects of chill and damp?
13. What personal grooming measure was recommended as protection for the throat and lungs?
14. As a home remedy for cold, what sweet ingredient was added to water?
15. What primitive medical method was still used to cure pneumonia in the Confederate army?
16. What was regarded as a cure-all, in the absence of better medicine?
17. What were "Waysides"?
18. What compassionate woman established a well-known hospital, which so impressed Jefferson Davis that he gave her a commission as a captain?
19. The disease known as "night blindness" or "gravel" was a complication caused by what other disease?
20. What disease was mistakenly believed to have a venereal origin?
21. What did "fighting under the black flag" refer to?
22. Health-wise, what part of "a complete and balanced diet" was most notably lacking, leading to disease?
23. What was the preferred (and fairly effective method) of ridding a uniform of body lice?
24. What contagious disease was believed to have been brought to the Confederacy by Yankees?
25. What was the most common skin ailment of the Confederate soldier?
26. What disease was treated (wrongly) with injections of ink?
27. What type of vehicle served as ambulances for the Confederacy?
28. What was the usual anesthetic for patients undergoing surgery?
29. What city was the site of hospitals established for soldiers from the separate Confederate states?
30. What was "camp fever"?
31. Why was influenza not a problem for the Confederate army?
32. What did "playing old soldier" mean?
33. How many years of medical school did doctors receive before the Civil War?
34. What was "laudable pus"?
35. Who many medical officers did the Confederate army have when the war began?

10. Venereal diseases, naturally.
11. Tar.
12. Flannel bands around the waist. (They were no more effective than the tar in the water, by the way.)
13. Letting the beard grow long—which was easy to do with little soap and water available for shaving.
14. Molasses.
15. Blood-letting—which was no help at all.
16. Alcoholic beverages, which, at least, did relieve some pain. Doctors were frequently teased about their own "medicinal" use of alcohol.
17. Voluntary agencies set up to care for ailing soldiers. They were also known as "soldiers' homes." They were the center of some controversy, since there were reports of the waysides' officials using donated goods for their own benefit (something that continues in modern-day charities).
18. The renowned Sally Tompkins, the only woman given a Confederate commission.
19. Probably scurvy, caused by a dietary deficiency (unknown at that time).
20. Smallpox. Doctors did not believe this, but apparently many soldiers did.
21. Killing body lice.
22. Probably fruit and vegetables, since the soldier's diet was often (bad) meat and (bad) cornbread, plus coffee. The soldiers rarely got fresh fruit, good greens, or juice.
23. Singeing it over a campfire—which some soldiers referred to as "popping corn," alluding to the large size of some of the lice.
24. Smallpox. In all seriousness, some Rebs did believe this, and it was true that many cases of the disease had been reported in the Union army before it became known among Confederates.
25. The "camp itch" or, simply, the "itch." It was hardly life-threatening, but in the days before skin ointment the camp itch could almost drive a man into frenzy.
26. Gonorrhea, believe it or not.
27. Canvas-covered wagons (no flashing lights or sirens at this time).
28. Whiskey or brandy, when available, and it often was not.
29. Richmond, the capital. Being near the thick of fighting, it naturally had more hospitals than any other city.
30. Possibly another name for typhoid, though the name is vague enough to apply to other diseases.
31. It was, in fact, but the actual name influenza wasn't used at the type. Some types of what were then called "pneumonia" were probably what we now call the flu.
32. Faking sickness at sick call.
33. Two.
34. The festering caused by infection—considered in those days to be part of the healing process.
35. About 24.

36. What sort of dance was the "Virginia quickstep"?
37. What kind of ailment was "the shakes"?
38. What did surgeons use silk thread for?
39. Why were most surgeons referred to as "butchers"?
40. Where did the name "general hospital" come from?
41. What Confederate facility had a 400-keg brewery, a soap factory, ice houses, and a bakery that could produce 10,000 loaves of bread per day?
42. What had to be done with soldiers whose families wanted them reburied near home?
43. What were "hop, step, and jumps"?
44. What Virginia city was home to Camp Convalescent, a center where Union men were sent after discharge from army hospitals?
45. What common prison disease caused men to lose their hair and teeth?
46. In what did North Carolina allow conscientious objectors to do in lieu of fighting?
47. In what branch of the Confederate army did hospital head Sally Tompkins receive her commission as captain?
48. Why were wounded soldiers sometimes allowed to go home to recuperate?
49. What valuable item did the CSS *Florida* capture from the Union ship *Harriet Stevens* in 1864?
50. What state's soldiers sometimes had to be separated from Virginia soldiers in Richmond's Chimborazo Hospital?
51. What Virginia hospital, with 8,000 beds, became the largest military hospital in America?
52. What group of people staffed the Wayside Homes and Hospitals?
53. What was the biggest complaint Confederate prisoners made about Union nursing chief Dorothea Dix?
54. What Scottish-born nurse published *Hospital life in the Confederate Army of Tennessee*?
55. Why did President Jefferson Davis give Sally Tompkins a commission as captain of cavalry?
56. What famous nurse traveled often through the Confederacy as she attended the Union wounded?
57. What was Dr. Hunter McGuire's medical specialty in his post-war career?
58. What color flags were used to mark field hospitals?
59. What disease was especially common in the New Orleans area because of the swampy terrain?
60. What essential part of the soldier's camp often went unused?

36. It wasn't. It was one of many names for a common camp complaint, diarrhea.
37. One of many names for malaria.
38. Tying off blood vessels.
39. About 3 out of 4 battlefield operations were amputations.
40. They accepted men regardless of which regiment they were from.
41. The Chimborazo Hospital in Richmond.
42. The corpse had to be disinterred, embalmed, then transported home in a coffin—often an expensive process.
43. A name for army ambulances. They gave a rather rough ride.
44. Alexandria. The camp was nicknamed "Camp Misery."
45. Scurvy.
46. Hospital duty or work in salt mines.
47. The cavalry, though, of course, she never actually served.
48. It relieved the government of the expense of nursing and feeding them.
49. Opium, desperately needed in the Southern hospitals.
50. Maryland's. Many Virginians had a snobbish attitude toward the Marylanders.
51. Chimborazo, in Richmond.
52. Women, mostly.
53. That she only employed ugly women as nurses.
54. The energetic Kate Cumming.
55. All hospitals in Richmond had to be run by military personnel, so to keep Tompkins' efficient hospital open, she had to have a military title.
56. Clara Barton, who later founded the Red Cross.
57. Gynecology and obstetrics—a tremendous change from his days tending the wounds of soldiers.
58. Yellow. The flags often had a large "H" in the center also.
59. Yellow fever.
60. The latrine. Most soldiers of the 1860s preferred to relieve themselves behind a tree or tent.

61. What office did Samuel Preston Moore hold in the Confederacy?
62. In what Tennessee city did women band together to open a hospital called the Southern Mothers' Society?
63. What name was given to the hospitals established by Congress at railroad junctions?
64. What important post was held by James Brown McCaw?
65. What was the specialty of the hospital in Kingston, Georgia?
66. Where was the Louisiana Hospital for mental patients?
67. What contribution did Dr. J. Julian Chisolm make to the Confederacy?
68. About what percentage of battlefield injuries resulted from sabers and bayonets?
69. What name was given to the infections that usually followed any surgery?
70. What disease was often treated by eating the herb sorrel?
71. What was the only Southern medical school that remained opened throughout the war?

⚑ Ridin' the Rails

South and North were like two different countries in some ways. Nowhere was this more obvious than in the railroads. Suffice it to say that the South had less, and less efficient to boot. As the Civil War dragged on, Confederates became painfully aware of the Southern railways' inadequacies.

1. What were "Sherman's neckties"?
2. What city, angry at Lincoln's call for troops, cut off its telegraph lines to D.C. and tore up rail tracks?
3. What obstacle was unexplainably placed on the tracks of the Baltimore & Ohio Railroad in Point of Rocks, Maryland?
4. What did President Jefferson Davis propose as a source for the iron needed for ironclad ships?
5. What was the name of the Confederate train captured by Federals in the "Great Locomotive Chase" of 1862?
6. What did Union troops occupying northern Alabama do to keep Confederate guerrillas from shooting at passing trains?
7. What Union general irked Tennessee residents by closing all the railways to civilian use?
8. What was the crew of the Confederate train the *General* doing when Union men seized the train?

61. Surgeon General.
62. Memphis.
63. "Way hospitals." These were especially used by soldiers on medical furlough.
64. Head of the large Chimborazo Hospital in Richmond, which he administered very well.
65. Men with severe venereal disease.
66. In Richmond, of all places.
67. He wrote the *Manual of Military Surgery for the Confederate States Army.*
68. About 1 percent.
69. "Surgical fevers," naturally.
70. Scurvy.
71. The Medical College of Virginia, in Richmond.

✎ Ridin' the Rails (answers)

1. Confederate rails, which Sherman's Union troops heated and wrapped around trees, making them unusable.
2. Baltimore, strongly pro-Southern.
3. A 100-ton boulder, supposedly placed there by the Confederates, though no one knew *how* it was done.
4. Railroad rails. His proposal was never acted on.
5. The *General.* This was the name of the Buster Keaton movie based on the famous chase.
6. Arrested local pastors and placed one on each train passing through—assuming that the guerrillas wouldn't want to accidentally kill a minister. They were wrong.
7. William T. Sherman.
8. Having breakfast off the train.

9. What Confederate general's men were responsible for torching Atlanta's munition dumps and railroad yards before evacuating?
10. What was the fate of the bold Union men who seized the Confederate train *General*?
11. When Tennesseans complained to Union general Sherman about his closing of the railroads to civilians, what alternate plan did he propose to them?
12. When the Rebel soldiers were paroled at the war's end, what was the chief obstacle in getting back home?
13. What did the Southern railroads *not* use when the war ended?
14. How were 22 Union men able to board the Confederate train the *General* before they seized it?
15. What was the standard width of railways tracks in the South?
16. How far did Jefferson Davis travel to get 250 miles from Jackson, Mississippi, to the capital at Montgomery, Alabama?
17. What was the average speed of trains on Southern railways?
18. What city had the Confederacy's only facilities for making railroad rails?
19. What railroad was crucial to the Confederate control of Virginia?
20. What brought the Union's daring Locomotive Chase to a halt?
21. What is the claim to fame of John W. Garrett?
22. What railroad line came close to being a "trans-Confederate" railway?
23. What Virginia railway was the first to play a strategic role in a Confederate victory?
24. What Georgia railway was the favorite target of Sherman's destruction?
25. What important railroad ran through Harpers Ferry, Virginia?
26. How many miles of new rail track were laid in the Confederacy during the war?
27. What 23-mile length of railway was the Confederacy's most important stretch of rail?
28. What was Henry Slocum's great contribution to the fight against the Confederacy?
29. What was the most famous hijacking incident of the Civil War?
30. What western Virginia railway was important to carrying salt and lead to the Confederacy from the region's mines?
31. What vital railway connected Richmond and Petersburg with North Carolina?
32. What was the purpose of the famous "Imboden Raid" in spring 1863?
33. What noted Confederate locomotive is found in Atlanta's Cyclorama museum?

9. John Bell Hood. The destruction was vividly portrayed in *Gone with the Wind*.
10. Most of them were executed.
11. Moving people and supplies by wagon train, just as people had done before the railroads came.
12. The horrid condition (thanks to the Federals) of the railroads.
13. Timetables—which would have been absolutely useless thanks to the condition of the railways.
14. They boarded as ordinary passengers and captured the engine while the crew had gotten off to eat breakfast.
15. There wasn't one, which was one of the key problems in the Confederacy's transport system. The North, by contrast, had one standard gauge for railways.
16. He went 750 miles—thanks to the poor rail connections in the South.
17. About 12 miles per hour.
18. Richmond.
19. The Baltimore & Ohio (B & O), which had 188 miles of track in Virginia.
20. The hijacked Confederate train, the *General*, had run out of fuel. The hijackers took to the woods.
21. President of the important Baltimore & Ohio Railroad, Garrett brought a curse on his company when he committed himself to helping the Federals. His railroad suffered continuous destruction by the Rebels.
22. The Memphis & Charleston, which would have linked the Mississippi with the Atlantic coast.
23. The Manassas Gap Railroad, which swiftly (for that day) carried Rebels to Bull Run, where they were victorious.
24. The Western and Atlantic.
25. The Baltimore & Ohio.
26. Not one.
27. The Richmond & Petersburg Railroad, connecting the capital with the vital rail nucleus at Petersburg.
28. The idea that Confederate railroad rails needed to be not just bent, but twisted to make them unusable. He was correct.
29. Undoubtedly the Union's bold capture of the *General*, a Confederate train. The plan came to a grinding halt when the hijacked engine ran out of fuel.
30. The Virginia & Tennessee Railroad, running from Bristol to Lynchburg.
31. The Weldon.
32. Cutting lines of the Baltimore & Ohio Railroad and capturing livestock for the Confederate army. Gen. John Daniel Imboden led the raid.
33. The *Texas*, used to pursue the Union spies in the "Great Locomotive Chase" after the stolen Confederate *General*.

⚑ Taxes, Taxes, and Taxes

Where there is war, there must be taxes to finance it. The Confederacy certainly found this to be so. And in wartime, as at all times, the unscrupulous find ways to profit from others' misery.

1. What official first proposed a direct tax on income?
2. According to the Confederate Constitution, what type of tax was to fund the federal treasury?
3. What was the highest income tax bracket for the Confederacy?
4. What name was given to the fund made up of the taxes imposed on army sutlers?
5. What much-hated law passed the Confederate Congress on April 24, 1863?
6. What was the lowest income tax bracket for the Confederacy?
7. Why were Federal authorities angry about West Point graduates joining the Confederate army?
8. How many Confederate states had a state income tax?
9. Late in the war, what income tax rate did Christopher Memminger want to impose on incomes over $10,000?
10. What percentage of grains, produce, and meats did the Confederate government lay claim to?
11. When did the Confederate Congress authorize the income tax?

⚑ Picture the Confederacy: Art and Photography

We are fortunate in having thousands of pictures from the Civil War years, not only paintings and drawings, but pictures from that new medium, photography. Confederate and Union soldiers were the first fighters in history whose images were captured forever by the camera.

1. Why were Civil War photographers unable to take action shots?
2. Who was "the photographer of the Confederacy"?
3. When Confederate troops were sketched by a Union artist in June 1861, where was the artist sitting?
4. What was a *carte de visite*?
5. Who was the only Confederate photographer to take numerous pictures of Rebel soldiers in the field?

✎ Taxes, Taxes, and Taxes (answers)

1. Secretary of the Treasury Christopher Memminger.
2. An export tax on cotton and tobacco.
3. For incomes over $10,000, the rate was 15 percent. (Compare that with today, if you like . . .)
4. The company fund. It was to be distributed fairly among the men.
5. The tax-in-kind law, requiring that 10 percent of agricultural products and livestock be given to the Confederate government.
6. For incomes under $1,000, it was only 1 percent.
7. It seemed ungrateful, the men having been educated at taxpayers' expense, then heading south.
8. Eight, ranging from .025 percent (Louisiana) to 10 percent (Virginia).
9. A whopping 50 percent. The Confederate Congress refused, fortunately.
10. Ten percent. This "tax in kind" hurt small farmers much more than plantation owners.
11. Spring 1863. This was long before the U.S. had a national income tax.

✎ Picture the Confederacy: Art and Photography (answers)

1. Photography at that time required long exposures, so only still shots were feasible.
2. George Smith Cook, noted for his dramatic pictures of Fort Sumter.
3. In a balloon—the first use of aerial reconnaissance in America.
4. The 1860s version of a wallet-size photo, about 2- by 4 inches. Many soldiers posed for these before they went off to war.
5. Jay Edwards.

6. How many newspaper photographers were there in the Civil War?
7. What did Missouri artist George Caleb Bingham accomplish with his painting *Order No. 11*?
8. What internationally known French artist painted the battle between the CSS *Alabama* and the USS *Kearsarge*?
9. What noted photographer covered the operations of the Union army in the South, collected the most valuable war photography ever made, then died in poverty?
10. English-born artist James Walker produced one of the war's greatest artworks in his huge painting of a Tennessee battle. Which one?
11. What English newspaper artist traveled with the Army of Northern Virginia and smuggled his sketches to England via blockade runners?
12. What Confederate soldier became famous in a painting by William Washington, an art professor at the Virginia Military Institute?
13. What contribution did *Frank Leslie's Illustrated Newspaper* make to the Civil War?
14. What role did photographer George N. Barnard play in the Confederacy?
15. One of America's greatest artists became famous for his painting of Union general questioning Confederate captives. Who was he?
16. What noted New York artist of Civil War battles was better known for his paintings of horses?
17. What member of "Stonewall" Jackson's famous "Foot Cavalry" went on to become the Confederacy's most renowned artist?
18. What English artist and journalist was a favorite visitor in the Confederate camps?
19. What Confederate officer and noted artist left his home in Italy to defend the state of Virginia?
20. What Union general had the honor of having his face painted inside chamber pots in New Orleans?
21. What noted Confederate photographer's wartime photographs are owned by the Valentine Museum in Richmond?
22. Where was Confederate soldier Conrad Wise Chapman living while he painted his famous pictures of Confederate camp life?
23. What was artist Adalbert Volck most noted for?

6. None. Photographs could not be reproduced on the printing presses of the 1860s.
7. Created sympathy for the Confederacy. The painting showed Missouri residents driven from their homes by Union troops.
8. Edouard Manet. The famous painting is in the Philadelphia Museum of Art.
9. Matthew Brady, whose war photos are a national treasure.
10. *The Battle of Lookout Mountain*.
11. Frank Vizetelly, one of the most famous Civil War artists.
12. Capt. William Latané, killed by Union troops and left to be buried by strangers. The painting *The Burial of Latané* depicted the touching scene and increased sympathy for the South.
13. It published war stories with woodcut illustrations, usually within two weeks of a battle. In a day when photographs could not be reproduced in newspapers, *Leslie's* gave the world its first look at the war.
14. As the first man to photograph such places as Chattanooga and Lookout Mountain, he gave people their first views of such beautiful areas.
15. Winslow Homer, who painted many pictures of camp life during the war. His later seascapes and woodland scenes are what really made him famous.
16. Edwin Forbes. Naturally his skill in painting horses served him well in painting war pictures.
17. Allen Redwood, who drew on his personal experience for his many Civil War paintings.
18. Frank Vizetelly, who at the end joined President Jefferson Davis's group as it fled Richmond.
19. Conrad Wise Chapman, whose nickname was "Old Rome."
20. The despised Benjamin Butler, the Union general in control of the city.
21. George S. Cook, who took over 10,000 photographs.
22. In Rome, Italy, with his family.
23. Political caricatures.

♫ Makers of Music

What is human life without music? Unthinkable, really. It certainly played a role in the South, both for soldiers and civilians. Music can rally the heart for battle, soothe jangled nerves, and recall the home that may be far away and long ago. In spite of the Confederacy's dire financial straits, music never became an unaffordable luxury.

1. What members of a regiment could be younger than the legal age for a soldier?
2. When a Confederate band played "Dixie" near Union troops, what song would the Union band play in reply?
3. What pro-Southern song, written in Louisiana, became a state song for a Union state?
4. What was the Confederate national anthem?
5. What well-known bugle composition was composed by a Union man encamped on a Virginia plantation?
6. What famous song was written by Englishman Harry McCarthy?
7. What general's death lead to a flood of sentimental songs and poems being written?
8. What brass musical instrument was widely used in military bands because its bell projected backward over the player's shoulder, sending the sound back to the troops?
9. What role did regimental band members play during battles?
10. What were "songsters"?
11. In what state was the composer of "Dixie" born?
12. What renowned American songwriter wrote the song "That's What's the Matter," mocking the Confederacy?
13. What general said, "I don't believe we can have an army without music"?
14. What patriotic song did Union authorities try to stop being printed when they occupied New Orleans?
15. What is the more famous composition of the author of *Emmet's Standard Drummer*, an army drumming manual?
16. What were the "ornamentals" taught to girls on Southern plantations?
17. What caused the much-loved patriotic song "The Bonnie Blue Flag" to lose some of its appeal?
18. What popular patriotic song was written by C. T. DeCoëniél and George H. Miles in 1863?
19. What better-known song was written by the composer of "Mac Will Win the Union Back," a song honoring Union Gen. George McClellan?
20. What devout general, who loved to sing hymns, was notoriously tone-deaf?

❧ Makers of Music (answers)

1. Fifers and drummers, who might be as young as 12.
2. "Yankee Doodle," naturally.
3. "Maryland, My Maryland," which Maryland-born James Ryder Randall wrote to convince his home state to join the Confederacy.
4. There wasn't one, officially. "Dixie" and "The Bonnie Blue Flag" were both popular patriotic tunes.
5. "Taps," composed by Dan Butterfield, which became the standard "lights out" signal.
6. The patriotic "Bonnie Blue Flag," an unofficial national anthem for the South.
7. Thomas "Stonewall" Jackson, killed at Chancellorsville in 1863.
8. The saxhorn, no relation to modern saxophones.
9. Either fighting, or serving as messengers, orderlies, and stretcher-bearers.
10. Small, cheap songbooks printed for soldiers' use.
11. Ohio.
12. Stephen Foster, who also wrote "Swanee River," which is Florida's state song.
13. Robert E. Lee.
14. "The Bonnie Blue Flag," unofficial anthem of the Confederacy.
15. "Dixie."
16. The "feminine arts"—piano, singing, drawing, painting, and French.
17. Its author, Harry McCarthy, abandoned the Confederate cause and moved to Philadelphia.
18. "God Save the South."
19. "Dixie," by Dan Emmett.
20. Thomas "Stonewall" Jackson—a great man, but a very bad singer.

21. In what Confederate states did the writer of "Dixie" travel to perform his song?
22. What patriotic song was found (without a title) in Confederate hymnals?
23. What song were J.E.B. Stuart's aides singing around his bed as he died?
24. What Southern city was (appropriately) the Confederacy's center for sheet music publishing?
25. What noted Southern song caused no end of embarrassment to its author?
26. What was the significance of the song "The Irish Jaunting Car"?
27. What was the claim to fame of Edward and Henry Blackmar?
28. What important items did Herman Schreiner smuggle into the Confederacy from the North?
29. What did William Shakespeare Hays contribute to the South?
30. What still-popular song was a favorite marching song for Confederate soldiers?
31. What song honoring a Confederate general was banned in Union-occupied territories?
32. What was the profession of Dan Emmett, the author of "Dixie"?
33. Where did Dan Emmett get the phrase "I wish I was in Dixie"?
34. What French song often appeared in Confederate band books?
35. What noted general used a young drummer boy to "beat the rally" in battle at Fredericksburg?
36. According to tradition, what did drummer David Scantlon of the 4th Virginia Regiment do to make sure he could keep drumming?
37. What flashy officer had banjo player Joe Sweeney in his entourage?
38. What popular folk song laments the sorry food of the Georgia militia?
39. What cheap and very portable instrument was just becoming popular when the war began?
40. What popular fiddle tune is still a favorite among fiddlers today?
41. What popular song was played at Jefferson Davis's inauguration?
42. Why was the song "The Homespun Dress" so popular?
43. What time of day was "Taps" normally played?
44. When "Taps" was played, what were soldiers required to do?
45. In what way did Confederate bugle calls differ from the Union's?
46. Who received breakfast first, men or horses?
47. What did the bugle call "Stable Call" signal?
48. What did the bugle call "Water Call" signal?
49. What bugle call was the signal to clean up camp?
50. What was the first bugle call used each day? (Note: It wasn't "Reveille.")
51. How many different bugle calls were used in camp each day?

21. None. Dan Emmett, a Yankee, did not perform in the South during the war.
22. "My Country, 'Tis of Thee." The song had the words changed from "Land of the Pilgrim's pride" to "Land of the Southron's pride."
23. "Rock of Ages."
24. New Orleans, always (and still) a very musical town.
25. "Dixie." Dan Emmett was a Yankee and very loyal to the Union.
26. Its tune became the tune for "The Bonnie Blue Flag."
27. They were the most prolific music publishers in the South, and the original publishers of "The Bonnie Blue Flag."
28. A font of music type essential in music publishing. Since New Orleans, the music publishing center, was now Union-occupied, Schreiner almost had a monopoly on Confederate music publishing.
29. One of its most popular songs, "The Drummer Boy of Shiloh." Hays was prolific, producing over 300 songs.
30. "The Yellow Rose of Texas."
31. "Stonewall Jackson's Way," published before Jackson's death but even more popular afterward.
32. A performer in minstrel shows.
33. From his wife, who frequently complained about Northern winters.
34. The French anthem, "La Marseillaise."
35. Thomas "Stonewall" Jackson.
36. At First Manassas he (so the story goes) turned his back to the enemy so they could not shoot a hole in his drum.
37. J. E. B. Stuart. Sweeney was noted for his comic parody songs.
38. "Goober Peas."
39. The harmonica.
40. "Hell Broke Loose in Georgia."
41. "Dixie," naturally.
42. It showed solidarity of soldiers and civilians. The song celebrated Southern girls who wore homespun and thus helped support the cause.
43. About 10 at night.
44. Put all lights out.
45. They didn't.
46. Horses. The bugle call for this was "Stable Call."
47. That men were to feed and tend the horses.
48. That men were to water the horses.
49. "Fatigue Call."
50. "Assembly of Buglers," followed by "Reveille."
51. Nineteen.

♫ Meeting the Press

Consider the importance of newspapers in the 1860s: They were the means of mass communication, as important as TV, radio, and print combined. Was the press biased? Always. Journalists in the Civil War era made no pretense of objective reporting. Writers both South and North aired their opinions happily—and not always with the sectional loyalty you might assume. Small wonder that the journalist's life could be a dangerous one.

1. What did the Confederate government do to censor attacks by the Southern newspapers?
2. When prostitutes advertised themselves in magazines, what would they claim to be seeking?
3. What totally false promise did the Richmond newspaper *Examiner* make in May 1861?
4. What type of paper sometimes had to substitute for newsprint?
5. What Northern city had five of its pro-Southern newspapers charged with disloyalty?
6. What propaganda move did Union general Benjamin Butler make in New Orleans in May 1862?
7. What notable Richmond riot was never mentioned in the Richmond newspapers?
8. What Midwestern city's newspaper was shut down for publishing pro-Southern statements?
9. How did pro-Union people in Raleigh, North Carolina, respond when Confederate soldiers wrecked the office of a pro-Union newspaper?
10. What substance was sometimes used as an ink substitute for newspapers?
11. According to New Orleans magazine editor J. D. B. DeBow, what did the South badly need to develop?
12. What contribution did Englishman Frank Vizetelly make during the Civil War?
13. What organization instructed newspaper reporters not to publish military details in their stories?
14. What was a key source for the Confederacy's knowledge of Union military movements?
15. According to a law of the Confederate Congress passed in 1862, what was to be published after each battle to recognize particularly brave soldiers?
16. What North Carolina city saw the trashing of a pro-Union newspaper office, followed by the trashing of a pro-Confederate newspaper?
17. What newspaper reporting association was splintered at the outbreak of the war?

✎ Meeting the Press (answers)

1. Nothing. In spite of nasty attacks from the press, the government did little in the way of censorship.
2. A "soldier correspondent."
3. It promised not to leak military information. It did, and so did every other newspaper, South and North.
4. Wallpaper. Thanks to the Union blockade, there was a shortage of practically everything, including paper.
5. New York, which was notoriously pro-Southern.
6. He took over the offices of the city's two newspapers.
7. The "Bread Riot" of April 1863, involving women looting the town. Troops had to be called in before the women dispersed.
8. Chicago. This caused a howl of protests about freedom of speech.
9. They wrecked the offices of a pro-Confederate newspaper.
10. Shoe polish.
11. Industry, in which it lagged far behind the North. He was right on target.
12. He covered the Confederate side of the war by his illustrations for the *Illustrated London News*.
13. The Confederate Press Association. Reporters did not obey.
14. The Northern newspapers, which published military stories in uncensored detail.
15. A Roll of Honor. This was important, since the Confederacy gave no medals.
16. Raleigh.
17. The Associated Press.

18. What South Carolina newspaper was the South's chief voice of secession?
19. How did Charleston newspaper editor Robert Barnwell Rhett respond to Secretary of War Pope's request that newspapers not publish military information?
20. What effect did the Union blockade of Southern ports have on the Charleston *Mercury*?
21. What popular illustrated newspaper in the North always depicted Confederates as seedy thugs in its pictures?
22. What Memphis newspaper declared that its owners would rather throw their equipment in the Mississippi River than endure a Union occupation?
23. What widely read Tennessee newspaper moved from Memphis to Jackson to Atlanta to Montgomery?
24. What was the "Raleigh newspaper war" of 1863?
25. When the Union occupied Memphis and the owners of the newspaper *Appeal* fled, what did the Union authorities do?
26. What popular illustrated newspaper was ordered shut down because it published pictures of Confederate defenses at Yorktown?
27. Who was the chief target of Charleston *Mercury* editor Robert Barnwell Rhett's attacks?
28. What monthly magazine was probably the antebellum South's most influential journal?
29. What journalist coined the term "Lost Cause" to describe the South's attempt to create a separate nation?
30. What Tennessee newspaper recruited and funded its own artillery battery in the Confederate army?
31. What New York newspaper was the first in the nation to try to report war stories objectively and without bias?
32. During the war years, what was the editorial slogan of the New York *Tribune* newspaper?
33. What venerable Virginia newspaper was noted for its consistent support of President Jefferson Davis and his administration?
34. What Union general was called a traitor by Northern newspapers for his generous offer of surrender to the Confederacy?
35. What was the most pro-Confederate newspaper in England?
36. What was the distinction of the *Southern Illustrated News* published in Richmond?
37. What noted magazine for Confederate veterans was published by the Kentucky branch of the Southern Historical Society?
38. What Unionist newspaper editor in Tennessee received his reward by being elected governor of the state after the war?

18. The *Mercury*, founded in 1822.
19. Rhett screamed "Censorship!" and said the public had the right to any war-related information.
20. The blockade caused a paper shortage, thus finally reducing the newspaper to 2 pages.
21. *Harper's Weekly*, which was notoriously pro-Union.
22. The widely read *Appeal*.
23. The renowned Memphis *Appeal*, one of the most famous Confederate newspapers.
24. Confederate soldiers trashed the office of a pro-Union newspaper, and pro-Union citizens retaliated by trashing a pro-Confederate newspaper.
25. Began publishing a new pro-Union paper called the *Union Appeal*.
26. *Harper's Weekly*. The censorship order was soon revoked.
27. President Jefferson Davis. Rhett constantly referred to him as an "imbecile."
28. *DeBow's Review*, which constantly urged the South toward secession.
29. Edward Pollard, whose 1866 book was titled *The Lost Cause*.
30. The Memphis *Appeal*, which funded the "Appeal Battery."
31. The New York *Times*.
32. "Forward to Richmond!"
33. The Richmond *Enquirer*, founded in 1804. Toward the war's end, a new editor became less pro-Davis.
34. William T. Sherman, who had been willing to guarantee property rights to the conquered Confederacy.
35. The *Index*, financed by the Confederate government and edited by the capable Henry Hotze.
36. It was the first illustrated newspaper in the Confederacy.
37. *Southern Bivouac*, published from 1882 to 1887.
38. William "Parson" Brownlow, who had had his presses trashed because of his pro-Union views.

39. What Southern newspaper was so consistently pro-Davis that readers believed its articles had been written by Jefferson Davis and his cabinet members?
40. What Confederate agent failed in his propaganda mission in France because he constantly antagonized the French people?
41. What Southern newspaper editor relocated more often than any other journalist?
42. Who wrote *Three Months in the Confederate Army* as a propaganda piece for Europeans?
43. What happened to the newspaper business of Kentucky anti-slavery publisher Cassius Clay?
44. What Irish-born journalist received praise for covering the war under Confederate artillery fire in Tennessee?
45. What Northern journalist covered the South during the secession crisis and barely missed being lynched a few times?
46. What British journalist angered both South and North for his reporting of early Civil War battles?
47. What Irish-born journalist became close friend and invaluable aide-de-camp to President Jefferson Davis?
48. What general spent his post-war years as a magazine editor, publishing *The Land We Love* and *The Southern Home*?
49. What general, formerly a Nashville newspaper editor, had fought a duel with another editor?
50. What name was given to soldiers who went from camp to camp after battles, exchanging news?
51. What Knoxville newspaper editor was banished to Union territory for his anti-Confederate views?
52. What Richmond newspaper's offices became a favorite meeting place for Confederate congressmen opposed to President Jefferson Davis?
53. How many newspaper photographers were there in the Civil War?
54. What magazine was founded in 1893 by Sumner Cunningham, a former sergeant in the 41st Tennessee Infantry?
55. What Knoxville, Tennessee, newspaper editor declared that he would "fight the secessionist leaders till hell froze over"?
56. What cavalry general's brigade printed a satirical magazine called the *Vidette*?
57. What anti-Jefferson Davis Richmond newspaper was more widely read outside Virginia than in the state?
58. What noted Yankee newspaper editor ran the headline "ON TO RICHMOND" to incite the Union army to action?
59. What was the second job of Confederate war correspondents?
60. What was war correspondent Albert Richardson's reward for his coverage of Southern battles?

39. The Richmond *Enquirer*, one of the few consistently pro-Davis papers in the South.
40. Edwin de Leon, who had been a successful journalist in the pre-war South.
41. Benjamin Dill, editor of the Memphis *Appeal*, which moved from Memphis to Jackson to Meridian to Atlanta to Montgomery to Columbus.
42. Propaganda-master and publisher Henry Hotze, who presented an idealized picture of Southern morale and patriotism.
43. Opponents dismantled his press and shipped it off to Cincinnati.
44. Joseph McCullagh, who published under his pen name "Mack."
45. Albert Deane Richardson, who became chief war correspondent for the New York *Tribune*.
46. William Howard Russell. Europeans saw him as the authoritative commentator on the war. He was booted out of America in 1862.
47. William Montague Browne, who went on to write a biography of Vice-president Alexander Stephens.
48. Daniel Harvey Hill.
49. Felix Zollicoffer.
50. "News walkers." These unofficial reporters were a great source of entertainment as well as information.
51. The infamous William "Parson" Brownlow.
52. The Richmond *Whig*, noted for its harsh criticism of Davis's war policies.
53. None. Photographs could not be reproduced on the printing presses of the 1860s.
54. *Confederate Veteran*, which was published for 40 years.
55. William G. Brownlow, one of the South's most famous Unionists.
56. John Hunt Morgan.
57. The Richmond *Examiner*, with editorials by its sarcastic editor John Daniel.
58. Horace Greeley (famous for his advice "Go west, young man").
59. Soldiering. Most wrote under pen names to keep their superiors off their backs.
60. He was captured and spent 19 months in Confederate prisons.

🏴 Mail Call

1. Who grudgingly accepted the postmaster general post after declining it twice?
2. How long had the U.S. Post Office Department been in service when the war began?
3. On what date did the postal system cease to be Federal and become Confederate?
4. In what way was the Confederate postal service designed to be different from the Federal service?
5. What shocking postal rate increase took effect in February 1861?
6. Mail service was daily when the war began. How was that schedule changed?
7. What important materials did Postmaster General Reagan obtain from Washington?
8. What longstanding privilege of congressmen was eliminated by the Confederate Postal Service?
9. What company was established to deliver mail between North and South at a reasonable rate?
10. What was the purpose of the Adams Express Company?
11. Where were most post offices found in Southern communities?
12. What did the postal service not have when it officially opened in June 1861?
13. What did the firm of Hoyer & Ludwig supply to the Confederacy?
14. Whose face was on the first Confederate stamp?
15. On what date did the first Confederate stamp go on sale?
16. Where did the Confederacy obtain its best stamps?
17. What three deceased U.S. presidents' faces appeared on Confederate stamps?
18. What city's mail service ground to a halt in August 1863 because of a wage dispute?
19. What motion was defeated in Congress in February 1862?
20. Other than mailing letters, why did many Confederates buy stamps?
21. The Congress proposed that a certain type of person be allowed to mail items for free. What type of person?
22. What type of transportation had to be used to deliver mail across the Mississippi?
23. Why would foreign countries not accept Confederate postage?
24. What generous exemption was given to postal employees?
25. Who was John Reagan's successor as postmaster general?
26. What noted states' rights advocate had his picture on a stamp?
27. What general's picture appeared on a Confederate stamp?
28. What private firm was responsible for most package delivery in the Confederacy?

✎ Mail Call (answers)

1. John Reagan of Texas.
2. Seventy years.
3. June 1, 1861.
4. It was to be financially self-supporting.
5. From three to five cents.
6. From daily to three times weekly in most areas.
7. Route maps of the Southern states and names of all postmasters in the South.
8. The franking privilege, sending out congressional mailings free of charge.
9. The American Letter Express Co. As the war heated up, it had to shut down.
10. It delivered Southern mail to addresses in the North—for 25 cents per letter, an outrageous rate for that time.
11. Usually a corner of a general store.
12. Confederate stamps. For a while, handstamps had to be used.
13. Stamps.
14. Jefferson Davis', naturally.
15. October 16, 1861.
16. England, which produced more consistent printing quality that the Confederacy could do for itself.
17. George Washington and Thomas Jefferson (Virginians) and Andrew Jackson (a Tennessean).
18. Richmond's. Some of the undelivered mail was, no doubt, important to the war effort.
19. Abolishing the Confederate mail and using private services. The motion came about because of frequent complaints about mail service. (Is anything new?)
20. For use as petty cash, since there were not actual metal coins in the Confederacy.
21. A soldier. The proposal was defeated. As a compromise, soldiers could send materials "postage due."
22. Small rowboats, which could pass quietly at night and avoid Federal patrols.
23. That would have implied accepting the Confederacy as a sovereign nation.
24. Exemption from the draft.
25. There wasn't one. Reagan was one of two original cabinet members to keep his post throughout the war.
26. South Carolina Senator and U.S. Vice-president John C. Calhoun.
27. Thomas "Stonewall" Jackson's. In fact, the ten-cent Jackson stamp appeared in 1867. It was a fake "collectible" that many people bought.
28. The Southern Express Company.

⚐ Collegiate Things

Colleges were mostly male in the 1860s. Not only were they male, but also military, since the martial spirit in the South was strong. Thus the war had a largely adverse effect on colleges, since teachers and students went off to war. But if the war caused the colleges to decline, the colleges certainly made a positive contribution to the war effort. The U.S. Military Academy, by the way, is in a category by itself and is covered in a separate chapter.

1. What Virginia battle is still commemorated every year by the Virginia Military Institute?
2. How many students did the University of Mississippi have when the war began?
3. What state university was almost completely burned by Union troops?
4. What important private school, founded by a Confederate general, burned during the war?
5. What state university was occupied by 4,000 Union soldiers at the war's end?
6. What university was turned into a refugee camp for families displaced by the war?
7. What men's college supplied more Confederate officers than any other school (with the exception of West Point, of course)?
8. What future Confederate general had opened the North Carolina Military Institute in 1859?
9. What future Union general was head of the Louisiana State Seminary of Learning when the war began?
10. What state's university had compulsory military training in pre-war days?
11. What military college sent its cadets out to repel Sherman's march through Georgia?
12. What Virginia college has a statue of Thomas "Stonewall" Jackson on its parade ground?
13. What famous Virginia college had its main building used as a horse stable by Union troops?
14. Who were the "Katydids"?
15. What state's university has the home of General Josiah Gorgas, the Confederacy's chief of ordnance?
16. What was the only Southern state having two state military schools at the beginning of the war?
17. What noted Southern military school had been modeled after the U.S. Military Academy at West Point?

✎ Collegiate Things (answers)

1. The Battle of New Market, May 15, 1864. The VMI cadets played a prominent role in the battle.
2. About 100.
3. The University of Alabama in Tuscaloosa.
4. The University of the South in Sewanee, Tennessee. Bishop Leonidas Polk, the founder, became a Confederate general and died in the war.
5. North Carolina, at Chapel Hill.
6. The University of Mississippi.
7. VMI, the Virginia Military Institute.
8. Daniel Harvey Hill.
9. William T. Sherman.
10. The University of Alabama.
11. The Georgia Military Institute in Marietta.
12. VMI, where Jackson was an instructor before the war.
13. Washington College in Lexington, later headed by Robert E. Lee, and finally named Washington and Lee University.
14. The brave VMI cadets who turned out to fight at the Battle of New Market.
15. The University of Alabama, which Gorgas served as president after the war.
16. South Carolina, with the Citadel in Charleston and the Arsenal in Columbia.
17. VMI.

18. What act had gotten partisan fighter John S. Mosby expelled from the University of Virginia?
19. What South Carolina military college was destroyed in the war?
20. What is the significance of the Fort Hill plantation in South Carolina?
21. What historic college in east Tennessee was used as Union officers' quarters in the Civil War?
22. What college's museum displays two of the largest Confederate flags in existence?
23. How many colleges did the South have at the beginning of the war?
24. What Virginia college had 94 percent of its alumni serving in the Confederate army?
25. On what university campus would you find the burial place of Robert E. Lee (and also of his horse, Traveler)?
26. What South Carolina college was occupied by black Union troops, then closed?
27. What former general succeeded Robert E. Lee as president of Washington and Lee College?
28. What historic Virginia college was vandalized by Pennsylvania cavalry?
29. What world-famous general alienated his father-in-law, a staunch Unionist and a college president?
30. What Virginia college saw seventeen of its alumni become Confederate generals?
31. What respected military college was burnt during the war and never reopened?
32. What state had only one public college, opened in 1860?
33. What college has Stonewall Jackson memorabilia, including his preserved horse, Little Sorrel?
34. What type of colleges generally remained opened during the war?
35. What large university was called East Tennessee University when the war began?

18. Shooting a fellow student who had made a "disagreeable allegation."
19. The Arsenal, which burned in the fire of Columbia in 1865.
20. It is a sort of shrine to secession and Southern nationalism, since it was the estate of John C. Calhoun. It became the site of Clemson University.
21. Washington College in Johnston City.
22. The Citadel's, in Charleston.
23. About 250, many of them shut down during the war.
24. The Virginia Military Institute.
25. Washington and Lee University in Lexington, Virginia. Lee died in Lexington, serving as president of what was then known as Washington College.
26. The Citadel.
27. His eldest son, Custis Lee.
28. The College of William and Mary, in Williamsburg.
29. Thomas "Stonewall" Jackson. Dr. George Junkin, president of Washington College, was the father of Jackson's first wife Eleanor.
30. The Virginia Military Institute in Lexington.
31. The Georgia Military Institute in Marietta.
32. Louisiana. It was the Louisiana State Seminary and Military Academy in Pineville. It had been modeled on VMI.
33. The Virginia Military Institute in Lexington.
34. Women's colleges. Most men's colleges closed, since students and faculty were all off fighting.
35. The University of Tennessee, in Knoxville.

ꙮ Money Matters

1. What two states supplied the foundation of the Confederate Treasury?
2. How did citizens cope with the worthlessness of Confederate money?
3. What was the monthly pay of a soldier, according to the October 1862 act of the Confederate Congress?
4. What incentive did the U.S. Navy give for capturing the infamous Confederate raiding ship *Alabama*?
5. What did the Confederate Congress ask the wealthy men of the South to contribute in August 1861?
6. What essential item cost $250 per pair in Charleston in January 1864?
7. What Rebel cavalry leader was blamed when his men robbed a Kentucky bank of over $18,000?
8. What did General Jubal Early's men demand from Chambersburg, Pennsylvania, as payment for not burning the town?
9. Who died with a bag of $2,000 in gold around her neck?
10. When Rebel soldiers invaded Vermont, what exactly did they accomplish?
11. What pro-Southern governor of a border state paid $60,000 for weapons that wouldn't fire?
12. Who boasted that he had done about one hundred million dollars worth of damage in the Confederacy?
13. Who received better pay, a Confederate soldier or a slave working in a Confederate munitions plant?
14. What did Confederate cavalry leader John McCausland demand from the city of Hagerstown, Maryland, as payment for the looting done by the Union in the Shenandoah Valley?
15. What was the real identity of the money-printing Southern Bank Note Company?
16. What did the Union print in an effort to debase the South's paper money?
17. What might religious conscientious objectors do in lieu of fighting?
18. What worthless pieces of paper littered the streets when Richmond was occupied?
19. What did army sutlers do to ensure a captive clientele?
20. What reward did the Union offer for the capture of the Confederacy's "David" torpedo boats?
21. What was distinctive about the Union ship *Jacob Bell*, captured by the CSS *Florida*?

🪝 Money Matters (answers)

1. Alabama and Louisiana. Both loaned $500,000 each to the new Confederate government.
2. Worked on a barter system, swapping salt for shoes, bacon for potatoes, etc.
3. Four dollars.
4. A $500,000 reward for its capture, or $300,000 for sinking it.
5. A loan of 100 million dollars to finance the war.
6. Boots.
7. John Hunt Morgan.
8. $500,000 in currency or $100,000 in gold. The town was burned.
9. Noted spy Rose O'Neal Greenhow, who drowned when her boat capsized.
10. They robbed three banks, making off with over $200,000.
11. Beriah Magoffin, who planned to give the guns to secessionists.
12. Union General William T. Sherman.
13. The slave, who received $30 per month. However, the money went to the slave-owner, not the slave.
14. $20,000.
15. It was simply a cover for the real printer, the American Bank Note Company of New York. No one wanted to admit that Confederate money was being printed in the North.
16. Counterfeit Confederate paper money, naturally.
17. Pay a $500 fee, or hire a substitute.
18. Confederate money, which had become completely valueless.
19. They issued change in tickets instead of money—tickets printed with their own name, redeemable only with them.
20. $30,000. The Union really feared these 50-foot wonders.
21. It was valued at $1.5 million, the most valuable ship taken by a Confederate cruiser.

22. What infamous American made off with the table on which Lee and Grant had signed the terms of surrender?
23. When, according to Confederate money, could the bill actually be cashed in?
24. What makeshift material was used for the Davis Guard Medal, the only military medal ever awarded in the Confederacy?
25. What important stash of papers was sold to the Federal government in 1871 for $75,000?
26. What was the first state to receive the Thanks of the Confederate States Congress in February 1861?
27. What reward did the Federals offer for anyone delivering President Jefferson Davis to the U.S. military authorities?
28. What did William George Davis of Florida give to the Confederacy to show his support?
29. What Cherokee leader captured a Union steamer carrying $120,000 worth of supplies?
30. Other than mailing letters, why did many Confederates buy stamps?
31. What did the companies of Archer & Daly and Keating & Ball provide for the Confederacy?
32. What gift did Col. Zachariah Deas give to his regiment, the 22nd Alabama?
33. What Confederate agent has been called "the greatest scoundrel of the Civil War"?
34. What Union general forced the loyal Confederates of New Orleans to contribute to a charity fund for the city's poor?
35. What were bank notes of low denominations called?

♌ Author! Author!

The Confederacy was more than men in gray. There were men—and women— of letters, too. In many cases the authors were men in gray, either writing of the war as they lived it, or writing it down afterward. The 1860s were a productive time in American literature, both in the South and in the North.

1. What world-famous American author spent less than a month in a Missouri Confederate unit?
2. What phrase did author David Christy contribute to the Southern vocabulary?
3. What was the Confederacy's version of "Sad Sack"?

22. George Custer, who bought the table for $25.
23. "Six months or two years after the ratification of a treaty of peace between the Confederate States and the United States"—which never occurred.
24. U.S. silver dollars, with their engraving scraped off and new inscriptions made.
25. The Confederate state papers, which had been hidden away by William Bromwell, a Confederate clerk.
26. Alabama, for loaning $500,000 to the Confederacy.
27. $100,000 in gold.
28. $50,000, directly to the Confederate treasury.
29. Stand Watie, the Confederacy's only Indian general.
30. For use as petty cash, since there were not actual metal coins in the Confederacy.
31. Paper money.
32. Enfield rifles, costing $28,000 out of his own pocket.
33. Jacob Thompson, who made off with all the Confederate funds stashed in Canadian banks. He lived in high style in Paris for several years.
34. The much-despised Benjamin "Beast" Butler.
35. "Shinplasters." The Confederacy had no metal coins, but lots of "paper coins."

✎ Author! Author! (answers)

1. Samuel Clemens, or Mark Twain. He wrote a humorous war story, "Private History of a Campaign That Failed."
2. "King Cotton," from his 1855 book *Cotton Is King*.
3. "Bill Arp," a creation of writer Charles H. Smith.

4. What noted American author fought in several battles in the South and wrote one of the best-known stories of a Confederate, "An Occurrence at Owl Creek Bridge"?

5. What Confederate memoirs, one of the best works written in the period, was not published until 1905, though its author had died in 1886?

6. What pro-Union author was noted for his hatred of both blacks and the institution of slavery?

7. What Southern author was captured while running the blockade to Britain to promote his own books?

8. Who was the "Poet Laureate of the Confederacy"?

9. What noted author of the Old South had served on the staff of cavalry general J. E. B. Stuart?

10. What does the Tennessee Battle of Shiloh have in common with the book *Ben-Hur*?

11. Who was the "Poet-Priest of the Confederacy"?

12. According to the author of *Uncle Tom's Cabin*, the great anti-slavery novel of the 1800s, who wrote the book?

13. What general's wartime memoirs were published posthumously to help support his ten children?

14. What Presbyterian clergyman wrote one of the first biographies of Stonewall Jackson, whom he had served under?

15. What rumpled general left a colorful *Autobiographical Sketch* that showed he was "unreconstructed" till the bitter end?

16. What famous general did Gen. Fitzhugh Lee write a biography of?

17. What general's autobiography is titled *From Manassas to Appomattox*?

18. What soldier's memoirs are titled *Make Me a Map of the Valley*?

19. What noted general's memoirs were titled *Destruction and Reconstruction*?

20. What Confederate biography was banned by Federals because they feared it would undercut Union morale?

21. Alabama novelist Augusta Jane Evans wrote *Macaria, or the Altars of Sacrifice*, which contained an account of the Battle of Bull Run. Which Confederate general gave her a report on the battle?

22. Who was the most popular novelist among the Confederates?

23. What was the most popular poem among Virginians?

24. What noted poet wrote "Ethnogenesis," a title meaning "birth of a people"?

25. How much traveling in the South did author Harriet Beecher Stowe do before writing *Uncle Tom's Cabin*?

26. What was the most popular European book read by Confederates?

4. Ambrose Bierce, whose *Tales of Soldiers and Civilians* was very popular.
5. Mary Chesnut's *Diary from Dixie*.
6. Hinton Helper, a North Carolina man who believed that slavery was wrecking the Southern economy.
7. Edward Pollard, famous for coining the phrase "The Lost Cause" for the Confederacy.
8. Henry Timrod, poet who waxed lyrical about the birth of the new Confederate nation. The title was not official.
9. John Esten Cooke, noted for writing the *Life of Stonewall Jackson*.
10. The author of the novel, Lew Wallace, was commanding a Union force at the battle.
11. Abram Joseph Ryan, Catholic chaplain and noted writer of patriotic Confederate poetry.
12. "God wrote it!" according to author Harriet Beecher Stowe.
13. John B. Hood, author of *Advance and Retreat*. Hood was 48 when he died of yellow fever.
14. Robert Dabney, who also gained fame as a theological author.
15. Jubal Early, "Old Jube."
16. His uncle, Robert E. Lee.
17. James Longstreet's.
18. Jed Hotchkiss, the South's most famous wartime mapmaker.
19. Richard Taylor, son of President Zachary Taylor.
20. John Esten Cooke's *Life of Stonewall Jackson*, published in 1863, the year Jackson died.
21. P. G. T. Beauregard.
22. Sir Walter Scott, whose historical novels of Britain impressed the Southerners with the long-lost world of chivalry.
23. Probably "The Sword of Robert E. Lee" by Confederate chaplain Abram Joseph Ryan.
24. Henry Timrod, sometimes called the Poet Laureate of the Confederacy.
25. Practically none—strange for a novel about plantation life. Most of her background material was taken from abolitionist tracts.
26. Victor Hugo's novel *Les Miserables*. Passages of the book in which Hugo condemned slavery were left out of Confederate editions.

27. What noted Georgia poet wrote *Tiger Lilies*, one of the first great novels of the Civil War?
28. What North Carolina author, who despised blacks, tried to convince Southerners that slavery made life miserable for non-slaveholders?
29. What poet of the conquered Confederacy later wrote "Reunited," praising the end of sectional bitterness?
30. What is the title of staff officer Henry Kyd Douglas' memoirs?
31. What controversial general's letters to his young wife are titled *Heart of a Soldier*?
32. What notable leader wrote *The Rise and Fall of the Confederate Government*, published in 1881?
33. Whose wartime diary gives a close-up view of the Confederacy from the viewpoint of a government clerk?
34. What talented woman wrote the 2-volume *Jefferson Davis: Ex-President of the Confederate States of America*?
35. What notable navy man wrote *Memoirs of Service Afloat*?
36. What author and soldier wrote literary sketches of famous commanders for the *Southern Illustrated News*?
37. What contribution did Marinda B. Moore make to children's literature?
38. What general left the memoirs with the longest title?
39. What controversial British journalist irked both South and North by his opinionated book *My Diary North and South*?
40. What patriotic poet had his family mansion burned by Sherman's troops?
41. What popular comic character was created by author George W. Harris?
42. What courageous Georgian, wounded five times in the war, later edited a twelve-volume *Confederate Military History*?
43. How many novels were published in the Confederacy?
44. What was novelist Sarah Anne Dorsey famous for?

27. Sidney Lanier.
28. Hinton Helper, whose book *The Impending Crisis* was widely hated by slave-owners.
29. Abram Joseph Ryan, a Catholic priest noted for such poems as "The Sword of Robert E. Lee" and "The Conquered Banner."
30. *I Rode with Stonewall.* Douglas was on Jackson's staff.
31. George Pickett's. His wife LaSalle was about half his age.
32. Jefferson Davis.
33. John Beauchamp Jones, whose 2-volume *Rebel War Clerk's Diary* is a classic of the Confederacy.
34. His wife, Varina Davis.
35. Raphael Semmes, famous as a Confederate sea raider.
36. John Esten Cooke, famous for his biographies of Lee and Jackson.
37. She wrote *The Dixie Speller* and *Geographical Reader for the Dixie Children.*
38. Joseph E. Johnston, who wrote *Narrative of Military Operations Directed During the Late War Between the States.*
39. William H. Russell, who peeved Southerners by his criticisms of slavery.
40. Paul Hamilton Hayne, famous for "The Battle of Charleston Harbor."
41. Sut Lovingood, who kept Confederates laughing during hard times.
42. Clement Evans, who also had an active career in ministry.
43. Fewer than 30. The chronic paper shortage caused problems in printing large books, which is why the Confederacy produced more poetry than fiction.
44. Not for her fiction. She willed Jefferson Davis her Gulf coast estate, Beauvoir, which was his home for his last twelve years.

Part 9

The
Criminal Life

⚐ Bars and Stripes Forever:
The Prison Life

When the Civil War began, both the Confederacy and the Union had prisons. By the war's end, there were many more prisons—and prisoners. A natural consequence of war is that traitors and suspected traitors are imprisoned, as are the captured men of the opposing side. One thing both South and North learned quickly: they were not prepared for the number of prisoners they received.

1. What were "shebangs"?
2. What pestilent animal often served as food for hungry prisoners?
3. What were "tunnel-traitors"?
4. What prison head was executed after the war because of the horrible conditions of his prison?
5. What name was given to the line of posts set in the earth, beyond which prisoners ventured at the risk of being automatically shot?
6. According to the rules for exchanging prisoners, how many enlisted men were the same value as a captain?
7. What were usually the only reading materials available for men in Confederate prisons?
8. What was the normal limit placed on any letters a prisoner might write?
9. How many chaplains did most Confederate prisons have?
10. What name did the Andersonville prisoners give to a freshwater spring that miraculously opened up within the prison?
11. In what Northern city was Fort Warren, the island prison home for many captured Confederates?
12. What noted leader was put in chains in Virginia's Fort Monroe after the war?
13. Why did the Confederate prisoners at Fort Warren refuse to speak to the prison commandant, Major Harvey Allen?
14. What prison had an enormous black dog named Nero, used to intimidate the prisoners?
15. Which Richmond prison was used especially for captured Union officers?
16. What kind of liquid was (supposedly) used as "secret ink" in prisoners' letters?
17. Why were men in some Confederate prisons forbidden to stand in front of a window?
18. With a 24 percent prisoner death rate, what was probably the worst Northern prison?

✎ Bars and Stripes Forever: The Prison Life (answers)

1. The crude huts used as prisoners' shelters.
2. Rats.
3. Prisoners who reported other prisoners who were digging escape tunnels—usually just before the tunnel was completed, and after weeks of strenuous effort.
4. Henry Wirz, commandant of the Andersonville Prison in Georgia, widely condemned for its bad treatment of prisoners.
5. The deadline. Most prisons, North and South, had a deadline.
6. Six.
7. Bibles and New Testaments, of course.
8. Usually one page or less.
9. None. The Confederate army had enough trouble keeping chaplains for its own soldiers.
10. Providence Spring, which is still flowing in the national park at Andersonville. The prisoners had long prayed for a source of drinkable water.
11. Boston.
12. President Jefferson Davis.
13. He was a North Carolina man, so they considered him a traitor for being in the Union army.
14. Richmond's Castle Thunder. Nero belonged to the commandant, George Alexander.
15. Libby Prison, a converted three-story warehouse.
16. Lemon juice or onion juice, which can supposedly be read when heated.
17. There was fear that they might be signalling to local Union sympathizers.
18. Elmira Prison in New York, near the Pennsylvania state line. Its cold winters were especially hard on Southerners.

19. Of all the Yankee prisons, which one was probably the healthiest for Confederate prisoners?
20. What Maryland prison held the largest number of Confederates?
21. What welcome item did Confederate authorities send under a flag of truce to Northern prisons?
22. What noted prison was in the James River rapids in Richmond?
23. What Yankee prison surgeon boasted that he had "killed more Rebs than any soldier at the front"?
24. What chemical compound was routinely used to treat all sorts of sicknesses among prisoners?
25. What was the curious fate of Richmond's Libby Prison after the war?
26. Which Yankee prison had observation platforms, used by local people to watch the harsh life of Confederate prisoners?
27. When prisoners attempted to escape by tunneling, where would they hide the dirt they excavated?
28. What unique escape method was used by the brilliant Confederate prisoner known as "Buttons"?
29. What was a normal part of every punishment of prisoners?
30. What were "sinks"?
31. What city had a slave market that was converted into a prison?
32. What was the previous use of Washington, D.C.'s most famous prison?
33. What was the "Fort Greenhow" prison?
34. What Southern fort, captured by the Union, became a prison for army deserters?
35. What Civil War site has prison escape tunnels on display?
36. What illness killed most of the Union soldiers in the prison camp near Florence, South Carolina?
37. What agreement was signed between the Confederate and Union governments in July 1862?
38. What Ohio politician was sentenced to two years in prison for defying a Federal order that no sympathy for the South was to be expressed?
39. What became of the Confederate prisoners being taken to a Union prison on the ship *Maple Leaf*?
40. Why did the Confederates bring out artillery to surround Richmond's Belle Isle prison in 1863?
41. Who was responsible for feeding the 13,000 Union prisoners in Richmond?
42. What was the purpose of the Union cavalry raid against Richmond in March 1864?

19. Probably Fort Warren in Boston. Only twelve deaths occurred there during the war. This was much less than other Northern prisons.
20. Point Lookout, the North's largest prison, which held about 20,000 Confederate prisoners, who lived in tents.
21. Cotton, to be sold to buy warm clothing, which Confederate prisoners badly needed.
22. Belle Isle.
23. The sadistic E. L. Sanger, surgeon-in-chief of New York's Elmira Prison.
24. Blue mass, a compound of mercury and chalk.
25. The entire building was carried off to Chicago in 1889 and made into a museum.
26. Elmira Prison in New York. The platforms were constructed by locals, not by the prison officials. Spectators paid 15 cents to watch the suffering Confederates. There were more women spectators than men.
27. In a nearby pond or stream, if possible. This was the only sure way of concealing it.
28. "Buttons" had himself pronounced dead and was carried out in a coffin. Its lid had not been completely nailed down, so "Buttons" escaped easily—after horribly frightening the black servant who was driving the wagon with the coffin.
29. They were denied regular food rations. So, in addition to whatever punishment they received, they were also half-starved.
30. Latrines.
31. St. Louis, Missouri. (Recall that Missouri had been a slave state.)
32. The nation's capitol. The Old Capitol Prison in D.C. had been the temporary capitol building for a few years after the War of 1812.
33. The Washington home of arrested Confederate spy Rose Greenhow, who was held under house arrest along with several other suspected Confederate spies.
34. Fort Jefferson, on Florida's Tortugas Keys in the Gulf.
35. Andersonville National Historic Site.
36. Typhoid fever.
37. An agreement for the exchange of prisoners of war.
38. Clement Vallandigham, a noted "Peace Democrat." He hoped to gain sympathy for his side.
39. They overpowered their guards, captured the ship, and forced it to drop them at Cape Henry, Virginia.
40. There was a rumor (probably with no basis) that the 13,000 Union prisoners were plotting an escape. Richmond did not need 13,000 Union men running around loose.
41. The Federal government, not the Confederates.
42. Freeing the Union prisoners in the city.

43. What Union general worsened the South's manpower shortage by ordering an end to prisoner exchanges?
44. What prison was widely known as the "Georgia Hell"?
45. What important Richmond buildings were converted into prisons for captured Federals?
46. What was the biggest drain on Richmond's inadequate food supply?
47. With the shortage of prison space at the beginning of the war, what was often done with captured enemy soldiers?
48. What did the Confederate government deny to the 13,000 Union prisoners in Richmond after December 1863?
49. What was the largest Confederate military prison in Texas?
50. What Confederate prison was managed by the colorfully dressed Charleston Zouaves?
51. Of the fourteen men who had served in the Confederate Cabinet, how many were imprisoned at the war's end?
52. What was the intention of the Dahlgren-Kilpatrick raid on Richmond in 1864?
53. What generous offer of the Confederate Congress did U. S. Grant accept in January 1865?
54. What Richmond prison had such a bad reputation that the Confederate Congress ordered an investigation of its commandant?
55. What Confederate prison was called the "Hotel de Zouave"?
56. What name was given to Confederate prisoners who took a loyalty oath to the Union and became Union soldiers?
57. After the Confederacy fell, what was the Confederate prison Castle Thunder used for?
58. What were "white-washed Rebels"?
59. What famous spy was noted for singing Confederate songs at the window of the Old Capitol Prison in D.C.?
60. What Richmond prison had its wards labeled by the names of the battles in which the Union men were captured?
61. In what position did men in the overcrowded Libby Prison have to sleep?
62. Where was the "Rat-Hell" in Richmond?
63. What Confederate-made items were sold at the New York Sanitary Fair in 1864?
64. What was the biggest complaint Confederate prisoners made about Union nursing chief Dorothea Dix?
65. What did William D. Wood, head of the Union's Old Capitol Prison in D.C., do on behalf of the Federal government?
66. What Union prison was sometimes called "the rat-catcher's paradise"?

43. U. S. Grant. Grant knew that the more Confederate soldiers stayed in Union prisons, the worse off the South was.
44. The crowded, unsanitary prison of Andersonville.
45. Tobacco warehouses.
46. The growing number of Union soldiers imprisoned in the city.
47. Parole, in which they took an oath to go home and not take up arms again.
48. The rations that had been supplied by the Federal government.
49. Camp Ford.
50. Castle Pinckney, in Charleston harbor.
51. Six (Hunter, Mallory, Reagan, Trenholm, G. Davis, Seddon).
52. The raiders would kill Jefferson Davis and the Confederate Cabinet, release all Union prisoners in the city, then burn the city down.
53. An exchange of prisoners between South and North. Grant had previously forbidden exchanges, hoping to keep the South's soldier power tied up as long as possible.
54. Castle Thunder, whose commandant, Capt. George Alexander, had been charged with "harshness, inhumanity, and tyranny."
55. Charleston's Castle Pinckney, which was run by the colorfully dressed Charleston Zouaves.
56. "Galvanized Yankees."
57. A Union prison for Confederates accused of war crimes.
58. Confederate prisoners of war who took a loyalty oath to the Union and became Union soldiers.
59. The colorful Belle Boyd, who was imprisoned there several times.
60. Libby Prison, which had the Gettysburg Room, the Chickamauga Room, and so on.
61. On their sides, to save space.
62. The east section of Libby Prison, which had more than a few rats.
63. Fans and rings made by Confederate prisoners at Point Lookout Prison in Maryland.
64. That she only employed ugly women as nurses.
65. Questioned Confederate prisoners to gain military information.
66. Point Lookout in Maryland. It was not the only prison where desperate men were known to eat rats.

67. How did captured Confederate spy Belle Boyd deliver messages to her accomplice "C.H."?
68. What Southern governor had to flee before Sherman's Union army and was imprisoned in D.C. after the war?
69. What anti-secession Tennessean was imprisoned after swearing that he would rather go to prison that live in the Confederacy?
70. What role did Ethan Allen Hitchcock, the author of bizarre books of philosophy, play in the Civil War?

⚑ They Spied

Spying in the 1860s was hardly the glamorous, high-tech activity we associate with James Bond movies. Even so, it had its adventurous and romantic side, and spies of both South and North did avail themselves of whatever technology was then available. Even so, the spy's life was a dangerous one, a fact that only added to the romantic glow of espionage.

1. What notorious Confederate spy killed a Union soldier who had insulted her mother?
2. What valuable material was sometimes smuggled into the Confederacy in the heads of dolls?
3. What public documents were major sources of military information for the Confederacy?
4. Which famous Confederate general sneered at the use of spies, saying "I have no confidence in any of them"?
5. Who was the Confederacy's chief spymaster?
6. What was the official name of the Confederacy's espionage bureau?
7. What special feature did spy boats have in their bottoms?
8. What disguise allowed Confederate spy Thomas Nelson Conrad to move freely among Northern troops?
9. What Union head of espionage had run a famous Chicago detective agency before the war?
10. What Union spy was able to enter Confederate camps disguised as a slave?
11. What Northern city was supposed to be burned in an 1864 plot by Confederate saboteurs?
12. In what public building of D.C. would Confederate spymaster Thomas Nelson Conrad meet with his spies?
13. When spymaster Thomas Nelson Conrad was arrested in Maryland, who did Union authorities think he was?

67. Wrote them on rubber balls and tossed them through her prison bars.
68. Joseph Brown of Georgia.
69. William "Parson" Brownlow, newspaper editor and clergyman.
70. He was commissioner for the exchange of prisoners between Confederacy and Union, a role that had an effect on many men who became prisoners of war.

✎ They Spied (answers)

1. Belle Boyd of Virginia, probably the Confederacy's most famous spy.
2. Morphine, desperately needed for pain relief in Confederate hospitals.
3. The Northern newspapers, which carried detailed accounts of Union movements.
4. Robert E. Lee. Gentlemen soldiers did not believe spying was a proper part of war.
5. William Norris.
6. The Secret Service Bureau.
7. Plugs, so the boats could be submerged and hidden when not in use.
8. A minister's garb. Conrad was, in fact, an ordained Methodist minister.
9. Allan Pinkerton, whose agency still exists.
10. The infamous Sarah Edmonds, who had served in the Union army disguised as a man.
11. New York. Fires were started, but little damage was done.
12. The Interior Department building. Conrad believed, correctly, that Union authorities would never expect Confederate spies to meet at a Federal building.
13. John Wilkes Booth, who was wanted for shooting Abraham Lincoln.

14. What form of communication was completely useless for sending secret messages?
15. What was the age-old European code system used by the Confederates called?
16. What was the name of the clever Union code system that so befuddled Confederate spies?
17. Who was the "Siren of the Shenandoah"?
18. What spinster gained fame as the Union's most famous spy in Richmond?
19. What vegetable substance was often used as a substitute for paper in carrying secret messages?
20. What would Union spies carry with them to put them in the good graces of Confederate officers?
21. What disguise did Union spy James J. Andrews use to penetrate Southern lines?
22. When young Confederate spy Sam Davis was captured bearing military secrets, which general was he headed for?
23. What was the fate of the captured spy Sam Davis?
24. What was the official title of the Union agency dedicated to spying on the Confederates?
25. What noted Union spy was arrested by the Pinkerton agency—his own employer—on suspicion of being a Confederate spy?
26. Where would Richmond spy Elizabeth Van Lew obtain the information she passed on to Union officers?
27. In whose household was black spy Mary Elizabeth Bowser employed?
28. What Union head of the Secret Service gained a nasty reputation in the North for harassing and arresting suspected Southern sympathizers?
29. What Union spy in the Confederacy was forced to earn a living lecturing after the war?
30. What was the true (and better-known) name of Union spymaster E. J. Allen?
31. What state had many of its citizens imprisoned for fear of their being Confederate spies?
32. What Washington widow was a notorious spy for the Confederacy?
33. What group of Southerners were eager and willing to pass on information to the Union?
34. Where did Confederate spy Rose Greenhow go after being banished from Washington, D.C.?
35. At the famous explosion of a Confederate bomb at a Union munitions depot, what container had the bomb been smuggled in?

14. The telegraph and its Morse code. Since the code was standardized and well-known, sending messages this way meant that enemy agents could tap into the telegraph lines and easily decipher the messages.
15. The "diplomatic" or "court" system, which was over four hundred years old.
16. The RTC—Route Transposition Cipher. The system apparently worked better than the Confederacy's system.
17. Confederate spy Belle Boyd, who had a host of colorful nicknames.
18. "Crazy Bet," the nickname of Elizabeth Van Lew.
19. Onionskin, which was cheaper than paper and easy to conceal.
20. Bits of information—usually useless—about the movements and strengths of Union troops. This would fool Confederate officers into believing they were sincerely pro-South.
21. He posed as a merchant selling contraband materials to Southerners, which opened up many doors to him.
22. Braxton Bragg.
23. Hanging. Davis had refused to betray his friends, thus becoming one of the Confederacy's youngest heroes.
24. The Bureau of Military Information.
25. The infamous Timothy Webster, who fooled—briefly—one of his fellow agents into believing he was a Confederate.
26. In Richmond's Libby Prison, where she regularly visited Union prisoners, who gave her information about the Confederate troops they had recently seen.
27. Confederate president Jefferson Davis'.
28. Lafayette Baker, who was more widely hated in the North than in the South.
29. Philip Henson, who was never adequately rewarded by the Union for his valuable services.
30. Allan Pinkerton, the Scotsman whose detective and security agency still exists.
31. Maryland, which remained within the Union but had many Southern sympathizers.
32. Rose O'Neal Greenhow, who regularly entertained prominent Union politicians.
33. Runaway slaves, naturally.
34. On a secret mission to England and France. The South had lost its best spy in Washington.
35. A wooden candle box, smuggled in by Confederate spy John Maxwell.

36. What Union Senator regularly passed on military information to spy Rose Greenhow?
37. What name was given to the Confederates' underground spy link operating between Richmond and Washington?
38. What pro-Confederacy group in Baltimore was infiltrated by Union spy Timothy Webster?
39. What was the ultimate fate of Timothy Webster?
40. What country was an operations center for Confederate spies?
41. What led the famous spy Sarah Edmonds to enter the army disguised as a man?
42. What Virginia-born Union spy plotted the "Great Locomotive Chase"?
43. What post was held—with great inefficiency—by John Henry Winder?
44. What Alabama-born Union spy was considered the most dangerous spy operating in the Confederacy?
45. What was the profession of noted Union spy Pauline Cushman?
46. What Union spymaster was captured, then succeeded in convincing Jefferson Davis of his Southern sympathies?
47. What man did spy Elizabeth Van Lew invite to tea when the Union troops entered Richmond?
48. What was the occupation of Union spies Thomas Boyd and William Lloyd?
49. What method did Union spy Henry Young use to misdirect supply trains away from Lee's army?
50. What noted Confederate spy passed on information that made Robert E. Lee alter his plans before Gettysburg?
51. What western Virginia spy, captured by Federals in 1862, took her guard's gun and shot him dead?
52. In what battle was executed Confederate spy Sam Davis wounded?
53. What Union official had the most extensive spy network in Europe—a constant thorn in the Confederacy's side?
54. Who died with a bag of $2,000 in gold around her neck?
55. What famous woman gave public readings titled *The Perils of a Spy*?
56. What Union general was the object of a kidnapping scheme by Union spy Rose Greenhow?
57. Who was the Confederate agent known as "C.H."?
58. Who said, "I would sooner die a thousand deaths than betray a friend or be false to duty"?
59. What Union spy and actress toasted President Jefferson Davis during one of her performances?
60. Who was the most famous member of Coleman's Scouts?

36. Henry Wilson, who knew a great deal since he was chairman of the Senate's Military Affairs Committee. He and the widow Greenhow were rumored to be more than just friends.
37. The "Secret Line."
38. The Knights of Liberty.
39. He was arrested and hanged in Richmond.
40. Canada.
41. She was running away to escape a marriage arranged by her father.
42. James J. Andrews. His ill-fated plan to capture a Confederate train led to his execution in Atlanta.
43. Winder was the Confederacy's chief of counterespionage, and quite incompetent.
44. Philip Henson, who fooled many a Confederate officer.
45. Actress. Cushman did some valuable spying for the Union in Kentucky and Tennessee.
46. Lafayette Baker.
47. Union general U. S. Grant, her employer.
48. They were transportation agents in the South, which enabled them to travel freely and gave them access to vital information.
49. Wiretapping of telegraphs. This occurred during the Appomattox campaign, when Lee's troops badly needed supplies.
50. James Harrison, an actor. A rather mysterious character, Harrison is sometimes called Henry Thomas Harrison.
51. Nancy Hart.
52. Shiloh.
53. Charles Francis Adams, U.S. ambassador to Britain. His spies worked to frustrate the Confederacy's efforts to purchase ships and armaments.
54. Noted spy Rose O'Neal Greenhow, who drowned when her boat capsized.
55. Belle Boyd, noted Confederate spy in Virginia.
56. George McClellan, "Little Mac." The scheme never materialized.
57. No one knows. He (or she) received messages from imprisoned spy Belle Boyd, who wrote them on rubber balls and tossed them through the prison bars to "C.H."
58. Confederate spy Sam Davis, executed by the Union at age 21.
59. Pauline Cushman.
60. Sam Davis.

61. What Confederate spy went on to become a Hollywood actress?
62. What spy despised the U.S. so much that she refused to sleep under prison blankets bearing the U.S. emblem?
63. What tourist attraction served as the usual meeting place for Robert Coxe?
64. What was the profession of agent John Palmer?

ꕔ Courts, Crimes, and Punishments

Boys will be boys, and soldiers will do bad things—from drinking too much to pilfering from civilians to desertion. The Reb soldiers learned very quickly that military life was more than a uniformed hunting spree. In the military, as in the civilian world, justice (and often injustice) is accomplished through the courts.

1. How many officers comprised a general court-martial?
2. How did a general court-martial differ from a special court-martial?
3. What was the common punishment for thieving soldiers?
4. What offense was punished by branding the man with the letter "C"?
5. What name was given to this punishment: tying a stick or bayonet in the man's mouth, then tying his hands together, slipping them over his knees and running a stick through the space beneath the knees?
6. What was the most common offense that brought a man before a court-martial?
7. What was the weight of the ball in a ball-and-chain?
8. What relief did many offenders receive in February 1865?
9. Where was a deserter often seated at the time of his execution by shooting?
10. What common punishment was done away with in April 1863?
11. Besides a red-hot iron, what other method was used to brand a man?
12. What schoolboy punishment was often given to offenders?
13. What tune was played when offenders were (literally) drummed out of the service?
14. In a firing squad, how many of the twenty-four guns were actually loaded?
15. What offense did the amnesty order of August 1863 pardon?

61. Ginnie Moon, who, like her sister Lottie, carried messages between Confederate officers and Southern sympathizers in the North.
62. Catherine Baxley, who also wrote a spiteful parody of "The Star-Spangled Banner."
63. Niagara Falls. Coxe lived nearby, and he would check the visitors' registry at the Falls Museum to see which Confederate agents had "signed in" to town.
64. A correspondent for the New York *Tribune*.

✎ Courts, Crimes, and Punishments (answers)

1. From five to thirteen, usually of rank higher than the man on trial.
2. Special courts-martial had only three officers and were concerned with non-capital offenses of privates.
3. The barrel shirt, an open-ended barrel worn over the bare torso, usually with such labels as "Thief" or "Robbed a comrade."
4. Cowardice in the face of the enemy. The brand could be on the face, the palm, or the posterior.
5. Bucking and gagging, a fairly common punishment, and much dreaded.
6. Desertion. It grew worse as the war dragged on.
7. Usually about 12 pounds, though some weighed as much as 32. The chain was about 6 feet, sometimes shorter.
8. President Jefferson Davis's general amnesty.
9. On his coffin.
10. Whipping, which was always done on the offender's bare back.
11. Indelible ink, which was just as permanent, but less painful.
12. Spanking with a paddle.
13. "The Rogues' March."
14. Half, usually. The other half were blanks, so no man knew if he had actually fired a fatal shot.
15. Desertion. The executive order said that any absentees who returned to their units within twenty days would suffer no punishment.

16. What name was given to a special space on the ground to which offenders were confined?
17. When a man was sentenced to carry a weight, what object would he have to carry?
18. What kind of diet was often prescribed as a punishment?
19. Besides having to wear a barrel, what other punishment involved a barrel?
20. What was the maximum number of days a man could be confined without a trial?
21. What punishment was called "being put on the roots"?
22. What was the punishment known as "grubbing"?
23. What was the unique punishment for stealing hogs from civilians?
24. What part of the body was sometimes shaved as punishment?
25. What name was given to men ordered to arrest or shoot shirkers?
26. When the punishment for a man was confinement to a guard-house, where might he be confined?
27. What was the maximum punishment for sleeping on guard duty?
28. From the standpoint of cost, what was the most sensible punishment for the Confederate army to administer?
29. What types of bags were sometimes tied to a man's legs as punishment?
30. Why did some officers object to imposing extra guard duty as a punishment?
31. What was a "wooden mule"?
32. In artillery units, what might a man be tied to as punishment?
33. Who could offer a pardon for a capital offense?
34. When an officer was convicted of cowardice, what was removed from his uniforms?
35. What was done with sword of an officer convicted of cowardice?
36. What two forms of capital punishment were administered by the military?
37. In a court-martial, how many votes were required for an execution?
38. What was the best outcome of the military's disciplinary problems during the Civil War?
39. What kind of brand was sometimes put on the hands of men who tried to smuggle slaves to free territories?

16. A bull pen, usually quite small, but with no actual walls or fences.
17. A rail.
18. Bread and water. (Consider that the bread might be barely edible and the water was likely polluted.)
19. Standing on the barrel with a placard stating the offense.
20. Eight.
21. Being assigned to extra guard duty.
22. Having to dig up tree stumps.
23. Officers took pieces of the pigskin, cut holes in them, and forced the thieves to wear the skins as collars.
24. The head, naturally. Sometimes only half was shaved, which would look even worse than a full-head shave.
25. "File-closers." Using their bayonets, they kept men in line and urged them forward.
26. To a tent, since an actual guardhouse might not be available, particularly if the regiment was on the march.
27. Death by firing squad, although in fact this punishment was never applied.
28. Forfeit of the soldier's pay, naturally, since the Confederacy was chronically strapped for money.
29. Sandbags, which can be quite heavy.
30. They believed that guard duty was supposed to be an honor for a soldier, and so inappropriate as a punishment.
31. The punishment of having to sit for several hours on a narrow wooden rail, with the feet not touching the ground. (Ouch!)
32. He might be tied, spread-eagled, to the wheel of a gun carriage.
33. The Confederate president, or the commanding general ordering the court-martial.
35. The brass buttons.
36. Hanging and firing squad.
37. A two to one majority.
38. After the war, most of the code of military justice was rewritten.
39. "S S" for "slave stealer."

⚑ Bars and Stripes Forever: The Prison Life (Part 2)

1. What single color of clothing were Confederate prisoners allowed to receive from family and friends?
2. Which Union general ordered that all prisoner exchanges cease between North and South?
3. What types of books were usually forbidden reading for prisoners?
4. What item were Confederate prison guards eager to exchange with Union prisoners?
5. What was the previous (and very Southern) purpose of Alabama's Cahaba Prison building?
6. What was the chief reason that Civil War prisons were so unpleasant?
7. What was probably the most secure Northern prison?
8. Which was more eager for prisoner exchanges, the South or the North?
9. What was the most crowded Union prison?
10. What particular type of prisoners were held in Richmond's Castle Thunder?
11. What was the most pleasant of Confederate prisons?
12. Roughly, how many Confederates died in prison camps?
13. In which Northern prison was discipline so lax that Confederate prisoners were allowed to wander through the town if they had taken an oath not to run away?
14. Which North Carolina prison was originally designed for Confederate prisoners?
15. What was the fate of North Carolina's Salisbury Prison after it was captured by Union forces in 1865?
16. What notorious Southern prison was built to alleviate overcrowding in the prisons of Richmond?
17. What Illinois prison had already been abandoned and condemned when the Union chose to use it to house Confederate prisoners?
18. Which Northern prison was scene of the most dramatic tunnel escape?
19. What filthy Washington, D.C., prison held such noted Confederate figures as spies Belle Boyd and Rose Greenhow?
20. At the Texas prison of Camp Ford, what deterred prisoners from escaping?

🔖 Bars and Stripes Forever: The Prison Life (Part 2)

(answers)

1. Only gray. As with prison uniforms today, a standard color insured that escapees could be easily spotted.
2. U. S. Grant, who believed that exchanging prisoners served to increase the Confederacy's fighting strength. Unfortunately, Grant's order resulted in thousands of Union soldiers languishing in Confederate prisons.
3. Military history, military treatises, and geography—all prohibited for very obvious reasons.
4. Money, of course, since U.S. greenbacks had much more value than the constantly depreciating Confederate money. Officially, prison guards were *not* supposed to make such exchanges.
5. A cotton warehouse.
6. Mainly because both North and South expected the war to be very brief. Thus most prisons were originally intended only for a few months use, not three or four years. Prisons often had to accommodate three times as many men as they were designed for.
7. Johnson's Island in Lake Erie had only twelve escapes. It was a half-mile from shore, and in winter the lake was frozen solid, so escapes were difficult.
8. The South, since the Confederate army desperately needed all its fighting men. The South also wanted to rid itself of its overcrowded and embarrassing prisons.
9. Probably overcrowded Elmira in New York. It held about 10,000 Confederates.
10. Political prisoners, particularly Union sympathizers who helped slaves escape to the North. With many spies, deserters, and murderers, the Castle Thunder crowd was an unsavory lot.
11. Probably Castle Pinckney, on an island in Charleston harbor. Living conditions were sanitary and comfortable, and no major complaints were lodged, nor were there any escapes.
12. About 26,500.
13. Camp Chase, near Columbus, Ohio. Eventually, as the war went on, discipline had to be tightened.
14. Salisbury Prison, which was supposed to confine deserters, spies, and disloyal Confederate citizens. Later, Union prisoners of war were confined there.
15. It was burned to the ground—appropriately so, since conditions there had become horrible.
16. Andersonville Prison in Georgia. It was thought wise to have prisoners further from the Yankee border and nearer adequate food supplies. Unfortunately, Andersonville eventually turned into a hell hole.
17. Alton Prison, which had been abandoned when the new Illinois state penitentiary opened at Joliet. The unsanitary prison was the scene of a major smallpox epidemic. The horrible place was demolished after the war.
18. Alton, in Illinois. The escapees tunneled through 8 feet of masonry and the 3-foot thick limestone foundation of the outer prison wall.
19. The gloomy Old Capitol Prison, which had been the temporary U.S. capitol after the War of 1812.
20. The location—rugged terrain and, more important, the constant threat of Indian attacks.

21. Which Ohio prison became a tourist attraction, with the public paying for tours of the prison?
22. What was the primary cause in Union prisons becoming harsher in their treatment of Confederate prisoners?
23. Where were Confederate prisoners confined in fairground exhibit halls?
24. Who was "General Terror"?
25. Which New York prison was home to many pro-Southern Northerners?
26. What offense was punished by branding the prisoner on the face with the letter "T"?
27. Which Confederate prison was mined in the event that the Union prisoners attempted a revolt?
28. What Union prison was the scene of much hostility because so many guards were blacks?
29. What horrible Confederate prison is now a pleasant city park in Richmond?
30. What Boston prison was home to Slidell and Mason, the Confederate diplomats captured in the notorious *Trent* affair?
31. What Southern association was formed to assist Union men escaping from Confederate prisons?
32. What woman doctor, working for the Union, spent four months in a Confederate prison?
33. What close friend and Confederate House member was President Jefferson Davis's fellow prisoner after the war ended?
34. What sort of men did Douglas Cooper use for tracking down escaped prisoners?
35. What general from Maryland led a raid on a Union prison in his home state?
36. Which member of the Lee family languished in a Union prison for nine months?
37. What did the Union do to intimidate fiery Confederate raider Hanse McNeill?
38. Why was Commissary General Lucius Northrop arrested by the Federals?
39. What aging general left the field to become head of the Confederate prison system?
40. What thankless job did Gen. John Henry Winder carry out in the capital at Richmond?
41. What dashing Confederate cavalryman escaped from Ohio Penitentiary by tunneling through the cement floor?
42. What Federal agency published a very biased report on the treatment of Union soldiers in Confederate prisons?

21. Camp Chase, near Columbus.
22. Mostly stories about the horrible conditions in the Southern prisons, particularly Andersonville. In the North there was a clamor for retaliation.
23. Camp Morton, near Indianapolis. The prison had originally been the Indiana State Fairgrounds.
24. Gen. Albin Schoepf, commandant of Fort Delaware Prison, noted for his harsh treatment of Confederate prisoners.
25. Fort Lafayette. Among the prisoners were some pro-Southern members of Maryland's legislature as well as Northern writers who had criticized the Union government.
26. Telling the guards that other prisoners were attempting to dig an escape tunnel out of the prison. The punishment was from the prisoners, not from the guards.
27. Libby Prison in Richmond.
28. Point Lookout, in Maryland. The animosity between black guards and Confederate prisoners was incredible.
29. Belle Isle in the James River rapids, connected to the shore by a footbridge.
30. Fort Warren.
31. The Sons of America.
32. Mary Edwards Walker. Oddly, she was captured while treating a Confederate soldier on a battlefield.
33. The loyal Clement Clay of Alabama. The two remained lifelong friends.
34. Indians, who excelled at the task.
35. Bradley Tyler Johnson, who hoped to free Confederates from Point Lookout Prison.
36. W. H. F. "Rooney" Lee.
37. Captured his wife and children and imprisoned them in Ohio.
38. He was charged with having willfully starved Union prisoners. He was not convicted.
39. Daniel Ruggles, whose high point was his performance at Shiloh.
40. He was responsible for Union prisoners in the city.
41. Gen. John Hunt Morgan, who escaped with six of his officers. They scaled the outer wall using a rope made of bed sheets.
42. The U.S. Sanitary Commission, which had no desire to make the South look good.

43. Why did prisoners always eat their rations quickly?
44. What Federal official was the real villain for every Confederate in a Union prison?
45. What common prison disease caused men to lose their hair and teeth?
46. What Northern prison official treated his captured Confederates so well that they commissioned a statue of him after the war?
47. What became of the released Union prisoners who left Vicksburg on the steamboat *Sultana*?
48. What offer did the U.S. War Department make to Henry Wirz, sentenced to death for his treatment of the Union prisoners at Andersonville?
49. What general, imprisoned after Lee's surrender, was released because his wife had some clout with President Andrew Johnson?
50. What notorious Richmond prison had its front door key auctioned off in New York?
51. What Northern prison was on a Mississippi River island between Illinois and Iowa?

43. Fear that the food would be grabbed by their messmates.
44. Commissary General William Hoffman, who had no sympathy for captured Confederates.
45. Scurvy.
46. Col. Richard Owen of Camp Morton in Indiana. The statue, a bust, was placed in the Indiana capitol.
47. The boat's boiler exploding, setting the whole vessel ablaze. Everyone aboard died by burning or drowning.
48. He would get a reprieve if he would implicate Jefferson Davis. He refused and was hanged.
49. Richard Ewell, whose wife had known Johnson in Tennessee.
50. Castle Thunder. The money from the auction was used to benefit orphans of Union soldiers.
51. Rock Island, generally regarded as one of the worst Yankee prisons.

Bibliography

Abel, Annie H. *The American Indian as Participant in the Civil War*. Cleveland: Arthur H. Clark, 1919.

Andrews, Matthew P. *The Women of the South in Wartime*. Baltimore: Norman, Remington, 1927.

Black, Robert C., III. *The Railroads of the Confederacy*. Chapel Hill, N.C.: University of North Carolina Press, 1952.

Chesnut, Mary Boykin. *A Diary from Dixie*. Cambridge, Mass.: Harvard University Press, 1980.

Cochran, Hamilton. *Blockade Runners of the Confederacy*. Indianapolis: Bobbs-Merrill, 1958.

Coulter, E. Merton. *The Confederate States of America, 1861–1865*. Baton Rouge: Louisiana State University Press, 1950.

Craven, Avery O. *The Growth of Southern Nationalism*. Baton Rouge: Louisiana State University Press, 1953.

Cunningham, H. H. *Doctors in Gray: The Confederate Medical Service*. Baton Rouge: Louisiana State University Press, 1958.

Davis, Burke. *Gray Fox: Robert E. Lee and the Civil War*. New York: Rinehart, 1956.

Davis, Jefferson. *The Rise and Fall of the Confederate Government*. 2 vols. New York: Appleton, 1881.

Davis, Varina. *Jefferson Davis: Ex-President of the Confederates States of America*. 2 vols. 1890. Reprint. Baltimore: Nautical & Aviation Publishing, 1990.

Davis, William C. *A Government of Our Own: The Making of the Confederacy*. New York: Free Press, 1994.

Douglas, Henry Kid. *I Rode with Stonewall*. Reprint. Chapel Hill, N.C.: University of North Carolina Press, 1940.

Dowdey, Clifford. *Death of a Nation: The Story of Lee and His Men at Gettysburg*. New York: Knopf, 1958.

————. *The Land They Fought For: The Story of the South as the Confederacy*. Garden City, N.Y.: Doubleday, 1955.

Eaton, Clement. *A History of the Old South*. New York: Macmillan, 1954.

————. *A History of the Southern Confederacy*. New York: Macmillan, 1954.

————. *Jefferson Davis*. New York: Free Press, 1977.

Freeman, Douglas Southall. *R. E. Lee*. 4 vols. New York: Scribner's, 1935.

————. *Lee's Lieutenants*. 3 vols. New York: Scribner's, 1944.

Harwell, Richard B., ed. *The Confederate Reader: How the South Saw the War*. 1957. Reprint. New York: Dover, 1989.

Hattaway, Herman, and Archer Jones. *How the North Won: A Military History of the Civil War*. Urbana, Ill.: University of Illinois Press, 1983.

Heaps, W. A., and P. W. Heaps. *The Singing Sixties: The Spirit of Civil War Days Drawn from the Music of the Times*. Norman, Oklahoma: University of Oklahoma Press, 1960.

Henderson, G. F. R. *Stonewall Jackson and the American Civil War*. New York: Longmans, Green, 1949.

Hesseltine, William B. *Civil War Prisons: A Study in War Psychology*. New York: Frederick Ungar, 1964.

Hood, John B. *Advance and Retreat: Personal Experiences in the United States and Confederate States Armies*. 1880. Reprint. Bloomington, Ind.: Indiana University Press, 1959.

Horn, Stanley. *The Army of Tennessee*. Norman: University of Oklahoma Press, 1941.

Jones, John Beauchamp. *A Rebel War Clerk's Diary*. Edited by Howard Swiggett. 2 vols. New York: n.p., 1935.

Jones, Katherine M. *Heroines of Dixie: Confederate Women Tell Their Story of the War*. Indianapolis: Bobbs-Merrill, 1955.

Jones, Virgil C. *The Civil War at Sea*. 3 vols. New York: Holt, Rinehart, & Winston, 1962.

Kane, Harnett T. *Spies for the Blue and Gray*. New York: Hanover House, 1954.

Lytle, Andrew. *Bedford Forrest and His Critter Company*. 1931. Reprint. Nashville: John S. Sanders, 1992.

Osborne, Charles C. *Jubal: The Life and Times of Jubal A. Early*. Chapel Hill, N.C.: Algonquin, 1992.

Owsley, Frank L. *King Cotton Diplomacy: Foreign Relations of the Confederate States of America*. 1931. Reprint. Chicago: University of Chicago Press, 1959.

Patrick, Rembert W. *Jefferson Davis and His Cabinet*. Baton Rouge: Louisiana State University Press, 1944.

Phillips, Ulrich B. *Life and Labor in the Old South*. Boston: Little, Brown, 1929.

Ramsdell, James G. *Behind the Lines in the Southern Confederacy*. 1944. Reprint. New York: Greenwood, 1969.

Robertson, James I., Jr. *Civil War Virginia: Battleground for a Nation*. Charlottesville, Va.: University Press of Virginia, 1991.

————. *The Stonewall Brigade*. Baton Rouge: Louisiana State University Press, 1963.

Shattuck, Gardiner H. *A Shield and a Hiding Place: The Religious Life of the Civil War Armies*. Macon, Ga.: Mercer University Press, 1987.

Stephenson, Wendell H. *A Basic History of the Old South*. Princeton: Van Nostrand, 1959.

Symonds, Craig L. *Joseph E. Johnston*. New York: Norton, 1992.

Taylor, Richard. *Destruction and Reconstruction*. Edited by Richard Harwell. New York: Longmans, Green, 1955.

Thomas, Emory M. *Bold Dragoon: The Life of J.E.B. Stuart*. New York: Harper & Row, 1986.

————. *The Confederate Nation, 1861–1865*. New York: Harper & Row, 1979.

Vandiver, Frank E. *Mighty Stonewall*. 1957. Reprint. College Station, Tex.: Texas A & M University Press, 1988.

————. *Their Tattered Flags: The Epic of the Confederacy*. 1970. Reprint. College Station, Tex.: Texas A & M University Press, 1987.

Walther, Eric H. *The Fire-eaters*. Baton Rouge: Louisiana State University Press, 1992.

Warner, Ezra. *Generals in Gray*. Baton Rouge: Louisiana State University Press, 1959.

Wharton, H. M. *War Songs and Poems of the Southern Confederacy*. Philadelphia: n.p., 1904.

Wiley, Bell Irvin. *The Life of Johnny Reb*. 1943. Reprint. Baton Rouge: Louisiana State University Press, 1978.

————. *The Plain People of the Confederacy*. Baton Rouge: Louisiana State University Press, 1944.